RULE BRITANNIA

PREVIOUS BOOKS BY THE AUTHOR

The Sea is a Magic Carpet
(1964)

The 'Titanic' and the 'Californian'
(1965)

An Agony of Collisions
(1966)

Aim Straight
a biography of Admiral Sir Percy Scott
(1966)

Broke and the 'Shannon'
a biography of Sir Philip Broke
(1968)

The Battleship Era
(1972)

Guns at Sea
(1973)

The Great Naval Race
Anglo-German Naval Rivalry, 1900–14
(1974)

Nelson's War
(1976)

The Lion's Claw
a novel (1978)

Tide of Empires
Decisive Naval Campaigns in the Rise of the West
Volume 1, 1481–1654
(1979)

The Unquiet Gods
a novel (1979)

RULE
BRITANNIA

THE VICTORIAN AND EDWARDIAN NAVY

PETER PADFIELD

ROUTLEDGE & KEGAN PAUL
London, Boston and Henley

First published in 1981
by Routledge & Kegan Paul Ltd
39 Store Street, London WC1E 7DD,
Broadway House, Newtown Road,
Henley-on-Thames, Oxon RG9 1EN and
9 Park Street, Boston, Mass. 02108, USA

Set in Century by
Input Typesetting Ltd, London SW19 8DR
and printed in Great Britain by
Unwin Brothers Ltd,
Old Woking, Surrey

British Library Cataloguing in Publication Data

Padfield, Peter

Rule Britannia.
1. Great Britain. Royal Navy - History - 19th century
2. Great Britain - History, Naval - 20th century
I. Title
359'.00941   VA454

ISBN 0 7100 0774 4

CONTENTS

INTRODUCTION   1

1 SHIPS AND ATTITUDES   7

2 MEN – AND A FEW WOMEN   18

3 OFFICERS   51

4 THE COMMITMENT AND THE MEANS   83

5 WIDER YET AND WIDER . . .   130

6 HIGH NOON OF NAVAL POWER   176

7 WAR NAVY   209

  REFERENCES AND SELECT BIBLIOGRAPHY   236

  ACKNOWLEDGMENTS   243

  INDEX   244

LIST OF ILLUSTRATIONS

The backbone of Britain's world power 2
HMS *Queen* 3
The ancient craft of a sailor 5
The battlefleet in the Crimean War 8
The Mediterranean fleet in Grand Harbour, Malta, 1860s 9
Bending the foresail 11
Model of a screw frigate 13
The gunnery training school, HMS *Excellent* 14
Jack aloft 19
Below decks in a home port: 'every excess of debauchery . . .' 22
Saturday night at sea 23
Turned in: berth deck at the end of the century 25
Aboard a gun boat in the China war 27
Drunkenness was not confined to the men 32
Dancing on deck 33
Sling the monkey 34
Mess table at the end of the century 35
Ship's concert party 36
Officer recreation on deck in the 1880s 37
Manning the capstan to weigh anchor 40
Petty Officers at the turn of the century 42
Brought by the lee 44
Taking in studding sails and reefing topsails 47
On board the *Highflyer*, 1855 49
Issuing grog at the turn of the century 50
Captain Sir Reginald Poore, Bt., and his Commander 52
Officers and Petty Officers of HMS *Shannon* 54
Officers' rank insignia on cuffs 56
Officers' tail coats, waistcoats and trousers 58
The Captain and Officers of HMS *Encounter* 63

HMS *Warrior*   65
Lieutenant's cabin aboard the battleship *Anson*   67
Admiral's cabin in HMS *Magnificent*   70
Midshipmen in a battleship's gunroom   72
A battleship's gunroom at the turn of the century   73
Christmas at sea in an ironclad   75
A quiet rubber in the battery   76
'Following your partner's lead'   77
'Why we enjoy going to dances in the navy'   78
Captain the Hon. Hedworth Lambton, Commander
A. P. Ethelston and Lt. J. Nicholas   80
Ironclads alongside the mole at Gibraltar   84
Burma War; squadron up the Irrawaddy   86
A mess in an ironclad's battery in the 1880s   88
The attack on Sidon, 1840   91
Coaling ship   93
The Hon. Henry Keppel   99
A Royal Navy corvette chases a dhow   111
Lieutenant Fegen boards a slaving dhow   112
A RN officer questions the Nakhoda (master) of
an East African dhow   120
Captured Arab slave traders aboard a British corvette   123
Mounting a field gun   132
Hauling a field gun in the 1840s   134
Shipping at Balaclava Harbour, Crimean War   136
'How Jack made the Turk useful at Balaclava'   139
The battle of Fatshan creek   144
Volage and *Hyacinth* against Imperial Chinese war junks   147
The gunboat *Cockatrice*, 1896   148
Firing an early Armstrong breechloader in the 1860s   152
Battery deck of the cruiser *Nelson* in the 1880s   153
An early Coles type turret   157
A battleship's forward turret in the 1880s   159
Open barbette mounting in the 1890s   161
Forward turret, bridge and twin funnels of the
battleship *Sans Pareil*   162
Quarterdeck of a battleship in the 1890s   165
'Spar' or 'outrigger' torpedo rigged for action   167
The Whitehead or locomotive torpedo   168
The Nordenfelt machine gun   170
Gun's crew in action   172
Bayonet charge   174
Divisions   177

Inspection bags and bedding	179
Jack ashore – Sally Point, Portsmouth	181
'Make and mend'	182
The water carnival	184
Infantry training at the gunnery school HMS *Excellent*	186
The naval square for repelling a charge	187
Ready for the final charge	188
Cutlass drill	190
Field battery exercise	191
Fleet regatta Mediterranean Station	198
The naval brigade of HMS *St George*	202
The cruiser *St George*	203
Sending a field gun ashore	205
An early torpedo boat destroyer	210
A destroyer attacking with a spar torpedo	211
Sir Arthur Wilson	214
Signallers on the bridge	217
Admirals 'Jacky' Fisher and Percy Scott	218
Naval field gun's crew firing	221
HMS *Implacable*, cleared for action	223
An early 'A' class submarine	224
Submarine coming alongside	225
HMS *Dreadnought*	226
Battle cruiser, *Inflexible*	228
The Dreadnought battleship *Colossus*	230
The watch below	231

'The squadron was very magnificent, a war vessel is indeed a brave object. In them men can enter all the seas, navigate the world, and display his country's power and glory when the circumstances demand, just like the British squadron. I felt all this so much that I determined to enter the Navy and devote the whole of my life to its service.'

Commander Okuda, Imperial Japanese Navy, after the bombardment of Kagoshima by a British Squadron in August 1863.

'I love the sea and have never regretted the step I took as a youngster when I joined the Navy.'

Petty Officer William Ashcroft, who joined as a boy in 1833.

'British mothers have wept over British sons who have chosen a sea life since British keels cut the waters . . . they will do it as long as there is a British boy to obey the call. And that call when it comes will induce him to leave the home circle and home comforts to live a life of hardship and danger from the tropics to the poles. And as his knowledge grows, he will curse the mistress who uses him so badly, but he will love her, and he will follow her despite her buffettings'.

Able Seaman Lionel Yexley, who joined as a boy in 1890.

'The Royal Navy is the salt of the sea, and the salt of the earth also.'

The last published words of the war correspondent G. W. Steevens, who died in Ladysmith, 1900; they conclude his description of the Naval Brigade there.

INTRODUCTION

The Royal Navy of the nineteenth and early twentieth centuries was a legendary force. It claimed supremacy in every ocean. The claim had been established during the great wars against France, when British fleets had subdued every coalition of naval power brought against them by Bonaparte – either locking the hostile fleets in their own ports while blockading squadrons rode outside, or destroying them in action. With the battle fleets neutralised, enemy shipping had been swept from the sea routes, and enemy colonies and overseas bases stripped from them. Britain had ended the wars in undisputed possession of what the French called the 'Empire of the Oceans' – such commanding fleets, such a tradition of victory wrought by persevering seamanship and disciplined great gun drill, such a chain of strategic bases along the sea routes of the world: her supremacy at sea was unchallengeable.

At the same time, due to this oceanic control, Britain's overseas trade had grown faster than ever before, and her industries had expanded, harnessing steam power. Meanwhile, those of her Continental opponents, cut off from overseas sources and markets, had been stunted. She had ended the wars not simply as the first naval power but as the greatest trading and manufacturing power, and well on the way to becoming a new sort of power altogether, the first industrial nation.

As the first industrial nation in the peace after the wars, her overseas expansion gathered momentum. New markets, new sources of raw materials and, after the appearance of steam-powered ships, new trading routes led to the acquisition of new bases from which to protect her interests both from local lawlessness and piracy and from the designs of rival European nations. Vast new sea and river areas and all the territories bordering them came under her authority, and the Royal Navy found itself adapting into an imperial police force operating chiefly in small ships on overseas stations. It still maintained battle fleets in the Mediterranean and home waters, and took great care to ensure that battleships in commission and reserve were more than equal to the combined fleets of the next two powers. While these great ships represented the real power factor behind Britain's position in the world most of the real work was done in the small ships of the overseas squadrons.

These were the ships that hurried to avenge violence against European life or trade, chasing pirate fleets at sea, hunting up tropical rivers, concentrating and landing naval brigades to fight overland. Their commanders, out of touch with higher authority for months at a time, needed to be local intelligence officer, ambassador and diplomat as well as policeman, making and interpreting treaties with local rulers, bearing gifts from the Great White Queen, 'showing the flag' as a reminder of the power that could be summoned to enforce her law, attempting to maintain stability and keep the traders' peace. Whenever a part of the Empire became embroiled in a border war, it was the overseas squadrons that first

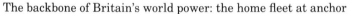

The backbone of Britain's world power: the home fleet at anchor

brought troop reinforcements – landing their own naval brigades and artillery to fight alongside the army – whose boats provided transport and gunships for the amphibious warfare in which they came to excel.

And it was the small ships that were used for the humanitarian goals the British imposed on themselves in the long Victorian peace; the attempt to put down the slave trade and to chart the coasts of the world for the seafarers of the world. These were new, indeed revolutionary concepts. Before the nineteenth century, navigation had been treated as a guarded craft secret, while British merchants had been among the greatest beneficiaries of the slave trade.

Behind the imperial and humanitarian roles, the energies of the service were fully occupied in mastering and harnessing the strange new phenomenon of runaway technological progress. As the European industrial revolution gathered way in mid-century, armaments and ship design were caught and swept along in its turbulent wake. In less than three decades the warship that had evolved, but

The towering height of their hulls presented an extremely majestic appearance, enhanced by a triple row of guns. This is HMS *Queen*

scarcely changed, over three centuries had been superseded by strange new types which bore little resemblance to the old ships save that they floated on water. With technical change went social and organisational upheavals which were even more difficult to assimilate. 'Little did I think,' wrote one Victorian admiral of his early years, 'that I was to live to see every familiar thing disappear, and to watch the growth of a new Navy.' The wonder, in that age before change had become familiar, was not that so many officers resisted it, but that so many rose to its challenges.

At the end of Victoria's reign, despite the new fleet and the new methods, the Navy's immense prestige remained undimmed; its officers and men regarded themselves as heirs to an *unconquerable* tradition, like Nelson's sailors, 'sea-rulers by birthright', while its bright and burnished battle fleets were more than a match in numbers and design for any three major powers combined, and its multitude of cruisers and smaller vessels girdled the world. A French strategist wrote in 1902, as one might have written in 1837, or any of the years between:

> For England the sea is not to be looked upon as a means of transport . . . but as a territory, a British territory of course. The English fleet which owns the Empire of the Seas, places its frontiers at the enemy's coasts, and will dispose of all commerce behind that frontier, just as any army disposes of the resources of a conquered province.

Such was the appearance of unchanged supremacy. Behind it in the highest councils there was growing concern. So far the Navy had shrugged off any foreign building challenges almost effortlessly by virtue of the country's industrial and financial lead. That lead had been shortened; all Europe, North America and Japan had undergone the same industrial transformation, and all were seeking markets, influence or colonies overseas and backing their claims with warships. The whole industrialised world was infected with 'navalism', and it was evident, at least at the Admiralty and Foreign Office, that the Navy could not long retain its supremacy by itself in every ocean.

The task of the Edwardian Navy was to come to terms with this new scale of challenge; it did so first by informal understandings with the United States, then by formal alliance with Japan, allowing a reduction in the numbers of ships outside European waters. Finally, as the German Navy rose clearly into view as the most single-minded and dangerous challenger, *ententes* were formed with

[4]

France and afterwards with Russia, and the naval building race narrowed into a duel between Great Britain and Germany. As the economic strain increased and warlike tension mounted, the Victorian Navy, with its host of small ships scattered for imperial policing, brightly painted and polished battle fleets, its peace-bred habits of complacent superiority, quite suddenly died. In its place there was a great grey armada prepared by constant warlike exercises and drill to unprecedented, almost mechanical efficiency, led in the important posts by men with technical minds, whose careers had been much concerned with *materiel*.

So much for the outline. This book is an attempt to fill it out in human terms, to penetrate the legends that must accumulate about any service as splendid and uniquely powerful – and as little analysed – and set down the reality – which of course was often very different – so far as possible in the words of those who served. It is not a comprehensive history of all those long-forgotten ships and campaigns, or even of many of them, rather a sample in depth

The ancient craft of a sailor: here 'serving' a rope after it had been 'wormed' with small stuff in the lay and 'parcelled' with canvas strip

of some of the most, and a few of the least, important to indicate how an expedition was mounted to punish an African tribe; how a slave dhow was detected, captured, punished; what a sailor was paid; how he was disciplined; what he ate; the diseases he suffered from; his pride in his craft; his arrogance as a Briton; his moments of frolic, and his exhilaration in chase.

CHAPTER ONE

SHIPS AND ATTITUDES

The British fleet in 1837, the year of Victoria's accession, looked very much the same as in Nelson's day. The great ships were painted with alternate black and white instead of black and yellow bands around the hull, but were essentially the same bluff, oak-built sailing castles mounting cast cannon on elm carriages little changed from Elizabethan times, manned and fought on the same principles exactly, 'rated' according to the number of guns they carried. The largest were the three-gun decked '1st rates' of over 100 guns, and the two-decked '2nd' and '3rd rates' of 80–92 and 74 guns; these were designed to lie in the line of battle.

> The neatness and order of the stately ships, the taut rigging, the snowy sails, the ropes coiled neatly down on deck: these things left an abiding impression upon my youthful mind.[1]

In company and under sail they were magnificent:

> England's oaken walls never looked stronger or grander than they did that evening, as these ships came tearing through the black water toward us. The warm, low sunlight glowing upon the piled-up canvas made them look like moving thunderclouds. . . . As each ship came up one thing looked even whiter than her creamy canvas, and that was the broad roll of curling foam which ran and played on the dark sea in front of her stem.[2]

As instruments of policy of an island empire they had no equal; here is Lord Palmerston:

> Diplomats and protocols are very good things, but there are no better peace-keepers than three-deckers.

Like all warships from the earliest days, the 'liners' had grown in size and they continued to grow. The latest so-called two-decked '2nd rates' – which actually had powerful batteries on quarterdeck and fo'c'sle above the two continuous gun decks – displaced 3,500 tons, which was as much as a three-decker – actually four tiers of guns – at the beginning of the century; the new '1st rates' displaced 4,500 tons and mounted 120 guns. There were few of them for they represented a prodigious expenditure of resources – perhaps 3,500 scarce trees that had taken decades to mature; 50,000 square feet of flax canvas, and 35 miles of cordage. They cost £120,000, which represented almost 30 per cent of total naval stores for building and repairs in the annual estimates, and each employed 900 men – five times as many as a small frigate, when sailors were one of the scarcest resources of all.

The increases in size were made possible by a stronger hull construction than hitherto; the great adzed ribs were now braced by diagonal timbers and by longitudinal 'stringers' and 'shelf pieces'

England's oaken walls during the first decades of Victoria's reign: the battlefleet in the Crimean War

The Mediterranean fleet in Grand Harbour, Malta, 1860s

which provided horizontal strength. There were more immediately obvious design changes; high timber bulwarks instead of low rails topped by hammock nettings ran all round what was in the newest ships a continuous upper deck in place of the former fo'c'sle and quarterdeck joined by 'gangways' along either side. Bows and stern were rounded all the way up to give greater arcs of fire for the guns and more protection against raking fire than the old square ends, although the large and vulnerable areas of stern windows were retained. Underwater, a shallow V shape had been introduced to replace the flat U bottom of earlier ships by Sir William Symonds, Surveyor of the Navy since 1832. His vessels, known as 'Symondites', were broader than formerly, with their maximum beam well forward and a sweet run to the stern; they were famous for their speed and grace of line. Sir William, unaware that the smoke columns visible all round the horizon presaged a whirlwind of change had standardised the designs of each 'rate' and the dimensions of their masts and spars, sails and rigging.

Armaments had already been made more uniform so that in place of the 32, 24, 18 and 12 pounder cannon and various larger carronades carried in the great wars, the latest ships carried only one calibre of cannon throwing a 32-pound ball, and one type of 8 inch shell gun. The trick had been accomplished by having three different lengths of barrel for a 32 pounder, thus three different weights;

[9]

the heaviest were carried on the lowest gun deck, the lightest on the highest, preserving stability while greatly simplifying the supply of cartridges and shot. The new 'liners' of Victoria's reign were more efficient and powerful than any Nelson had known.

Below them were the '4th', '5th' and '6th rates', mounting from 50 or even 60 guns down to 28, and termed frigates; they carried much the same canvas as battleships but on a lighter hull, hence they sailed faster. They were designed for use either as auxiliaries to the fleet, seeking out and keeping touch with the enemy fleet, or independently on trade protection and attack on enemy trade. On most overseas stations where there were no ships of the line they were the capital units in the area. Frigates carried their main armament on a single gun deck with lighter pieces and carronades on the quarterdeck and fo'c'sle above; like the liners the new classes had rounded ends and continuous upper decks with high bulwarks; the largest of them had timbers and armament equal to the upper tiers of earlier '3rd rates'; the latest 'Symondites' mounted forty-four 32-pounders and six 8 inch shell guns – heavier armament than the traditional '3rd rate's' upper batteries.

After the frigates came the sloops, some of which came to be called corvettes later, either three-masted and ship-rigged, or two-masted brigs; they carried all their light guns – between eight and twenty – on the upper deck, nothing below. They were economical in cost and manpower and well suited to the inshore and river operations which formed the bulk of day-to-day work; they were the most numerous ships on the overseas stations.

Each ship of whatever rate carried four deep, tapering 'square' sails on her fore and on her main mast, and three above a 'fore-and-aft' gaff-rigged sail, known as the spanker, on the mizen. Between the masts she set four staysails, and right forward three jibs leading from the foremast to the bowsprit and jib-boom. This was 'plain sail', and she carried two suits. She also had a suit of studding sails which could be boomed out either side of the square sails on the fore and main to increase the area of canvas in chase with a light wind astern.

Under plain sail, as the wind freshened, the first canvas to be taken in would be the uppermost, known as the 'royals' on each mast, and the outermost or 'flying' jib. If the wind continued to rise, the very deep topsails – in fact the sails next above the lowest sail on each mast – would be braced round to spill the wind, slacked and rolled and tied at the first line of reef points, then re-set. A further rise in the wind would mean a further reduction of the area of the topsails to the second reef points and the spanker in. If the

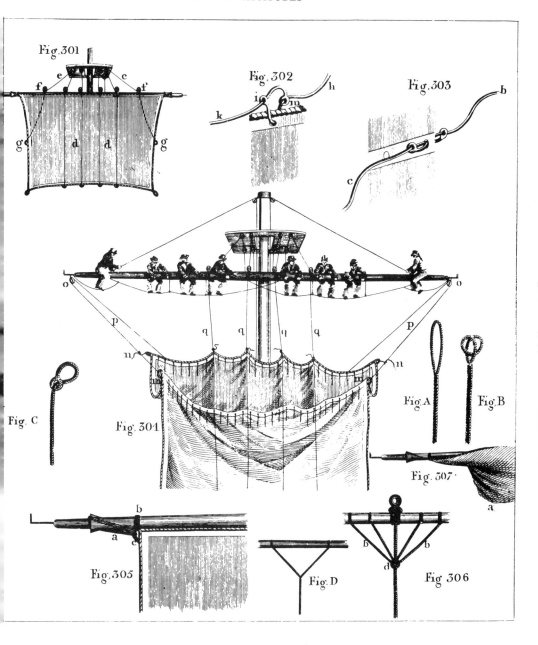

Fig. 301

Fig. 302

Fig. 303

Fig. C

Fig. 304

Fig. A

Fig. B

Fig. 307

Fig. 305

Fig. D

Fig 306

Bending the foresail, Napoleonic War period

[11]

wind was forward of the beam the topgallant sails just above the topsails would be taken in instead.

Those who have only been to sea in iron or steel ships can have no idea of the strange voices of the wooden ship as she strained and lurched under a press of sail against a head sea.[3]

Further rises in wind force would mean the topgallants in and a third reef in the topsails, then a reef in the 'courses' below the topsails, finally a fourth reef in the topsails and the mizen topsail perhaps taken in. If the wind reached gale force, the main course would be taken in and the reefed fore topsail, after which further increases would be met by taking in the main topsail, setting tiny storm staysails and taking in the last of the 'plain' canvas, the reefed fore course. Officers who drove their ships hard had the canvas torn from the sheets.

Because of their apple-cheeked bows and stubby shapes, ships of the line seldom made more than seven knots in the best conditions of wind and sea and a clean bottom; frigates could reach ten knots and 'Symondites' more: daily runs of nearly 240 miles were accomplished by some in steady force 5 trade winds. Nevertheless, for most a speed of 8 knots was 'rattling away'.

In addition to the sailing classes familiar to generations of seamen, were some twenty-seven curious-looking steamers with single tall funnels between their masts and elliptical paddle-wheel sponsons projecting either side amidships. Most were employed as tugs or as mail packets and despatch boats. Few were armed for there were serious objections to their use as fighting ships: the exterior paddle wheels were vulnerable besides masking much of the broadside space normally occupied by the main armament, arguments which applied equally to the ponderous engines and great crankshafts which crossed the upper decks, spilling oil as they revolved. Even more serious for a Navy which relied on a battle fleet strategy of close blockade off the enemy's ports for months at a time, and whose trade needed protection over thousands of miles of sea, was their very short endurance under power. Marine steam engines still worked at little over atmospheric pressure, at temperatures little over boiling point, and consequently consumed huge amounts of fuel for the small horsepower they produced, fuel that like the engines took up valuable space and was exhausted all too quickly. One steamer which made a passage of eighty-eight days from Falmouth to Bombay in 1837 spent twenty-five of them coaling at various ports en route.

Nevertheless, while the steamers were looked on chiefly as ancillary to the fleet, not as prototypes of a new kind of Navy, there were obvious uses for them both for coast defence at home, and for active river and coastal operations overseas, particularly against slave traders. For these warlike purposes they were equipped with shell guns on pivot mountings which could command both broadsides from the upper deck.

By 1837 these small gunboats had proved their value on many occasions, and that year was in some respects a turning point. Although it saw the Admiralty reject the Swedish designer Ericsson when he came with designs for a screw propeller that would do away with at least one of the steam-warship's disadvantages, it also saw the establishment of an engineering branch of the Service on a permanent footing, with engineers appointed by Warrant to rank just below the other practical heads of department, boatswains, gunners, carpenters, instead of being supplied by the firm that provided the machinery. And apprenticeships were established to provide future engineers – sought as fitters rather than theoreti-

Model of a screw frigate

cally educated men. The overall head of the new department, Chief Engineer and Inspector of Machinery, had been appointed two years previously from outside the Service. Undoubtedly the steamer had arrived.

Another, less obvious herald of transformation from the old Navy was the gunnery training school, HMS *Excellent*, moored in Portsmouth harbour. There had been nothing like her in the great wars; drilling men at the great guns and in small arms had been a matter for individual Captains and had varied according to their experience and inclination, while the business of preserving the powder in the damp old ships and making it up into cartridge of the correct weight for each calibre of gun at each stage of an action had been a matter for the Gunner and his mates, relying on strange formulae handed down through centuries. Now, in the *Excellent*, the Service had an establishment which had begun to replace individualism and craft lore with standardised training and scientific experiment. Although it was concerned chiefly with spreading the best of the old methods

The gunnery training school, HMS *Excellent*, established 1840

it was a natural focus for testing new inventions in every field, not only gunnery. Above all, it was a seed bed for those twin attendants of the industrial age, regimentation and specialisation. As the engineer was infiltrating below decks, chipping away at the sailor's ancient art and pride in managing the whole ship, so the *Excellent* was breeding a special class of seaman-gunner and specialist officer who would do much the same with the ship's armament.

What will you do with your sights at sea where there is motion and the distance is known?
I will raise my sights to the degree required, and lay my gun so that the bore may pass as much above as below the object, and look out to fire the moment it is brought on by the motion.[4]

It was an innocent enough beginning. Yet there were those who perceived the dangers to the Navy as they knew it.

'Pray, sir, what is the meaning of the word impact?' a Lord of the Admiralty asked when shown an *Excellent* examination paper. 'And what in the name of good fortune is meant by initial velocity?'

'I'll be hanged if I know', replied another – Admiral Sir John Beresford. 'But I'll tell you what I think we had better do – we'll just go at once to Lord de Grey' (First Lord) and get the *Excellent* paid off. The Chancellor of the Exchequer is very anxious to get a reduction in the Navy Estimates.'

The Admirals gave Lord de Grey a graphic account of their naval exploits, how they had knocked away masts and yards, riddled hulls, and all the damage they had done. Lord de Grey listened with exemplary patience to all that was said, and rising from his seat assured them that he thought their proposal to pay off the *Excellent* admirable, and then patting Sir John on the back, added, 'But I'm afraid my dear Beresford, I cannot sanction it, for you have no idea how d—d scientific that House of Commons has become.'[5]

It was a curious, intermediate period between the old certainties and the new ideas of material progress. Both were very evident, but they seldom interacted. Naval strength was measured in ships of the line and frigates, naval skill in seamanship and great gun drill – particularly seamanship, which was the preoccupation of all ambitious officers. The times of the various competitive evolutions with which the art was nurtured during the early Victorian years are not recorded, but about mid-century a crack ship could start

[15]

with lower yards and topmasts down and make all plain sail inside five minutes. This was the real Navy; the overwhelming majority of officers and all the prime sailors imagined it would go on for ever; steamers and steam engines were not only beneath their notice, but actively disliked for the smoke which spread soot over sails, rigging and decks, and the coal which spread everywhere below.

Yet the steamer had its enthusiasts among serving officers, even its theorists. Here is Captain Sir John Ross, writing in 1828:

> The ancient rule of forming the line of battle [must] be utterly changed; since the nature and direction of the wind will no longer form the same elements of calculation. . . . Still more a steam vessel may be rendered a single offensive weapon in herself on a system similar to that of the galleys in the time of Rome. . .running down its antagonist by the mere impulse of a fortified stem accompanied by a superior weight and velocity.[6]

Theorists were not confined to steam; 'every ship of those days was pursued by experimentalists' and inventors anxious to bring old methods into line with the possibilities of that bright dawn of technology. New styles of gun carriage were produced; new sights, shells and shell guns, new patterns of anchor, iron chain cable, iron water tanks alongside the old timber casts – even scientific methods of writing up the Log with a scale of wind force invented by the Hydrographer of the Navy, Admiral Beaufort, and a simple code for describing the state of the weather instead of the old generalities.

Still there was no organisation, apart from the tiny nucleus aboard the *Excellent*, for evaluating the riot of invention, or co-ordinating and directing individual effort and disseminating the results – chiefly because there was no need to change in response to experiment – only in response to the French. Most of the new features were in reply to, or imitation of, the old naval rivals. It was not so much that the Admirals at the head of the Service were averse to practical improvements but their habits of mind were naturally pre-industrial; they did not seek technical change to gain advantages, but reacted to each new development or challenge from abroad, and used it – the steam engine, or the shell gun – in the way which appeared to suit its capabilities best while changing the established ways of the Service least. This comfortable, common-sensical attitude suited the conditions well; the practical compulsions of all Boards of Admiralty, at a time of government insistence on economy, were to keep expense to a minimum and at the same time preserve known superiority by retaining existing ships and armaments and dockyards and skills.

This they did. In the dockyards of southern England and up nearby creeks some 58 ships of the line and many more frigates and lesser craft were laid up 'in ordinary' as a reserve. Their condition varied; a few 'demonstration ships' had lower masts and rigging and all internal fittings; most were hulks. A report at the end of 1837 suggested that of the 'line' ships in ordinary only 25 were in a perfect state, 15 needed 'substantial repairs'; the rest were hopelessly decayed. At the same time there were 20 battleships in commission and 11 building. Against these totals the two principal rivals, France and Russia, whose combined naval strength had been used as a yardstick for British strength since the end of the great wars, had 63 line ships in commission or reserve and 36 building. On paper, the 'Two-Power Standard' had been maintained, just; in practice, as the majority of the rival ships in commission belonged to Russia, whose sailors were not sufficiently exercised to be a match for the British it probably had been. But the rotten state of many of the ships in ordinary, the size and power of 20 French ships of the line nearing completion, and the great efforts the Russians were putting in to their Baltic fleet caused alarm at the Admiralty, and prompted increased building programmes of '1st' and '2nd rates'. Such scares about French or Russian building were a constant feature of the Victorian Navy.

CHAPTER TWO

MEN – AND
A FEW WOMEN

Sailors and methods of recruiting them had changed less than ships. There was an unofficial hard core of men-of-war's men at the naval ports, but they were not continuously employed by the Admiralty; they signed on for the duration of a ship's commission and were paid off – those who survived it – some three, or perhaps, four years later. When their money had run out, and it rarely took long, they signed on another vessel, not necessarily a warship. The only concession the Admiralty made to the idea of regular service was to provide a pension of from 10d. to 1s. 2d. a day for anyone whose period of service on naval ships totalled twenty-one years, a smaller pension for those invalided from disease and a larger one for the limbless and wounded; they also offered inducements of extra pay for those trained as gunners aboard the *Excellent*, or rated as Petty Officers; these provided a nucleus of dependable men.

This voluntary system worked because only some 25,000 men and boys were needed for the small proportion of ships in commission in peacetime, and there were over 190,000 sailors and fishermen in the country as a whole. It was recognised that it could not work in a major war and the lack of a reserve of men for the fleet was quite as much of a problem as the poor state of so many reserve ships. 'Pressing', by sending parties aboard merchant ships and around the inns and streets of seaport towns to conscript men forcibly was still legal, but it had been the cause of so many evils and so much unpopularity that it was believed to be impractical. The Admiralty had worked out a modified form for national emergencies by which sailors would have to serve a limited – instead of limitless – term of five years in the Navy on a roster basis; to this end a register of all seamen in the country had been compiled.

These slight shifts from the haphazard ways of the eighteenth century made little difference to the practical matter of manning a

Jack aloft

ship; this was still the Captain's individual responsibility when he took over the vessel he was to commission. What he took over in fact was the stripped down hull of a vessel without masts, armament or stores, which he had to man, then rig, fit out and provision. He was provided with a detachment of Royal Marines, the only ratings for the sea service who were established as a permanent force and who lived ashore in barracks when not serving afloat, and a number of boys from the Royal Navy School for the sons of pensioners at Greenwich, or from the Marine Society, a charity which cared for orphans and other stray children. But for the sailors who would rig and sail and maintain the ship he had to apply in the time-honoured way with handbills posted at the large sea ports.[1]

WANTED, Petty Officers and Able Seamen for His Majesty's Ship
CHILDERS
Commander Henry Keppel
Now fitting out for the Mediterranean Station
N.B. – None but the Right Sort need apply.

The 'right sort' came from the seafaring community based very largely on the naval ports of the south of England, Chatham, Portsmouth, Devonport, an unmistakable breed whose way of life had marked them out from their fellows ashore.

> The men had great arms and shoulders. They could climb but they could not march. They had steady heads aloft, and very unsteady heads ashore. They were artisans in rope and leather and canvas. They were tailors, embroiderers, cooks and washermen. Nothing in them or about them had accurate limits. There was no greatness of soul that they might not ascend to; there was no temptation so light that they might not yield to it. They were artists, not mechanics: and being in constant interchanges of combat and alliance with the uncertain and fickle elements of wind and weather, they were apt to think that everything that occurred was an emergency, so that they themselves partook of that emergent character.[2]

The description by Admiral Colomb, probably the most powerful and sensitive intellect of the nineteenth-century Navy, brings out the marvellous adaptation of man and timber ship; neither had accurate limits, both struck a natural balance between mastery and respect for the elements among which they worked – the very flexible products of art and unpredictable hazard.

'The soldier's uniformity and precision were wholly unsuited to the sailor', another Admiral wrote of those years,

> The sailor had to be capable of instant independent action. . .at any moment he might have to tackle an emergency on his own initiative. If a seaman of the old days noticed anything wrong up aloft, up he would run to put it right without waiting for orders. Life and death often hung upon his promptitude of resources.[3]

[20]

Aloft, the sailors were as quick and agile as monkeys, swarming with bare feet and prehensile fingers and toes amongst the rigging, running out along the yards without holding on to anything, falling sometimes but usually catching hold of a rope or spar and swinging up again; occasionally crashing to their deaths. In the competitive evolutions between ships which they entered with as much zest as the Captain or officers whose reputation and prospects were at stake they were careless of life or limb: 'I once saw the Captain of the Maintop hurl himself bodily down from the cap on a hand who was slow in obeying an order,' Admiral Lord Beresford wrote in his memoirs. 'Certainly,' one sailor wrote,

any officer who had insisted on the precautions laid down by the Regulations would have found his ship eternally last and would have earned the contempt of his men for being a milksop.

Another wrote years later,

I am doubtful if there are many men in the Navy today who would stand bolt upright upon the royal truck of a line-of-battle ship. I was one of those who did so. But in those days fear never came our way.

Every memoir and contemporary account stresses the total absence of fear of the hands and the wild spirit of competition with which every evolution was carried out, against other ships, mast against mast – always against the clock. Every morning aboard an active ship the first evolution would be to cross the upper yards which had been sent down the previous evening. On each mast the leading hand of the royal (or uppermost) yard would perch on a small iron bar known as the 'jack' projecting some 12 to 18 inches either side at the t'gallant masthead, 150 feet above the deck. In one hand he would hold his open knife fastened to a lanyard around his neck, in the other the ring for the rigging which had to be fitted on the royal yard when it reached him. His only support would be a leghold on the thin rope which ran from the royal truck (top) to the 'jack' on which he was poised. The yard itself, lashed vertically to its halyard with a strand of yarns, would rise towards him as the men on deck ran away with the rope.

As the yard came within reach of the leading hand, the strand was cut and the knife left swinging on the end of the lanyard, the ring of the lift and brace was slipped over and a hand came out to let the officer on deck know all was ready. Then came the order 'Sway across!' . . . as the order rang out the leading hand tightened his hold of the yard rope [halyard] and was whipped off his feet into space. He knew that a few feet above was the sheave and that if the swaying yard was not stopped in time his hand would be dragged through and he would be dashed to the deck below. But he had confidence in the watchful eye of the officer and his opposite number attending the stopper. It was just a wild, delirious ten second's gamble with death, then the Boatswain's pipe shrilled out 'High enough!'[4]

Carelessness in its highest form was a feature of these men which was noted with something like awe by most commentators from socially higher backgrounds. Carelessness of danger: 'I saw one of our Jacks make a low bow to a shoot that he saw coming directly at him: at the right moment he bobbed his head, and it passed about a foot above his body'. Carelessness of the future, carelessness of health, turning in with clothes soaked from work on deck, turning out to face biting winds in light cottons; indescribable carelessness with money, taken in and skinned alive by all varieties of land shark and bumboat women who hovered about the ships in port – and equally generous with everything they possessed to any ship-mate on hard times. These were the qualities most often remarked. 'I do not think any one can come up to the bluejackets for selfsa-crificing acts of kindness on behalf of shipmates or friends,'[5] wrote Agnes Weston, the founder of a Sailors' Home for the men of the fleet in Portsmouth.

Below decks in a home port: 'every excess of debauchery . . .'

Saturday night at sea

And naturally they were as careless of the consequences of raw spirits in their brief and riotous periods ashore as they were of the prostitutes that teemed in all seaports, and who swarmed aboard the men-of-war lying out at anchor, with all the hands confined aboard lest they desert. Nevertheless some men managed to desert – disguised as prostitutes. The orgies that took place in the low and ill-lit decks in these circumstances have been described often: release from the rigours and routine, rough spirits, music of fiddle and fife and drum, female company, encouragement to braggadocio, gusty dancing and singing combined to create a heady atmosphere of carnival which resulted inevitably in their prisoned and deprived

[23]

circumstances, in 'every excess of debauchery that the grossest passions of human nature can lead to'. The phrase comes from a *Statement of Certain Immoral Practices prevailing in HM Navy*, written by a naval officer of 1822, but still valid, as the conditions had not changed. Equally valid is the observation from the lower deck: 'What they did during that time was simply the swing back of the pendulum – a phase of that law of compensations which seems to govern everything on this old planet.' Venereal disease – especially syphilis – was rife, and from the scanty figures available appears to have been much more prevalent in the Navy than in the comparably confined and hard-used soldiers ashore. Treatment – not always successful – was by application of mercury ointment.

It would be a libel to suggest that such gross generalisations applied to all sailors: many came from moral homes or were instilled with the rigid religious code of institutions like the Marine Society. Here is one commander of a small vessel:

> The men were a very decent lot and never gave trouble, and the Gunner, a serious-minded man who only wanted to go ashore occasionally on a week-day to attend some extra prayer meeting. . . [6]

And here is the last letter home of a young private of the Royal Marines Light Infantry, written before the battle of Graspan in the Boer War, in which he was killed:

> Well I can still say I am perfectly happy as I am still on Jesus' side, and He makes me to be peaceful and happy. . . . I am in God's hands. God bless you all. Praise God I am still happy, and I am hoping to have a Gospel meeting in camp tomorrow. Good-bye and God bless you. [7]

A few sailors were married, although these were older men, Petty and Warrant Officers, some of whom seem to have taken wives to sea with them; there were also a few female nurses aboard line ships, at least in the early years of Victoria's reign. It would have been impossible for an ordinary seaman on one shilling a day or an Able Seaman on 1s. 2d. a day to have supported wife and family in any conventional sense, particularly as they were not paid the bulk of their wages until the very end of a ship's commission. In a less conventional sense there were perhaps a number of well-married men like George Bolt of the *Asia* in 1836. While lying at the Nore, Bolt asked the Commander to allow his wife on board. [8]

'Which is she?' asked the Commander. Bolt pointed her out.
'That is not your wife.'
'Yes, sir. I am lawfully married to the woman.'
'But that is not the woman you had aboard at Sheerness.'
'No, sir. This is my Portsmouth one.'
'How many have you got?'
'Five. One in Plymouth, one at Portsmouth, one at Sheerness and two in Cork,' said Bolt. And it was true.

Similarly with drink, many knew their limits from shocking youthful experiences or remained sober and steady by conviction despite all difficulties amidst a system designed to encourage rum as the safety valve for bare conditions and harsh discipline, and in an age when drunkenness was fashionable for men. So much was this the case that after the short and infrequent periods of leave allowed, those who were not carried back insensible and hoisted aboard usually shammed drunkenness.

When the temptations of the shore were left behind, and they could practise their master craft with canvas, hemp, fid, seizing twine, marlin-spike, knife, Stockholm tar, leather palm and sail-maker's needle in the clean breeze with the sky and sea open in every direction these simple, usually unlettered and mostly very young, hard-muscled, taut-bellied men saw more clearly than most

Turned in: berth deck at the end of the century

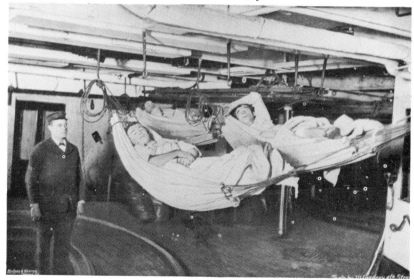

'what a little puny devil man is. The fact is there is a deep sense of religion in those who go down to the sea in ships. Every Minister of God, irrespective of the denomination to which he belongs is treated with respect.[9] Working aloft they sang and swore; they rarely blasphemed.

Off duty they berthed between decks as fighting men had for centuries, slinging hammocks from hooks in the deck-head beams usually less than eighteen inches apart all the way along the forward half of the ship between the guns in rows unbroken by any partition.

> When the men are extended in their beds their bodies are in contact. When at sea with a watch on deck, the accumulation and pressure is reduced by half; but when in secure harbours 500 men perhaps sleep on one deck, their bodies touching each other over the whole space laterally, and with very little space room lengthways. The direct results of elevated temperature and deteriorated air may be conceived. . .[10]

One Surgeon spelled it out: 'in a few minutes after the men have retired to rest the atmosphere around them becomes charged with carbonic acid and animal exhalations'. Warships with small crews were no better off as the berthing space was similarly limited. The Surgeon of one complained of 130 men sleeping in a space 54 feet by 6 feet, giving them less air 'than is enjoyed by the inhabitants of the lowest lodging houses in the narrowest alleys of London', conditions that were shared in most ships with the pigs for the Captain's table, kept in a manger right forward. At sea in foul weather the situation was at its worst for although one watch might be on deck, the only means of ventilation through open gun ports and open hatches with windsails rigged above them to catch the breeze could not be used; everything was battened down. The only lavatory area was at the 'head' of the ship out over the bows, where 'seats of ease' – as one Admiralty draft has it – and urine gutters were fashioned on a grating between the cathead and the bowsprit. These could not be used without some hazard and discomfort, and as dysentery was a common complaint, the conditions below decks may be imagined.

It is easy to exaggerate this picture. Accounts from the lower deck itself seldom mention either sanitary arrangements or overcrowding; for one thing most ships were stationed in the Mediterranean or tropical areas where prolonged foul weather was not such a feature as it would have been in the North Atlantic. Intense heat was more memorable, and then the men slept on the upper deck or wherever they could find a soft plank; for another there was nothing quite as clean and bright as a warship under normal conditions. Decks were scrubbed every morning, paint was washed, brasswork polished – all before the breakfast half-hour at 6.30, and the men took great pride in the neatness and order of the particular section of deck allotted to their mess – consisting of eight people – indulging the same kind of rivalry as they did over sail drill. 'Our lower deck was well worth looking at', one sailor wrote of his first ship in 1836, 'and many Captains and officers were quite astonished when they saw it.' Compared with the poorer quarters of the large towns, where sewage ran down the streets or overflowed from backyard cesspits, a man-of-war was a model of hygiene; naval surgeons spent a great deal of time trying to persuade Captains *not* to wash the decks so often as it kept the timbers constantly damp between decks and aggravated the numerous rheumatic and bronchial complaints.

Food was as sparse as the accommodation, and the official ration which never varied from week to week or winter to summer, from polar to tropical zone except at ports where fresh meat or vegetables were taken aboard, was sickeningly monotonous. Breakfast was a pint of cocoa or chocolate without milk, together with bread, termed 'biscuit' – the notorious 'hard tack', baked at the home victualling

Aboard a gun boat in the China war

[27]

establishments to a tooth-breaking brittleness and stored in ships' holds or on foreign stations often for several years until it was alive with weevils and maggots. The tales about it are legion: 'there was never any necessity to ask anyone to pass the bread. . .all that had to be done was to have a piece placed on the table in the right direction and it would walk over to its required destination'; 'the only fresh meat we got was in the biscuit'. 'In reality,' a midshipman of those years remembered, 'we never ate the weevils if we could help it. The biscuit was always well baked before being brought to table, and before eating it a few hard taps on the table brought out the little browned carcasses.' A sailor's memoir suggests that this was not so on the lower deck: 'You had to get into a dark corner so as not to see what you were eating.'

Dinner was piped at noon; at sea on salted rations it was a pound of beef one day, pork the next in endless alternation.

> Most of the salt beef and pork had been in barrels knocking about the station for years, and was so tough and stringy, especially the beef, that it required strong teeth and still stronger appetites to deal with it at all as food. The beef, when cold, was as hard as wood, and resembled nothing so much as fine-grained mahogany or rosewood. Indeed it would take a splendid polish and could be made into snuff boxes or other fancy articles.[11]

With the pork went a thick pease soup, with the beef a quantity of flour, and once a week suet and raisins which could be mixed into a duff – and always 'biscuit'. The preparation of this diet was the responsibility of the men themselves; each mess elected a 'cook' for the week and during the early morning, while the hands were cleaning the decks the 'cooks' would go with their mess tubs at the pipe, 'Hands of the mess for meat!' to collect the rations. The meat would be weighed out from the evil-smelling casks by the butcher, with the Purser or an assistant in attendance to read out the quantities due to each mess, and a Petty Officer and a Corporal of Marines as representatives of the ship's company. Each 'cook' would return to his mess, a collapsible table with benches either side between the guns, and prepare the lumps of gristle and fat and the pease or flour as best they could with whatever extras or seasonings the mess had been able to buy from the Purser's private store or 'canteen', or from the bumboats at the last port of call. When they had done what they could among the brooms and swirling water they would take their preparations up to the galley situated by the foremast and leave them with the one-legged or otherwise invalided Ship's Cook, who would deposit all the offerings in one enormous copper, any vegetables, pease or puddings also going in, put into duck bags bearing the mess number. On fresh meat days in harbour the same system applied except that the meat was taken up to the cook in tin dishes for baking instead of boiling.

> The Ship's Cook, not having sufficient time or oven space to bake all the dinners in time did the following: in the centre of the large square copper lid is a small round lid for the purpose of letting out steam without entirely uncovering the copper. Taking off this small lid the Ship's Cook would pile the dishes of meat round and over it pyramid fashion, then cover the lot with sacks to keep in the steam; just before seven bells (11.30 a.m.) they would be taken off and popped in the oven to 'brown off'. I shall not attempt to describe such a dinner as an eatable article; readers must bring their own imagination to bear. . .'[12]

That description comes from later in the century, but it is unlikely that things had changed; in any case it conveys well the attitude to food and cooking facilities for the hands. It can be parallelled by the facilities provided for the cheapest class of emigrants, the steerage, in merchant ships of the time.

Tea, called 'supper', taken between 4.30 and 5 p.m., consisted of tea without milk and the ever-present biscuit; after that there was nothing save the evening 'grog' ration until breakfast at 6.30 the following morning.

These official rations provided some 2,900 calories a day – that is on the assumption that they could all be eaten, although it is clear from all accounts that they could not. By modern standards, this is about three quarters of the calorie intake required by a hard-labouring man. As it sometimes occurred that ships on long cruises had to go on short rations, and as labour was both hard, and in bad weather almost continuous, it is no wonder that the prevailing feeling at sea was a gnawing hunger. Many sailors still chewed tobacco to assuage it, although the habit died out gradually through the century, and invariably the first thing on signing off a ship or on their infrequent shore leave was to go for a mighty 'feed'. They chose establishments which provided hard drink as well, and it sometimes occurred that they literally ate and drank themselves to death.

But once again the picture was not always as grim as a recital of official figures suggests. At most ports fresh fruit and other foodstuffs were bought or bartered from the bumboats that crowded around, and fresh meat was often taken aboard on the hoof, not solely for the Captain and Officers. 'At the Cape we shipped thirteen bullocks for fresh meat as a change from salt pork,' wrote one sailor of a line-of-battleship of 1841. And here is an account from a sloop on the east coast of Africa:

> Having received some 20 or 30 bullocks, besides sheep, pigs etc., which made our main deck appear more like a farmyard than a battery, we sailed from Zanzibar . . . I remember, after sailing from Johanna, once having as many as 50 bullocks between the guns on the main deck, besides sheep, etc. the hay being stowed under the spanker boom.[13]

Then there was fishing, permitted from certain positions, and on the anti-slave and anti-piracy patrols that occupied the smaller vessels on distant stations the men spent days and sometimes weeks at a time in the ships' boats when fresh fish and fowl provided a full and satisfactory diet. Netting fish with the huge seine nets provided for all ships by the Admiralty was another source of fresh and tasty food, as well as providing splendid sport for all hands. The delights of 'seining' parties are mentioned in many memoirs.

> An officer always viewed a beach with two thoughts, one for sand for holystoning the decks, two for its availability for hauling the seine net. . .when we arrived a haul was in progress and I and the other officers 'tailed on' to the lines in duty bound. As the net approached the shore the fish began to spring and jump like wild things – it was the largest haul yet made, but the rush to escape was so great and continual, and the fish were so large, that we began to dash after individuals, and to capture them in the shallows. In the heat of the proceedings I found myself doubled up on my hands and knees in the water endeavouring to collar two enormous, violent, unruly fishes and to keep my watch from being wet at the same time, while all around fish were leaping and splashing, men yelling and shouting and a general chaos of fun, fish and confusion.[14]

Another reason why the official rations do not tell the whole story was the system of drawing an allowance of money known as 'savings' in lieu of rations. This money was then used to buy more edible foodstuffs from the Purser who took stocks to sea with him as a private commercial venture. In other ships the men themselves clubbed together to buy a quantity of provisions on credit in the name of the ship's company while the ship was commissioning, appointing Managers for the stock and fixing retail prices. This was known as a 'canteen'; but it was not universal as some Captains would not allow it. However the system grew steadily until it was actually written in to the King's Regulations and Admiralty Instructions with rules designed to safeguard the men from exploitation by the canteen managers, and to ensure that profits went to form a fund for the benefit of the ship's company. Of course it was not possible to divorce the management of the canteen from the authoritarian structure of the lower deck, where discipline was maintained by the Master at Arms and Petty Officers, and there is little doubt that these men did exploit the hands, and take what they regarded as the legitimate perks of their status out of high canteen prices. Nevertheless, with a well-run canteen men had a great deal more variety than the official diet suggests.

In addition to food, which they cut up with the knives they used about the rigging and ate with iron spoons helped with fingers as no cutlery was supplied, all hands were allowed a gallon of beer a day, or local wine if the beer ran out or became sour, and a quarter of a pint of rum which was mixed with water in the proportion two to one and served twice a day: half after dinner, half after supper. In the tropics it was perhaps mixed with lemon or lime juice dispensed to prevent scurvy. Men were allowed to take 'savings' instead of grog but were not allowed to give or barter it to others. Needless to say the rule was unenforceable; tots of rum were a prime article of exchange, particularly for services rendered, and despite all precautions and ceremonial with which the grog issue was attended it was always possible to buy a bottle of the neat stuff on the lower deck. For one thing Warrant and Petty Officers drew their ration, and probably rather more, from the rum barricoe before it was watered for general issue to the cooks of the messes at 12.30. Many men, by all accounts, saved up their dinner ration to have in the evening after the day's work, or even saved it in bottles for days, and then drank themselves insensible. Drunkenness was not confined to the men.

Two geese were pets of the ship's company. One day the Captain. . .came across the geese unable to stand and apparently drunk. He sent for his steward and asked him what was the matter with the geese. 'Drunk, sir, they attend the grog tub every day and nearly all the cooks of the messes give them

The Old Hunks goes to Night Quarters
(A libel on Parmaster North)

Drunkenness was not confined to the men

grog'. The Captain said, 'You know the rule; if a man is found drunk his mess's grog is watered for three days. If I hear of the geese being drunk again I will water both yours and the boys' grog.'[15]

While there were many cases of insubordination, and many accidents, caused by drunkenness at sea, the majority of men amused themselves for most of the time without indulging in excesses. Some of the accounts of days spent running down the trade winds suggest an idyllic state of affairs after the routine of the day ended with supper. One officer's journal from 1843 records:

This has been a beautiful day. If we had not a foul wind I should enjoy it above all things. At 6 p.m. we turn the hands up to dance and skylark, and the men on one side are dancing to the bugle and fiddle; on the other they are playing at two or three different games, all looking so happy![16]

Dancing on deck was popular throughout the Victorian and Edwardian eras

That this is not just a view from the quarterdeck is demonstrated by a parallel account from the lower deck of the line of battle ship *Asia* in the Mediterranean in 1840.

> Every night after quarters at sea or in harbour it was 'Hands to dance and skylark!' The fiddlers were on the main deck and the band sometimes on the quarterdeck. The band played on the poop every evening at 8 o'clock and the drum and fife band as well, until the 9 o'clock gun. On the forecastle and gangways you would see games of all sorts, such as 'Beat the bear', 'Sling the monkey', 'Hunt the slipper', 'Follow my leader', 'Jump back leapfrog' and many other games. The officers would have their games on the quarterdeck.[17]

'Sling the monkey' was a game popular with officers as well, and was played on quarterdeck and fo'c'sle well into the twentieth century.

Sling the monkey

In this game one of the players is made to put his head and arms through a loop at the end of a rope fast at the masthead. It is not quite long enough for the feet to rest upon the deck, and with every push the occupant of the loop, the 'monkey', is set swinging away, to receive whipping blows from the others as he passes to and fro. They are all armed with large handkerchiefs rolled up very tightly and fastened at each end to prevent them unrolling. The 'monkey' is also armed with a similar weapon, and if he can succeed in touching one of his tormentors with it, the latter has to take his place.[18]

These descriptions raise more doubts about the supposed calorie intake of Victorian men-of-war's men – hard work from 4.45 a.m. until 4.30 p.m., hard play from 5 p.m. until nightfall, all on less than 3,000 calories!

Not all leisure was spent so physically; sing-songs on deck are a feature common to most accounts.

Mess table at the end of the century; knives and fingers

Ship's concert party: Widow Twankey and the Magician and The Grand Vizier, his son and 'Pekoe's Pal'

In the evening the men always sang, and it was very fine to hear a chorus of about 800 men and boys, many of the latter with unbroken voices. We had one young man who used to sing 'A che' la morte' and other tenor songs from Verdi's operas as well as many singers that I have heard on the stage. The songs however were not always of this high class . . . we midshipmen knew all the men's songs, and their parlance which was sometimes strong; many of their comparisons and similes were often witty and original.[19]

That reminiscence of Admiral Sir Percy Scott refers to the 1860s. In the very early years of Victoria's reign few if any conventional airs would have been rendered, only the traditional sea songs, known as 'Fore-bitters' after the rostrum, the fore bitts, on which the soloist stood. The rest of the company squatted on deck or on coils of rope or gun carriages, and joined in the choruses.

There was something moving in the contrast between the perfect silence with which a crowd of men closely packed in a small space listened to each stanza and the volume of sound put forth by earnest voices in chorus. In the Fore-bitter the singer had no accompaniment. He trusted to his voice alone. The songs

[36]

Officer recreation on deck in the 1880s: deck hockey. Note the exceptionally high deckheads of the transitional battleships, especially in comparison with the old wooden walls

were almost always of great length, and any failure of memory on the part of the singer was practically unknown. As they were not written down they could have been learnt only by listening to them often and attentively.[20]

During later Victorian times, as the sailing community became less of a class apart, and steamship fo'c'sles provided a subtly different atmosphere the old Fore-bitters went the way of other ancient customs, swamped by popular airs and the *double entendres* of the music hall.

Putting on plays or music hall turns was another popular activity, especially in the Mediterranean where there was a large fleet of 'line' ships whose time was spent largely cruising or in harbour, not on the more active duties of the smaller ships outside European waters.

We used to have a play aboard once a week, to which the Governor [of Malta], the Admiral and all the gentry would come. . . . Everyone wanted to know where we kept the women in the ship as they were never seen ashore; they were all young topmen dressed in female clothing.[21]

[37]

Two particular occasions set aside for revelry were Christmas Day and Crossing the Line; both had their established ritual although each ship's company played out minor variations. At Christmas the mess deck was hung with elaborate decorations made by the sailors themselves and each mess displayed mottoes and verses with strong patriotic messages, comments on characters and events of the commission, or wry statements of grievances which the men hoped might be attended to. Here is one from the liner *Asia* in 1836:

> A Another Christmas day we greet
> S Success attend our noble fleet
> I In friendship let us all be seen
> A And united sing 'God Save the Queen'[22]

All routine was suspended from after supper on Christmas Eve until Boxing Day and the cooks of the messes busied themselves through the night preparing Christmas dinners from delicacies bought and saved up for the occasion. Efforts were always made to ensure fresh beef or other meat for the feast, and there was inevitably raisin-stuffed duff. On the day itself the senior hands, Boatswain's Mates, Quartermasters, Captains of the Tops took over the duties of the boys, while the youngest became captains of tops for twenty-four hours. After church service the band played 'The Roast Beef of Old England' while Captain and officers walked the mess deck admiring the decorations and mottoes. This was the traditional time for a crew to show displeasure with unpopular regimes by sullen silence, but for respected Captains and officers there were chairs to carry them around the deck to the strains of 'For he's a jolly good fellow' – often declined in favour of the youngest midshipman aboard – and invitations to share tots. After dinner and an extra allowance of grog the men enjoyed total absence of restraint; it was the one day smoking was permitted on the lower deck, and there were the usual games, drinking, music, dancing; often ending up with the majority insensible. Here is a description of a Christmas sing-song aboard a small ship in the tropics:

> Once singing was started the general discomfort was forgotten
> and men who had not given voice during the commission joined
> in . . . from song we passed to choruses only, then as the spirit
> of the occasion gained sway swung off into a wild dance around
> a midship stanchion. The mess tables were cleared away and
> round and round we went, now 'Marching through Georgia',

now trolling the last popular chorus learnt before leaving England, later letting the whole world know 'We'll rant and we'll roar like true British seamen', carried out in letter and spirit. Clothes except silk handkerchiefs for loin cloths long since cast aside, and as we swung round in wild abandon and a thick fog of tobacco smoke, a wet track was left on the deck from our reeking bodies.[23]

The hands were left very much on their own at Christmas, but Crossing the Line was a ceremony in which both officers and men mixed freely and roughly. Here is a description from a small 16-gun brig in the 1850s. The evening they approached the Equator the sailor who was to play the part of Neptune dressed and hid himself under the bowsprit, while a Quartermaster with a good voice was sent into the chains with a hand lead line – although of course there was no bottom for a thousand fathoms. Meanwhile, fire hoses were rigged, buckets full of water placed in the fore top and a tar barrel lashed at the lee cathead.

The Quartermaster called out ever-reducing soundings; 'By the mark five – and a half four – by the deep four –' at which all hands were piped on deck to shorten sail. Neptune, under the bowsprit, cried,

'Ship ahoy! What ship is that?'

'Her Britannic Majesty's Brig, *Siren*.'

'Where are you bound?'

'Rio de Janeiro.'

'Heave to and I'll come aboard!'

As all hands were grouped below the fore top hauling on the buntlines, leechlines, clew garnets and braces to bring the brig to, the water buckets were emptied over them and the fire hoses directed at them; in the shouting and confusion Neptune climbed up over the bows with his trident and bright crown, and made his way to where the Captain was waiting to receive him on the quarter-deck. There he delivered a short and flowery speech asking after the health of the Queen, her consort Prince Albert and the royal family, and about the latest news. The Captain replied, asking in his turn what ships had passed – to which Neptune answered with the name of a vessel that had left port shortly before them. The Captain's steward then produced a bottle and they toasted the Queen, after which Neptune made his way back to the fo'c'sle and departed the way he had come, calling out that he would be back at nine the following morning to initiate those of the crew who had not previously entered his watery dominions. As he departed in the

Manning the capstan to weigh anchor

dusk, the tar barrel at the cathead was set alight and dropped into the water.

The next morning at breakfast time we battened down all hatches except the companion, got up a studding sail from the nettings, secured it to the gunwale of the pinnace and filled it with water, placed plenty of buckets of water near the hatchway and draped a flag over the field gun carriage to be used as Neptune's car. As each victim appeared on deck blindfolded he got it in the neck; any who turned rough got a double hose. The 'Barber' (the 1st Lieutenant) was ready with his 'razor' made out of a rough piece of hoop iron, his paint brush and his 'lather' pot; while shaving his customers he asked them questions and every time they opened their mouths to answer, in went the lather brush. The 'Doctor' was there with his pills, medicine and 'smelling salts' bottle with a lot of pins stuck in the cork. The 'Secretary' called out the names, the 'Constables' stood by with treenails for staffs, and the 'bears' hauled the carriage to the music of a fife and drum; on it were seated Neptune brandishing a trident, 'Amphitrite' (his 'Queen') and a small boy, all the actors dressed in their different rigs. After 'shaving', each victim was tipped backwards into the sail, then unblindfolded and soundly ducked; some who had given trouble or were unpopular bore the marks of it for days.'[24]

These glimpses of leisure and the few age-old customs which provided a break in routine soften the outlines of life on the lower deck of a man of war, but scarcely affect its stark essentials. The men lived under a code of discipline sanctioned by physical brutality. This ascended from informal 'starting' by the Boatswain's Mates – chasing men about their tasks with a rope's end, or more formally making a man run the gauntlet of several Boatswain's Mates with knotted ropes on the upper deck – right up to the ancient ritual of a flogging at the gangway, a ceremony attended by all the ship's company and officers in full dress. The miscreant, bare-backed and with a leather pad to bite on, was lashed spread-eagle to an upright grating and given from a dozen to four dozen full-weight athletic blows with a cat-o-nine-tails, which lacerated his flesh and scarred him for life. And beyond summary corporal punishment there were still twenty-two offences for which a Court Martial might pronounce sentence of death; on occasions they did so. Execution was carried out in the time honoured way: from a noose at the starboard fore yardarm:

> At 8 a.m. the *Rodney* fired a gun and the men ran away with the rope. There was a toggle about a fathom from his neck but he went up with such force that it carried away the toggle and stranded the rope.[25]

While this was exceptional, a flogging at the gangway was more or less routine on most ships, awarded for leave breaking, drunkenness, insolence, leaving post of duty, stealing a boat with which to desert. Admiral Colomb recalled:

> The practice was to clear off old scores, and shake off the

Petty officers at the turn of the century

lethargy of smooth harbour residence by a good flogging match the first time after leaving the land. And while there were generally blue jackets [sailors] in a condition for the exercise, it was certain there would be a large batch of marines. It was then the custom of the service, and no one minded it much. There was a certain art in being flogged which was taught on the lower deck, and a fine marine in good practice would take four dozen with a calmness of demeanour which disassociated the lash from the idea of infliction of pain by way of punishment and warning, and connected it up in people's minds with any of the ordinary and routine operations to be carried out on board ship, such as scrubbing decks.[26]

That was one officer's view. Here is another; it comes from the journal of a young and intelligent Lieutenant a week or so out from home in a newly commissioned ship in 1843:

The Captain flogged that man (found drunk) this morning; gave him three dozen, and wound up with a short and appropriate speech. We were all much pleased with the Captain's behaviour as the first flogging is generally taken as a criterion of his future conduct towards the ship's company in the way of supporting his officers.[27]

The lower deck could inflict equally brutal punishment when its own code of conduct was outraged — for instance by stealing from a shipmate.

Two chests were placed amidships, one atop the other and securely lashed to stanchions either side, and two hammocks were lashed to these, one up and down, one crosswise. The victim sat looking on with a blanched face, and was then seized and lashed spreadeagle across the hammocks and given four dozen with a hammock clew, in effect a cat of 22 tails made of special kind of rope called 'nettle stuff'.[28]

Other official punishments were confinement in cells, extra duty, putting men on a 'black list', stopping leave — of which there was little enough in any case — diluting grog with six parts of water ('sixes') or any device the Captain could think up to suit the crime or his own temperament. Keeping the whole ship's company short of water, half a pint per day in the torrid heat of the West Coast of Africa, was one Captain's way of showing his dissatisfaction. Another had halters made weighing forty-two pounds with hinges and padlocks to fit around men's necks. Probably the commonest way of showing general dissatisfaction with the smartness or efficiency of a ship's company was to make them repeat their drills, or even to keep them continuously at different drill. Here is an extreme case which occured in one small and unhappy ship after the hands had refused to sing one evening when the Captain requested it.

> The hands were turned out at 4 o'clock in the morning to scrub decks though it was not a Saturday, and from then on right through the day we weighed anchors, dropped anchors, made plain sail, unbent sail, went to general quarters, etc. until we realised the 'Old Man' was getting his own back with a vengeance. At 4 p.m. the hands went to supper, after which we were piped to evening quarters and ordered to 'Man and arm boats!'[29]

So it went until the Captain, inflamed with drink and passion, went too far and tried to have two of the larger boats hoisted together. This proved impossible with the number of hands available, and when the men 'as though at some pre-arranged signal threw the boats' falls on deck and walked forward', he lost control completely. The upshot was that the 1st Lieutenant had to arrest him to get him off the deck – after safeguarding himself by asking each officer separately, 'Is the Captain drunk or sober?' Eventually the besotted man was invalided home instead of being court-martialled. It is interesting that until he had taken that last step over the edge of what was possible the men had done all he had required of them for more than twelve hours without a thought of disobeying indeed 'the general feeling [had been] one of unexpressed admiration of the way the Captain had retaliated'.

More pervasive forms of discipline than those meted out by the Captain were instilled by the Ship's Police and Petty Officers, and by the men themselves; in such a close-crowded community of har-

Brought by the lee

dened, *careless*, often wild characters living in hazard from the elements and with a constant sense of emergency generated by officers whose ideas of smartness were closely connected with the speed at which everything was done, the slow, the unhandy and the weak could not survive the censure of their fellows. Handling a sailing ship was an exercise in team-work; a man's life often depended on the whole crew fighting her through foul weather. Added to this, in a man-of-war, was the constant competition between ships and between different divisions in a ship so that team work became ingrained and team discipline, mostly self-imposed as a desire to be well-thought of by the other team members, was a dominant factor. Standards of excellence were set by the best *men*, not by the officers: 'the upper yard men were a specially picked elite, to be referred to as the smartest royal man in the fleet was to reach a pinnacle of fame.'

Below these heights of daring and agility a man was allocated to a 'division' according to his ability: the most experienced sailors were the Forecastlemen who manned the fore yard and worked the foresail, staysail, jibs and all the forward gear; they wore their hats a little differently from the common run. Then came the fore topmen, main topmen and mizen topmen who manned and worked the upper yards on these masts, the Gunners, generally old and steady men who worked the main yard and mainsail as well as looking after the guns and their carriages and lastly the afterguard, the least efficient section which worked on the quarterdeck under the eye of the Commander and officers. With such differences in status and constant rivalry between the divisons, discipline in much of the work about the ship came more from individual and team self-respect than from authority.

It was another matter with the petty rules necessary at other times to govern such a large number of men living such a confined existence. The administration of this kind of discipline was the province of the ship's Police or ship's Corporals, known as 'Crushers', men recruited from Marines or Able Seamen of good character.

They enjoyed the status of Petty Officers and their chief, the Master at Arms, known as the 'Jonty' or 'Jaunty' from the French *Gendarme* was overlord of the lower deck. Their position between the Officers and the hands in a Service and an age in which respect for superior rank was ingrained, gave them immense powers of patronage, and they ran their dominion between decks with a blend of blackmail and violence, turning a blind eye or granting favours in return for money or services or simply to be 'in' with the natural leaders of the lower deck. At the same time they wielded their canes or ropes' ends freely in the atmosphere of 'rush' which had become an integral part of the system. In lower deck accounts they have an unenviable reputation, accused of running espionage organisations, even of provoking offences so that they might report men and justify their otherwise 'useless idle lives.' One explanation from the lower deck accounts for this in terms of the type of men who applied for the job.

> Able Seamen who could never hope to become seamen Petty
> Officers or whose temperament did not fit them for the
> strenuous life on deck, would change their rating to ship's
> Police. . .and immediately commence to lord it over those who
> had hitherto treated them with the contempt that a 'failure'
> always receives.[30]

Certainly many seem to have enjoyed their power and the opportunities for brutality. Here is one who was found out:

> The Master at Arms one day tied a boy to two hammock hooks
> above a gun and every time he passed gave the boy a stroke
> with a cane. Someone saw it and told Joe, the Boatswain's Mate
> who was looking after the boy, about it. Joe got the Commander
> down and he was caught in the act. Next morning the hands
> were turned up, the Master at Arms was disrated, the corner of
> his discharge cut off and his jacket turned inside out. The ship's
> Corporal had to put a rope around his neck. They beat to
> division and he was led around all decks and as he was going
> over the side the Captain said, 'You blackguard, you are
> leaving the ship with a halter around your neck and that is the
> way you will go out of this world.[31]

Besides illustrating the way boys were looked after and taught their business by an older hand, not necessarily a Petty Officer, who constituted himself a 'sea daddy', the account disposes of any

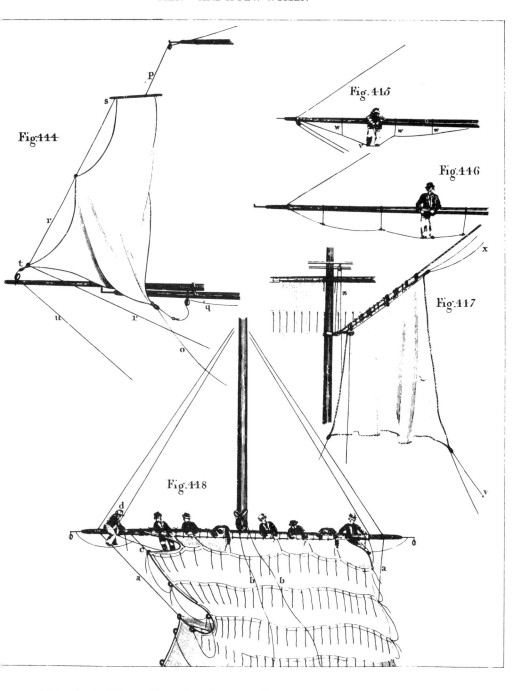

Taking in studding sails and reefing topsails

idea that sadism was a normal ingredient of discipline in a man-of-war. There were sadistic and insensitive officers who could use the savage sanctions of the Articles of War to support tyranny; there were Ship's Police who used their positions to bully or to pick on every petty infringement, yet the normal régime was far less dramatic: rough, certainly, because the hands were rough, arbitrary yet loose fitting in many areas like a familiar coat, worn usually with tolerance and good humour on both sides of the dividing line.

> Had they [Ship's Police] conscientiously carried out the harsh and stupid regulations that existed in the name of discipline the Navy would have been in a blaze of mutiny long since. In selling favours they broke the regulations into fragments and so made life for the men possible.[32]

As for the men, they did not know discipline in the modern or military senses of the word. If a sailor was called up before the Commander for some offence,

> he did not stand to attention like a marine, but shifted from one foot to the other, hitched his breeches, fiddled with his cap, scratched his head. 'Well, sir,' said he, 'it was like this. . .' and he began an interminable yarn. 'That'll do my man,' quoth the Commander. But, not at all. 'No, sir, look here, sir, what I wants to say is this. . .' and so on until the Commander had to order a file of Marines to march him below.[33]

He did not wear a uniform, although the rig he made himself from blue, white or check material bought from the Purser had developed into something very like one. The trouser legs were wide at the bottom so that they could easily be rolled above the knee for washing decks and did not strain at the knees when a man was climbing aloft. The loose upper garment known as a frock was tucked into the waistband of the trousers and had a white collar which was said to have been pulled up around the head and held in position by the hat against wind and weather in former times; now it was usually decorated with rows of white tape around the edge.

A pocket at the breast held a knife, whose lanyard went around the neck over knotted black, silk neckerchief – used in action to bind around the ears and shut out some of the deafening roar of the cannon. On his head he wore a round straw hat tipped back so that he could see aloft, or one covered with duck and painted a shiny black. His feet were bare. For inspections and shore he wore a short blue jacket – which earned him the title 'bluejacket', although some officers called him simply 'Jack' — and a pair of shoes, often with shiny buckles. These garments looked generally similar because all Purser's supplies, known as 'slops' were similar, but there were almost as many variations in cut and decoration as there were men to wear them. One Admiral remembered 'they used to embroider their collars and their fronts with the most elaborate and beautiful designs'. Some Captains encouraged these fancies, others wouldn't have them; still others had their gig's crew or the whole ship's company rigged in livery of their own design and colour like coachmen or footmen.

Such in essence, but without accurate limits, was 'Jack', the man-of-war's man. He accepted the privations as he accepted the hazard of his life, and the rewards, never measured in financial or material terms, but real enough. His skills provided him with deep satisfaction, his environment with wonder and challenge. His spirits rose when it came on to blow; he sang most under stress of

On board the *Highflyer*, 1855

weather, and in between long periods of monotony he packed in more unusual incident and adventure than he could hope to meet in a shore berth. If he served for long enough to enjoy his pension – a privilege accorded few others in his position – he could:

> recall many pleasant memories as well as many hardships and privations. I love the sea and have never regretted the step I took as a youngster when I joined the Navy.[34]

The Lords of Admiralty believed his conditions 'superior to that of almost any class of person who must earn his subsistence by the sweat of his brow'. Most of his officers – who were often very attached to him, an attachment repaid in full – believed him well looked-after by comparison with merchant ships and foreigners, and his predecessors of the great wars.

> I partly remember one of our Captain's little speeches to the men before going on shore: 'Well, men, you are going on shore again with a good suit of clothes and plenty of money in your pockets. Write home and ask any of your friends if there is any nation under the sun which treats their men like England. I am sorry to say some of you will not be very long on shore before you will be rolling about beastly drunk. Oh, that cursed drink!'[35]

Issuing grog at the turn of the century

CHAPTER THREE
OFFICERS

The Captain of a man-of-war was a monarch within his ship. His power was not absolute, but nearly so. He could not declare war – at least against a European power. He could not sentence a man to death, nor since a humanitarian outcry in the press and service journals could he have a man flogged without recording it in a punishment return which had to be sent to the Admiralty. This seldom deterred him. When in company with other ships he had to follow in line and his crew had to perform evolutions ordered by the Admiral or senior Captain – who would come aboard from time to time to inspect and comment on his ship and company. When sailing alone he would be under orders from the senior Officer on the station – yet these could not be more than general directives; communications were far too slow to permit particular orders to meet the changing situations he might meet. He made his own decisions. He had few constraints.

He dispensed the patronage and enjoyed the ceremonial of a monarch. When he came aboard to the shrill and quaver of a Boatswain's pipe, the Marine Guard snapped to the present, assembled officers uncovered their heads, side boys and quartermasters were rigid, and any hands employed about the deck stood away forward. He lived in solitary state in a spacious – sometimes leaky – area under the poop at the after end of the quarterdeck. This was partitioned into a day cabin extending the width of the deck at the extreme stern, commanding a splendid view through the row of stern windows, with a lavatory off on the quarter, a dining room and a night cabin. The doors of this suite, guarded night and day by a Marine sentry, led out on to the quarterdeck by the wheel; one side of the deck was reserved for his exclusive use. Except on urgent matters of duty he was not addressed unless he made the first approach. He did not select his commissioned or Warrant Officers

Captain Sir Reginald Poore, Bt., and his Commander aboard the
battleship *Illustrious*, 1901

but he had absolute power over them when aboard, and the rest of
the crew and the aspiring 'young gentlemen' were his men, to 'rate'
or disrate as he judged, to punish as he thought fit, to work for as
long as he liked at whatever tasks or drills he devised. It followed
naturally that he could make or break a ship; no generalisations
will do. Each Captain was an individual rendered more than usually
individualistic by his lonely position and unbounded powers. He did
his duty to the Service and to his crew but the solitary mind without
opposition or constraint could be prey to any delusion of duty. One

of the most tyrannical Captains of the age wrote in his private diary:

> I proceed in charity with all men, not perfect myself, and
> willing to overlook all faults in others provided they do not,
> when I tell them of it, still continue to tread upon
> my corns.[1]

This man's ship was in a state of continual incipient mutiny, with officers confined to their cabins and not on speaking terms when freed. A more common type, 'fairly plentiful in the Navy', was represented by Captain 'Charlie' Brownrigg:

> Bluff of speech, impulsive, passionate, a bit of a tyrant and
> bully, generous to a degree, and simply idolised by the ship's
> company.[2]

The sketch was by a member of the ship's company. These sort of qualities occur time and again in memoirs of the period, and at the highest level they fused into a kind of paternalistic leadership which was so thoroughly in tune with the age, with the men's character and with the Navy's policing tasks as to be inspired. Here is a sketch of Captain Edward Chichester of the *Immortalité*, a little later in the century:

> He was then in the prime of life, and of unbounded energy. In
> face and figure he might have sat for *Punch's* cartoons of 'John
> Bull'; fierce, truculent and hot-tempered, he was as warm-
> hearted, single-minded, obstinate and unreasonable as a child.
> Every characteristic of him, good and bad, was big, and the
> biggest things about him were his love of England and of his
> own West country, his love for his wife and family, his whole-
> hearted pride in the Royal Navy and his devotion to his own
> ship.

> If he could read what I have written, he'd bang on the desk
> with a huge fist, stick out his great jaw and thunder at me,
> 'You've made a fool of "Old Chich"; scratch all that rot out; and
> the old *Immortalité* wasn't *his* own ship either! she was *our*
> ship, Umph! Umph!'

> That was perhaps one reason of his extraordinary
> popularity. . .Even on the quarterdeck, when seeing defaulters,

it was the same. I remember a wretched little ordinary seaman being brought before him for continual drunken leave-breaking. 'Umph! Umph! You miserable little rat,' he growled, 'What are you giving all this trouble for? Why don't you steer clear of those lousy drink shops? Aren't you man enough to know when you have had enough? You're bringing disgrace on the *Immortalité* – your ship – our ship.'[3]

The path to the Captain's exalted station began, as it always had, in the Gunroom; up to 1837 a few aspirants had learned a certain amount of theory at the Royal Naval College, Portsmouth, before being drafted to ships, but after that year the College entry was stopped and all were pitched straight into the rough and tumble of a sea-going ship as First Class Volunteers at the age of twelve or thirteen. The rules for entry were simple; the first was to find a Captain willing to take a lad into his ship, after which the Admiralty had the right to approve; a simple test in writing and arithmetic, and a medical examination were formalities. Later the Admiralty increased its own powers by first regulating the number of boys any Admiral or Captain could 'nominate', then by increasing the academic qualifications and imposing a competitive examination, thereby weeding and selecting.

Officers and petty officers on the quarterdeck of HMS *Shannon*, 1857

But in the early Victorian years it was still a matter of securing the patronage, known as 'interest', of individual officers, and the only real qualification required – though unwritten – was a professional or aristocratic background. During the great wars men of humble origin had been patronised and obtained commissions through ability; now in peace there were drastically fewer opportunities, and openings to commissioned rank had become far more exclusive. Up to mid-century it seems that over 50 per cent of officer entrants were from a professional home – not surprisingly over 60 per cent of these were sons of naval officers, most of the others divided between the Church and the Army – while nearly all the rest came from the gentry or aristocracy, none from humble and almost none from commercial backgrounds. The figure may not be accurate as there are no complete records, but they correctly reflect a trend towards a higher social class.

Once aboard, the hopeful Volunteer began to acquire a sailor's skills naturally by working alongside the men on deck and aloft. Meanwhile his bookwork was looked after, more or less, in between the demands of the ship's active service, by a Warrant Officer 'Schoolmaster', often in the Captain's fore cabin: 'We looked upon it as a waste of time. . .we always tried to evade it by being on duty, any old excuse.'

After two years the Volunteer would expect to be rated Midshipman by the Captain, and would serve in this capacity for at least another four years before taking his examination for Lieutenant; the total sea time required was six years. However, such was the bottleneck of Lieutenants caused by the run-down in the active fleet after the wars that he would not necessarily, or even probably, obtain a commission for several years after that – many never did obtain one and lingered on as very mature, deteriorating or drink-sodden 'Young Gentlemen' well into middle age. Some Midshipmen tried an alternative route to a commission via the navigating branch, passing an examination and being rated 'Master's Mate'. The Master, as of old, was the sailing Master or pilot, and although he was appointed by Warrant and could never hope to be more than Master, the rating Master's Mate had evolved by custom into a possible, though far from certain, path to commissioned rank. There was another kind of 'mate' too, who had entered as Volunteer 2nd class and was genuinely on the way to becoming a Master with no hope of a commission.

All these, the Volunteers, Midshipmen and Mates of both types, together with the Clerk – hoping one day to be a Purser – and the Assistant Surgeon, messed in the Midshipman's berth. In a ship of

[55]

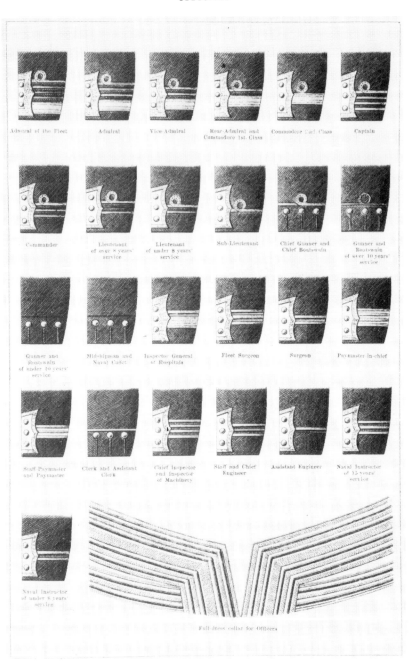

Officers' rank insignia on cuffs, 1900

the line this was a compartment on the lower deck aft, known as the Gunroom, a term which came to be used to describe the Midshipman's mess in a single-decked craft, where it was usually a small side cabin further forward. Much of the space was occupied by a table, around which were lockers whose top surfaces provided a continuous seat. At the start of the voyage the space under the table was often completely occupied by provisions bought to vary the official rations – which were the same as the men's. Light from one or two small scuttles was augmented by lamps burning cocoanut oil and by 'Purser's dips', tallow candles stuck in bottles; 'they repeatedly fetched away when the ship rolled if not steadily looked after.' There was no other heating.

Beneath, on the orlop deck below the waterline in a dark and barely ventilated area known as the cockpit – or in smaller vessels on the same deck just outside the Gunroom – the 'Young Gentlemen' slung their hammocks, each above his own sea chest containing his belongings and basin for washing.

We never washed, because if you spilt a drop of water by your sea chest in which was a basin holding a pint of water, you had to dry holystone the deck, a holystone being a bath brick, and you rubbed the sand into the deck till the wood was spotless white! When the first bathroom was introduced into one of Her Majesty's Ships I heard the First Sea Lord myself say to the Second Sea Lord [scandalised by the innovation] 'Did you ever wash when you went to sea?' 'No,' replied Sir Sidney Dacres. 'No more did I,' said Sir Alexander Milne.'[4]

This reminiscence of Admiral Lord Fisher was no doubt heavily embroidered, according to the custom of the Service, but conveys the authentic attitude.

With the mixture of age and background among the 'Young Gentlemen' and with the older members passed over for promotion with nothing to hope for and 'soured, poor chaps, by the daily sight of backstairs influence at work in pitchforking youngsters over their heads into berths to which they felt they had a just claim' the youngsters were frequently bullied unmercifully, and subject to organised fagging. Despite the ancient custom of jamming a fork in a beam overhead, when all youngsters had to scramble out and leave the mess to the oldsters, they also witnessed scenes of drunkenness, foul language and gross behaviour.

My messmates were of various weights and ages. The oldest

[57]

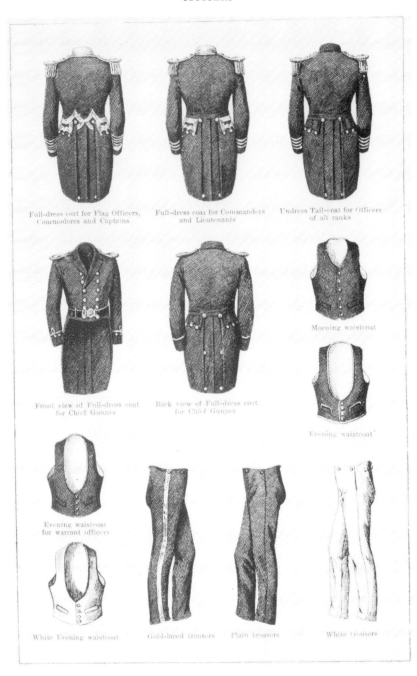

Officers' tail coats, waistcoats and trousers, 1900

was about 36 and the youngest 14. We youngsters were partly made use of for keeping in good condition the muscles of the seniors, and some of them always carried a 'colt' specially prepared for bringing to their senses such juniors as they thought required thrashing. The colt consisted of a piece of rope with a hard knot at one end which, when not in use, was stowed away in the jacket pocket. One of the oldsters was very fond of throwing things at us – especially our own things, and one day I had out my desk and was dutifully writing home when he seized it and flung it at me as hard as he could, the contents going flying and the ink running all over me. But there didn't seem to be anything strange or unusual about it all, or anything to complain of.[5]

It was a way of weeding out the weak, the too-sensitive and others not suited to the rigours of a sea life, and perpetuating the qualities which had made the Royal Navy supreme. Those who flourished in such an environment had to be fearless, spirited, quick-witted, self confident; while of course the practical work with the sailors under all conditions from such an early age made them superb seamen. These were the qualities which distinguished the best Victorian naval officers. Here is Sir William Hewett V.C. portrayed by the hyper-critical Admiral Percy Scott:

In handling a ship under sail he was a master sailor: under fire he was absolutely fearless; and his boldness and swiftness in decision were equalled by his readiness to take any and every responsibility.[6]

This was the kind of man the Navy wanted, and, by and large, the kind of man it got: narrow-minded, intolerant, insensitive, pig-headed, loud-mouthed and tyrannical as many may have been, these also were necessary qualities – over-sensibility and too questioning an approach would not have suited the conditions nor have been respected by the men. The wonder is that there were so many who survived without showing these traits.

Not all gunrooms were gross. The smaller ships particularly often seem to have had happy gunrooms where a rumbustious kind of order and justice was maintained by the oldsters without overmuch arbitrary violence. Here is a view from outside – an Engineer:

This evening I was much pleased to see young Baird, the Sub., reading his Bible before going to sleep. There are many things I observe in him which really speak well of one so young; the more so since he has been brought up in a gunroom, a place as a rule where things having any moral tendency are laughed at. Most of the members are wild, harum-scarum, but at the bottom thoroughly good-hearted and genuine, who in general turn out the good officers and true men, of whom I think W. Baird is a specimen.[7]

It is the *variety* of conditions between gunroom and gunroom and the spirit of 'anything was good enough and nothing was too bad, we thought little of what we had to put up with, and carried everything off with a light heart' which is marked in most accounts. Here is one such which views the 'Old Mates' in a more sympathetic light:

> The duties of these elderly gentlemen were mostly nominal; they were styled mates of the hold or stores, etc. They seldom appeared on deck except on Sundays when they took their week's exercise. Their uniform was a blue coat, in shape like our plain evening dress, anchor buttons and a small white cord edging, white pantaloons, hessian boots, cocked hat and sword. It was considered a compliment to be spoken to by them. . .Down in the Midshipman's berth they reigned supreme, spoke very little before grog time.[8]

By the time a boy was rated Midshipman, he was familiar with the Sailors' work and he would be given responsibility as Midshipman of a 'top' or of one of the ship's boats. Although he had to rely largely on the Petty Officer concerned it provided him with valuable experience of using judgment and initiative in often ticklish, perhaps hazardous situations at an age when his fellows ashore would still be at their books. In the smaller ships on slave or piracy patrol an experienced Midshipman might find himself in command of a 'prize' to be sailed into port or in charge of an armed cutter in an expedition up-river. Independence and the practicalities of command were learned as naturally as seamanship.

> In a sailing ship the Midshipmen were brought into very close contact with the seamen, always working with them aloft, on deck and in boats. . . [they] acquired at an early age that knowledge of the men's customs and ideas which is really the key to managing them.[9]

Midshipmen also stood watches or more usually paced them in

an officer-like manner with the officer of the watch at sea and in harbour, running messages, checking on lookouts' reports, signals or tasks about the ship; bright lads were selected as aides to Captain or Commander.

Official punishments from the Captain or Officers were less painful than the unofficial ones in the gunroom. One was to stand for a long period on the main bitts, massive columns of timber by the mast, on which topsail halyards and other heavy ropes were made fast. 'To keep one's footing for an hour or so was no light punishment.' Stoppage of leave was another punishment, but probably the favourite was 'mastheading'.

'Go up there, sir and stay till you're called down' he shouted.

Up I mounted the rigging nothing loath, in fact rather inclined to congratulate myself. . . . My joy, however, was of short duration. A tornado was brewing. I saw the black clouds on the horizon and knew what was coming. I thought for a moment the old man's heart might soften as I watched the great black wall advancing on us with its line of seething white water below and the lightning playing between fantastic flashes; but no summons came from the quarterdeck for me to descend.

Presently the squall struck with a howl, and I clung to the ropes about the mast as I felt the wind rushing past with a force that, with a less strong hold of the cordage about me, might have sent me overboard. It was a wonderful sight, with the sea whipped into foam which flew with the wind over the ship in clouds of mist like steam. It was over in a few minutes, and then down came the rain, a veritable deluge. In a second I was soaked through to my skin.

The rain ceased, and then came a hail from below, 'Masthead there!' 'Aye, aye!' I promptly answered, as in duty bound. 'Come down!' I reached the deck and stood before the grim-visaged Commodore. 'Are you wet?' he asked. The answer was needless for I looked like a drowned rat; but I meekly said, 'Yes, sir!' 'Then go and stand there until you are dry,' he ejaculated as he pointed to the main bitts.[10]

Ambition to get on in the Service was a more potent spur to smartness than any punishment, for there was no orderly career progression. All promotion and appointments in the early stages were by 'interest' – the patronage, that is, of senior officers in a position to recommend a man or ask for his appointment to their own ship. Admirals, for instance, could select most of their own officers when they hoisted their flag, and the Flag Lieutenant received promotion at the end of the commission: 'naturally enough they chose their own sons and nephews first – then those of other Admirals who could return the same favour, with the result that naval careers became almost a monopoly of certain families'. While this was true to a great extent, it is also true that smart and able young men without family connection could get on if they succeeded in catching the eye of one of the great. That balanced and intellectual Admiral, Philip Colomb, even suggested that this was the most important form of 'interest'. Here is an extract from his biography of Admiral Cooper Key:

> The boy began to create for himself those friendships which go to build up what in the Navy is called Service interest', which determines almost surely the rate of advancement, and have at all times been of more importance than family or political connection – without which, indeed, family or political connection is almost powerless.[11]

Whatever the precise balance between family influence and Service reputation a young Officer simply could not get on without 'interest' of some kind – and even with this precious talisman the numerical odds seemed against him. A 'commission' was not a general commission as a Lieutenant or as a Commander in Her Majesty's Navy, but a specific appointment in a certain rank to a particular ship; when the ship's commission ended, the officer's commission ended with it, and he became unemployed on 'half pay'. To become eligible for the next rank up he had to have put in a certain number of years sea time in the rank below; therefore rapid promotion meant almost continual employment. Yet there was a vast pool of officers acquired during the hugely expanded fleets of the war years seeking commissions in comparatively very few active ships. Of some 3,000 Lieutenants not more than 800 to 900 were employed at any one time; of over 800 Commanders – second in command of a ship of the line, or Captain of a lesser vessel than a frigate – fewer than 150 were employed.

The situation was even worse for Captains, as some 90 per cent were unemployed on 'half pay'. However, the promotion struggle was over for those who reached this rank, as it was the bottom step of a continuously ascending escalator which could carry them without any effort on their part – without even the necessity of going to sea – up through the Captain's list, then on to and through the

Rear-Admiral's, Vice-Admiral's and Admiral's lists as vacancies were caused by deaths above. They could never be overtaken by those below, nor could they overtake anyone above; their only struggle was to obtain a ship to command or a fleet in which to hoist their flag.

As no one ever retired and no one was ever advanced for special qualities, the rate of ascent was tortuously slow. The average age of the Admirals was seventy-six; there was no Admiral who was not a veteran of the great wars; many had been Captains of ships of the line in one or more of that famous series of battles since 1797 to 1805 which had given the Royal Navy mastery. Even the top end of the Captain's list was composed of men who had commanded frigates in the great wars; the senior fifty dated their Captaincies from 1802. In these static conditions, the prime requirement for an officer who wished to reach the flag list before he was in his dotage was to fly through his Midshipman's, Lieutenant's and Commander's time and be made up to Captain at a very early age. For this, he needed copper-bottomed interest and continuous good luck. The vast majority commanded neither, and for them the Navy was not so much a career as a part-time occupation, interspersed perhaps with service in merchant ships, some kind of employment ashore,

The Captain and Officers of HMS *Encounter*, 1862

or simple inaction and penury. For every sour 'Old Mate' rotting on board ship there were scores of Midshipmen and Lieutenants rotting on half pay ashore.

'Half pay' was not so drastic as the term implied; a Lieutenant in employment was paid between £119 and £129 a year – £149 if he was commanding a small ship; 'half pay' was nearly as much, sometimes over £90 a year. However, in those days a man needed at least £150 to support the station of 'gentleman' – indeed a skilled mechanic's wages amounted to more than this. It is easy to see why marriage was discouraged for anyone below Captain's rank; it tended to soften a man and make him think more of the comforts of home than of his duty – 'We don't want the Navy manned with tame cats and domesticated spaniels' – and marriage was virtually impossible for anyone without private means.

If the difficulties facing individuals were enormous – and how can the sum of frustrated hope, inaction and broken pride be measured? – the Admiralty was not without its own problems. Where were the Admirals young and vigorous enough to command its fleets in emergency? And had the few young enough the necessary experience – indeed had they been employed *at all* since ascending the escalator of promotion?

The commissioned officers of a two-decked ship of the line consisted of Captain, Commander and five Lieutenants; there were also commissioned Marine officers, but they were not trained as seamen and were not a part of the executive. The Commander was the chief executive under the Captain, responsible for the maintenance of the ship and all her gear alow and aloft, the organisation and discipline of the men, their proficiency at all drills and evolutions. In frigates and smaller ships with no Commander, this overall responsibility was discharged by the First Lieutenant. Naturally he delegated – cleanliness and maintenance to the Boatswain, of the hull and spars to the carpenter, of the guns and magazines to the Gunner and Gunnery Lieutenant, who had passed through a course at the *Excellent* – but there was nothing about the ship, her sails and armament which he did not know intimately. There was no specialist to whom he needed to defer. All had mastery of every power of motion and fighting quality of the ship; he had grown up as part of them. And for their duties they needed chiefly alertness, prompt decision, presence and a fine voice. They cultivated their voices to the limit of human lungs until they could be heard from the weather gangway to the jibboom and over the trucks of the royal masts in a gale. A Midshipman in the three-decker *Marlborough* recalled in later years that the gunnery lieutenant 'was gifted

[64]

with so great and splendid a voice that when he gave his orders from the middle deck, they could be heard at every gun in the ship.'

The art of shouting orders was not simply to be audible at the furthest extremities of the vessel, but also to inspire urgency and gain a reputation for smacking things about.

It was the universal belief of naval officers that unless the men were kept constantly on the rush, they were doing nothing and learnt nothing. Our own gunnery lieutenant who was without doubt an exceedingly zealous officer, devoted all his energies to seeing how many projectiles he could crowd into a gun in a given space of time. . . . It must not be thought that there was any friction between officers and men. The continually rushing around and hurling of orders like stones from catapults were looked on by everyone as such necessary parts of naval life that they were accepted as a matter of course.[12]

Abuse was also accepted; it was part of the unquestioning deference to authority inculcated from the day a boy joined a man-of-war. 'He was considered a smart officer who could put the fear of God into everyone, including his own second in command.' There is an amusing account in one memoir of a First Lieutenant known as 'Chaw-finger Jack'; his nickname derived from his habit of 'doubling up the first finger of his right hand, putting it into his mouth and biting it hard across the knuckle to prevent himself from swearing at the men', so leaving a deep, permanent scar. 'Chaw-finger Jack' received regular abuse from his Captain – 'after which he would be seen going forward with his knuckle in his mouth.'

'My Lords desire to call attention to all officers to . . . the necessity that exists for working their ships without the aid of steam . . . not only on the score of economy, but for the important purpose of ensuring the efficiency of screw ships as sailing ships' HMS *Warrior*

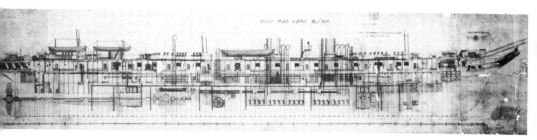

He was representative of the 'tarpaulin' or 'Boatswain-type' officer – familiar to previous generations of sailors, and still to be found in the Service, although doomed to disappear for lack of replacements. His predecessor had been another; one of the breed of socially superior Midshipmen which was about to render his type extinct found him drinking hot gin and water with his wife, 'a lady who appeared to my unsophisticated judgment to be about the same social class as the bumboat woman.'

It would be wrong to leave an exaggerated picture of loud-mouthed officers who cared only for 'rush'. Here is the most famous Arctic explorer of the day (later Admiral) Leopold McClintock as a Lieutenant:

> Quick in his movements as in his decision he was always quiet
> and perfectly calm, seeing everything done himself without
> noise or fuss. While all his orders were carried out promptly
> McLintock included in his idea of duty consideration and
> kindness to everyone on board.[13]

Besides executive officers, there were the commissioned officers of Marines – on a ship of the line usually a Captain and two Lieutenants. Although they enjoyed continuous employment in a permanently established corps, their position on board was far from satisfactory. They could never rise to command even the most humble ship; they had no executive status except over their own contingent of Marines, and even there the ultimate sanctions of discipline were in the hands of the executive branch. They had no watch-keeping duties to keep them employed, and appear in most accounts to have wiled away tedious hours doing very little. They were known as the 'Soldiers', or from their scarlet uniforms, 'Lobsters'.

The other officers were regarded as non-combatant as they did not have charge of men to fight the ship, although they could scarcely avoid being physically present in action. They were appointed by Warrant from the Admiralty. Most important was the Master, an ancient title that had once carried responsibility for the management and sailing of the ship and her men, but had narrowed down to specialist navigator with a small coterie of assistants that scarcely constituted a department, and no executive responsibility. In the open ocean his skill with sextant and chronometer was unquestioned; when it came to a landfall or coastal passage, where the hand lead and a sharp look-out were still the best aids – especially in those many as yet uncharted and unlit regions of the world – the Captain who bore ultimate responsibility for the safety of the ship sometimes took matters into his own hands.

One morning nearing Sierra Leone, the Captain asked me where I thought we were. I said, 'Nearly up to the anchorage sir.'
'What can you tell by?'
'The look of the land.'
But he was not convinced although the Master seemed to think I was right. He called one of the Kroomen (natives of the coast):
'Here Tom Bottle Beer, where Sierra Leone lib?'
'Daah, sir he lib,' said the Krooman, pointing.
'Where the lights?'
'Can see no lights.'
'Here, Jack Frypan, where Sierra Leone?' Jack Frypan showed him, but he still would not believe him. But when daylight came we were a long way past the town.[14]

Another officer of long-standing – seldom a 'gentleman' and notorious as an artful juggler of ship's accounts – was the Purser; he

Lieutenant's cabin aboard the battleship *Anson* at the turn of the century

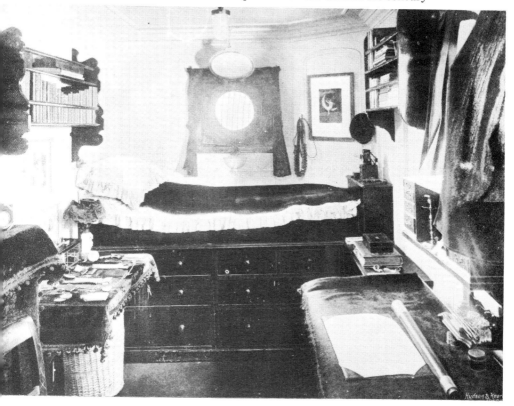

was responsible for the food and drink and all domestic provisions like tallow candles, articles of clothing, soap and so on, their issue to the men, and replenishment. He had graduated from Captain's Clerk. His pay was less than half that of a Lieutenant but he was confidently believed to make more than anyone else on board – including the Captain – from official and unofficial perquisites. Chief of the official kind was an allowance of two ounces in every pound of rations he dispensed; a 'Pusser's Pound' was fourteen ounces. In addition he carried private stocks of provisions which he sold on his own account, and he also made a profit from the domestic articles, or 'slops' which he managed on a credit basis.

> Once every three months we had a muster by the Open List
> and got our slop tickets. As each man's name was called the
> Clerk would read out his rating and how much duck, soap or
> tobacco he had drawn, how much he was in debt to the Purser
> or how much money was due to him. Then he would give each
> man his 'slop ticket' with all the articles marked on it and ask
> him how much money he wanted to draw. An AB or Petty
> Officer could draw from one dollar to ten if he wanted it and
> had not been before the Captain for any misconduct during the
> quarter. Some men would say 'Five dollars, sir', and the
> Captain would say, 'No, no money here for drunkards.' When
> another man asked for five dollars, the Captain would say,
> 'Give him two and consider me a good friend to you as it will
> save you three dozen off your back!'[15]

Apart from these small 'subs' a Purser did not handle the men's wages; these were still paid in the time-honoured way by a team of Admiralty Clerks who came aboard when the ship reached a home port at the end of her commission.

The practical heads of the other departments, the Boatswain, Gunner and Carpenter, who lived usually in cabins close by their stores and messed separately, were officers, but did not mix socially in the wardroom; the only others who did were those trained in a civilian profession, Surgeon, Chaplain, Schoolmaster. The Service had difficulty in attracting sufficient of these men, which is not surprising considering shipboard conditions, low pay, lack of opportunity and low status as mere Warrant officers. It is doubtful if many of those attracted were of the highest quality, although it is certain they must have possessed rare fortitude and the ability to rub along with all sorts of men. The Surgeon in particular had to serve a hard apprenticeship. Despite having qualified from one of

[68]

the Royal Colleges of Surgeons, generally Dublin it seems, or Edinburgh, and entering the Service with the Warrant rank of Assistant
Surgeon, they berthed with the Midshipmen in the squalor of the
cockpit and messed with them in the gunroom, as the historians of
the medical branch put it 'with no facilities for study, no reference
books, no intellectual stimulation, no status'. There they stayed for
years before the step up to full Surgeon. Here is the account of one
middle-aged Assistant Surgeon as late as 1848:

> We sleep in hammocks amongst boys between the ages of 11
> and 19. At 6.0 we must start from our hammocks, perform a
> morning ablution in the presence of boys and private Marines
> on a chest containing library, toilet and wardrobe. At 7.0 the
> sick are seen and prescribed for; that over we return to
> breakfast. At 9.0 a.m. the sick report is prepared for the First
> Lieutenant's inspection, which is provided for quarters, at
> which we have to stand like automats.[16]

Such an apparently humiliating position was not unique to doctors
at sea; ashore they were socially inferior to the gentry. As to their
professional skill, it is probable they killed rather more than they
helped. Their outlook was in general quite as traditional and un-
scientific as the most unlettered Gunner aboard, and they used a
similar jargon to disguise their real ignorance. Scurvy, for example,
the answer to which had been discovered and lost and re-discovered
many times during the preceding centuries, appeared and was
actually more prevalent at the end of the nineteenth century than
at the beginning. The various fevers which caused havoc among
crews on tropical stations were scarcely classified, let alone inves-
tigated in an analytical spirit. Of course there was no germ theory
to provide the clue; disease was believed to be spread by bad air;
thus *An Outline of Naval Surgery* published in 1846 suggested that
a man was safe in an African forest by day, but not by night:

> death, then, in the form of fever or miasm, lurks in every
> corner, hovers around every bush . . . miasm, condensed and
> concentrated, through the absence of light and heat, rises,
> emanating from the debris and decomposition around.[17]

Individual Surgeons and Assistant Surgeons, separated from each
other by sea and the slow pace of the sailing ship, practising the
witchcraft taught at Medical Schools in crowded and difficult con-

[69]

ditions, their spirit often broken by their lowly status, can scarcely be blamed for failing to perceive the error of their remedies. There were an enormous number of variables and no system. Besides with the miasma theory of disease, it was natural that all effort should go towards rooting out the sources of miasma. Hygiene and ventilation were the Surgeons' chief concern, and in these important fields they accomplished much. And yet – where were the sceptics?

A naval Captain – not a Surgeon – had written as early as 1823 that his experience suggested that 'to bleed was to kill', and he remarked that the Surgeon's treatment was not 'such as is justified by successful practice, but rests wholly on theory'. Surgeons surely noticed the same thing, yet bleeding and blistering and purging continued to be standard and too often terminal treatment for sufferers from the fevers described as 'intermittent', 'remittent', 'continued' or 'eruptive' which lurked in the tropical zones, while a variety of drugs, some of which were 'not only unnecessary, but have actually killed far more people than fever ever has', according to one experienced African explorer in 1854, were used promiscuously.

Much the same could probably be said about the Schoolmasters who had the unenviable task of instructing spirited 'young gentlemen', most of whom seem to have considered their lessons a waste of time made passably interesting only by ragging the 'Schoolie'.

Admiral's day cabin, HMS *Magnificent* at the turn of the century

Certain it is that professional subjects such as mathematics applied to navigation were the mainstays of the teaching, and there was little if any attempt to give a wide general education. As for the higher aspects of professional knowledge, theories of tactics, analysis of strategy, these things were scarcely formulated at the time, hence could not be taught. There had been theorists during the eighteenth century – mostly French – but the impression was that the British Service had prevailed by virtue of the splendid instincts of its officers, the courage and steadiness of its sailors, and overall superiority in ship-handling. Naval history, where it existed, was heroic, never analytical.

Judging by the lack of space devoted to the Surgeon, the Schoolmaster and the Chaplain in most memoirs, these worthies – the only conventionally 'educated' men aboard – made remarkably little impression. When set alongside the hundreds of thousands of words describing the 'characters' and the extraordinary habits and adventures of the commissioned branch they scarcely seem to have existed. Occasionally one of them bobs up, usually in a negative way:

> The Chaplain had two hobbies, fishing and smoking. His
> Marine servant told me that his cabin was stocked with pipes
> placed in racks fixed to the side of his cabin. He brought
> enough pipes from England to last the commission. We used to
> go rather far from the ship when fishing . . . I fancy I can see
> him now, settling himself in the sternsheets of the skiff with
> his billy-cock hat and long frock coat, which he always wore
> winter or summer. There he would sit with a line in each hand,
> and remain wrapped up in his own thoughts without saying a
> word; smoking away and only moving either to refill his pipe
> from a huge pouch or else to haul in his line.[18]

This ship had a very religious Captain, and services conducted by the Chaplain 'were as much part of our routine as piping dinner'. Most of the smaller vessels – and some of the larger ones, had no Chaplain, such was the shortage – in which case the Captain took Divine Service every Sunday morning. One Captain of legend conducted his in shirt sleeves; with his uniform on he recognised no higher authority!

The men generally detested Sunday morning; it started with a rush to get the decks cleared up, a rush to get breakfast over, a rush to get their best uniform on and was followed by a seemingly interminable two hours or so while the Captain in full dress, accompanied by a retinue of officers, Petty Officers and Midshipmen aides inspected them as they were drawn up in their divisions, then descended and poked into every corner and compartment below, searching for dust or disorder, while they remained standing silently.

All the officers of a man-of-war messed in what was known as the Wardroom, immediately below the Captain's accommodation – except in small, single-deck ships in which case it was forward of the Captain's quarters. They slept in cabins either side whose doors opened out into the Wardroom which consequently had no daylight except from the row of stern windows. A long, good-quality table ran along the centre of the room with chairs of equal solidity and quality placed around it. Decorative oil lamps were suspended above.

Accounts of Wardroom life are scarce; it was everyday and so normal compared with the bizarre atmosphere and rituals of the Gunroom that few thought to record it. At the start of a commission a mess caterer would be chosen from among the officers. He would be responsible for buying the extra provisions and delicacies for the table from 'mess money' contributed by all members – perhaps £3 a month, the first instalments paid in advance. Each officer would have his own servant, either a boy or a Marine, who in addition to his normal duties would look after his tiny cabin, be his valet, fetch his washing water, rouse him for his watches, serve him at table

Midshipmen in a battleship's gunroom in the 1850s

for a small extra pay. In general standards of behaviour were those of the gentry ashore; breakfast was probably a silent meal; a light luncheon was taken in the middle of the day and a heavier dinner in the early evening. This was a formal occasion – so far as conditions allowed – with the President of the Mess, the Commander or 1st Lieutenant, taking the chair at the head of the table, which was spread with a white cloth, agleam with silver cutlery and glasses; the servants stood behind their officers to attend them. Grace was said by the Chaplain; afterwards conversation was confined to sport, times past, characters remembered and well-embroidered, leg-pulling and badinage. It was not done to use swear words, discuss Service matters or mention ladies' names, much less amatory affairs. In large ships with a band music was played during the meal. Wine was served by each officer's servant and marked down to his wine account – separate from his mess money – and after the meal the port and madeira circulated clockwise around the table. The formal part of the evening was concluded by the President calling on his Vice, usually the most junior officer, to propose the loyal toast.

'Gentlemen, the Queen!'

All would raise their glasses remaining seated – a dispensation granted by William IV because of the low deckhead beams – and repeat, 'The Queen! God bless her!'

A battleship's gunroom at the turn of the century

Sometimes the Captain was invited to dinner as a guest of the Wardroom; on other evenings he would invite certain officers to dine with him. Conversation was apt to be strained on these occasions unless the great man was unusually adept socially. In one account of a remarkably unhappy ship where the Captain was detested by all his officers, none would accept his invitation; when at length he ordered them to his table, they came but refused to eat.

More popular were guest nights; guests were always male, officers from other ships or friends or officials from ashore. In many ships it was the custom to invite the Gunroom for a guest night once a week, but this was not always the case. While starting with all formality and decorum, guest nights often ended up as boisterously as a Gunroom evening with singing or high-spirited dancing on deck; like the men, few officers needed female partners to enjoy a wild dance.

More usual probably were the evenings spent yarning over the table through pipe smoke. Many officers were accomplished raconteurs, and those who could tell the tallest stories with the most conviction were greatly admired.

Some acquired reputations throughout the Service; Captain Broad of the *Cormorant* was one such; one evening while his ship was at anchor he invited two of his officers to dine and witness a contest between him and the Captain of a US corvette who also had a considerable reputation for drawing the long bow.

It would be difficult for me to say which of the two really deserved to take the cake, but it was extremely funny to see the look of disgust upon Captain Broad's face when returning to his cabin after expediting his American competitor. He took up his whisky and soda saying, 'My word, what a champion liar, Woods. I saw you gaping with wonder as you swallowed those tough yarns. But most of them stuck in my throat, and I must wash them down.'[19]

Another notable raconteur was Commander P. W. R. Rimington.

This jaunty, high-spirited navigator had a fund of the most extraordinary yarns, so highly improbable that he quickly earned the title of 'The Dockyard Liar'. The following yarn is a specimen of his marvellous gift. We believed he invented it on the spot to prove that 'crocodiles have more than average intelligence' – which we had been debating at dinner with the

Christmas at sea in an ironclad. Illustrations by Col. Field

usual entire ignorance of the subject, and with the usual
heated, abusive observations on each other's intellect. 'My dear
chaps,' he began, 'I can tell you a slight experience of mine
which may assist.' Everyone listened; even the heavy-handed
wardroom servants ceased to clatter the plates. 'My brother in
law put me up for a week's shooting three years ago; he
commanded the 58th Punjabis you know. The village tank –
pond my dear chaps – simply swarmed with muggars – crocs
you'd call 'em, my happy ones. On our way out to a bit of a
snipe marsh one morning we saw a muggar lying in the slime,
such a whacker that my brother in law – fine old chap he was –
it was his 51st birthday I remember – shot him and sent him
up to the mess to be skinned. In the evening they showed us a
tiny monkey they'd found inside him.[20]

The story continued to describe how he had found the secret of the
crocodiles' meal by hiding near the tank at sunset. Five huge muggars had come out of the water and scraped holes in the mud at the
edge; then, putting their tails in the holes and patting down the
mud around them they had planted themselves bolt upright.

'with their legs stuck at different angles and their jaws wide
open, looking, my innocent old dears, just like trees struck by
lightning. Down went the sun and presently out came a troop of

A quiet rubber in the battery of the cruiser, *Nelson*, in the 1880s; note
the high deckhead

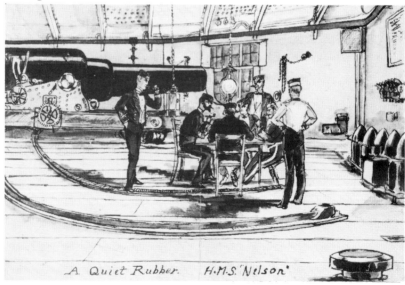

A Quiet Rubber. H.M.S. 'Nelson'

[76]

little rascals [monkeys], from the dusky forest; nervous as cats they were till they found the coast clear. Not a movement from the muggars, not a sound, till twenty or more of those nippy little chaps were at the edge, drinking. Then one of them made a noise – coughed gently. My Aunt! You should have seen those monkeys bolt; they made for the nearest trees and scrambled up those lightning-struck crocs like riggers. And my dear old sportsmen, as they went up, so those big jaws opened and shut and they went down inside 'em! I think, gentlemen, you will agree with me that crocodiles have *some* intelligence,' and Rimington, calmly accepting the salt cellar we pushed across to him, beamed on us.[21]

Whist was another favourite way of passing the evening, while in fair weather on deck there were more energetic pastimes, sling-the-monkey, single-stick and for the younger officers – probably only those from the Gunroom – 'skylarking', a form of follow-my-leader played up and about the rigging.

In port the recreations were chiefly shooting wildfowl, fishing, riding on borrowed or hired mounts, or simply going for a ramble. There were comparatively few of the organised sports like cricket, football, tennis or racquets until facilities were available later in the century, although fox hunting was indulged by those who could afford it in home ports and some English-speaking colonies. On

'Following your partner's lead'

foreign stations, where the small European communities were isolated from news and contact with the larger world, the visit of a warship was always a great occasion and the officers were entertained lavishly to riding parties, picnics and in the evenings banquets and dances, hospitality which was always returned by the ship. On those coasts where there were no Europeans picnics were still organised among the officers, sometimes for the whole ship's company, and held on a pleasant-looking beach or island with swimming afterwards. Hauling the Seine net was ever-popular and boat sailing was another diversion although that again was not so competitive and organised as it became later in the century.

If all else proved stale there was, at least for the younger spirits of the Gunroom, the prospect of raising hell with the natives.

In the business part of Whampoa, as in Canton, there were big paper lanterns and sign boards hanging outside the shops. Landing with stout sticks in our hands, we would march down that large street, smashing each lantern as we went along. Oh, the excitement and the chattering Chinese, as they rushed out

Why we enjoy going to dances in the navy

[78]

to pick up the remains of their cherished lanterns, cursing us 'foreign devils' as we were with all their might, and calling down upon us the vengeance of their gods![22]

Recreation was not the fetish it was to become later in the century; for one thing all ships, except perhaps in the Mediterranean, were at full stretch on duties which provided as much interest, excitement and tight and unexpected situations as any sportsman could wish, for another a ship's rigging was a natural gymnasium and sailing-ship life in itself provided the chance to exercise nice skills every day – as well as challenge and real hazard.

In about ten minutes the wind was blowing nearly a hurricane. The Captain was on deck the whole time looking up at the sails and masts, so the full force of the light was shining on his face. No one could help admiring the calm, firm look he had. We have spoken of it since with great admiration. He was simply watching for a shift of wind and preparing in case the vessel was taken aback. In a few minutes the hands were turned up

Captain the Hon. Hedworth Lambton, Commander A. P. Ethelston and
Lt. J. Nicholas, 1st Lieutenant of HMS *Powerful*

and every man at his station. As soon as the squall was over the wind did change, in quite an opposite direction! Had not everything been prepared it would have turned out most serious, but thank God we have a Captain who thoroughly understands his profession.'[23]

That was a small vessel; the majority of ships in commission were small. Here is another, the 16-gun brig *Childers*, first command of the Hon. Henry Keppel, sailing for Malta in dirty weather and a freshening wind.

About noon an extra heavy squall struck the brig, throwing her over on her beam ends, main yard under water. The First Lieutenant, standing on the hammock netting holding on to the topmast backstay, was thrown off his legs. He sang out, 'Put the helm up!' I, sticking to the weather quarter like a limpet, called out, I am afraid, 'The helm be d—d! I see the keel!'[24]

For their duties at sea, officers wore dark blue jackets without tails, described as 'round' or 'ship' jackets and similar to the ones modern naval officers wear although with a different cut, no epaulettes, usually a black cravat, dark blue trousers, black boots and a black cloth peaked cap with a gilt band, crown and anchor badge at the front – and a very skimpy top. Probably some officers still wore glazed black hats with wide brims and a gold loop and cockade at the side. For ceremonial occasions a dark blue tail coat was worn, double-breasted for the commissioned, single-breasted for the warrant ranks, with a black leather sword belt outside and a white waistcoat beneath, white or dark blue narrow trousers, black boots and the familiar cocked hat. A Lieutenant, Master – who ranked as a Lieutenant – Surgeon and Purser wore a gilt epaulette on their right shoulder only; Commanders and above wore a balanced pair. Sleeves had buttons near the cuff and only Flag Officers had distinguishing gold lace stripes, although without the curl familiar today. What officers actually wore was often a good deal more individual than the descriptions imply.

Some Captains allowed officers to wear any fancy uniform they liked; others insisted on their wearing a blue frock coat, even on the West coast of Africa. One Admiral always wore a white billycock hat, another wore a tall white Ascot hat.[25]

Like the men, the naval officers of Queen Victoria's reign were not to be confined within accurate limits; the haphazard training and career structure was probably 'productive of more individuality, originality and self-confidence', as one experienced Admiral put it, than the more orderly and scientific systems which evolved later. At the same time it tended to a narrow mental outlook; the old type of officer received generally critical memorials from later generations of scientifically-minded men for their lack of interest in tactics or strategy and for clinging to methods and glories of the past instead of seizing on the technical innovations crowding in from every side. Of course they were the products of their environment. Yet there were among them highly cultivated, well-read individuals, excellent artists in pen and ink and watercolour, sensitive observers, entertaining yarn-spinners and accomplished diplomats. There were also enough forward-looking men and experimentalists, just as there were among the later 'scientific' officers some who wondered, as all now must wonder, just where technology was taking them.

Probably only two generalisations are worthwhile: they were superb sailors and they were uncompromising in their conception of duty, whatever eccentric or occasionally certifiable forms it took. They handed on to the late Victorians not only a tradition of smartness second to none, but also a selfless belief that the good of the Service was the only thing that mattered. This sketch of one of those later Victorian officers, Commander George Cherry, who had absorbed the doctrine will serve for them.

Although the chance of his being promoted to Captain was but small and the chance of his ever becoming a Rear-Admiral on the active list was absolutely non-existent, he did his job as if his life depended on it. The men liked him; he was very strict but he was utterly fair and just; he never made favourites, and he always saw that meal hours, make-and-mends and watch belows were religiously observed. They admired his ability; they admired the way he never spared himself, and they were interested by his grim contempt for popularity. But he shook the officers and especially the Midshipmen from the crowns of their heads to the soles of their feet. I shall always look on him as one of those many who have made the heart of the British Navy what it is.[26]

CHAPTER FOUR

THE
COMMITMENT
AND THE MEANS

Great Britain spent astonishingly little money on her world-wide Navy and the chains of bases which sustained it. The public and successive governments had lost interest in the Service after the immense efforts of the war years; economists of the Manchester school had persuaded many that Free Trade would mean the end of the succession of European wars caused by rivalry over national trading monopolies. Merchants and manufacturers believed indus-trial and financial strength as important as naval strength; in any case neither they nor anyone else wished to pay for a large Navy while there were no obvious threats from other naval powers. As for the House of Commons, it either knew or cared little for the needs of the sea-scatter of bases and entrepôts that the nation had collected during the great wars and since.

All the bases had been taken and held for strategic reasons con-nected with trade routes, mainly to the east where the East India Company controlled a vast commercial and political empire extend-ing 'from the banks of the Indus to the frontiers of China, from the mouths of the Ganges to the mountains of Tibet'. Despite the naval needs of this elaborate jigsaw of treaty and concession, and the needs of new areas being opened to the products of British factories, despite the crusade the British people had taken upon itself to destroy the slave trade by sea, politicans looked on the Navy largely as a home defence force and unique backing for British statesmen in the concert of European powers. It was only the necessity of maintaining a 'Two-Power' standard that kept the Navy in funds at all.

As bases and dockyards were not such an obvious measure of strength as ships of the line they were run down, especially over-seas. Trincomalee, headquarters of the East Indies station, which Nelson had called the finest harbour in the world, was allowed to decay on £1,350 a year – less than the pay and allowances of a single Rear Admiral. The base at the Cape of Good Hope was run on little over £1,000 a year, Gibraltar dockyard on £400, including £41 'for postage and regulating the dockyard clock'. These figures are not the whole story; they take no account of the military garrisons – although Trincomalee had none and the Cape only a small one – nor the stores, victuals and repairs. And there is a sense in which it is incorrect to detail them separately as the whole naval force in the area was available to concentrate and protect any one threatened, just as they were there for the succour of that force or any part of it. Nevertheless, it is significant that one of the major home ports, Portsmouth or Plymouth, cost more to run than all the overseas naval bases, dockyards, victualling and medical establishments put together. In 1837 the home establishments together cost £527,000, the overseas £44,000 – about half the cost of a two-decker ship of the line.

This was still too much for the economists who believed overseas attachments cost more to defend than they produced in trade. This was not the experience of the men on the spot. From China and the

Ironclads alongside the mole at Gibraltar

Indonesian archipelago, from the Pacific – where the Navy had no base but relied on hired facilities and local purchases at Valparaiso, store ships from England, or on the other side, Sydney, from Mexico, Valparaiso and Peru, from northern Brazil and the equatorial coasts of Africa, traders were calling for more protection for life and property against piracy, native attack and internal disturbances. To meet all these and other more pressing demands caused by revolts in Canada and on the borders of India in that age of slow communications and passage times dependant on local weather, the Admiralty had 10 ships on the East Indies station, which also embraced China, Australasia and the Pacific, 15 on the Cape of Good Hope Station, which took in east and west coasts of Africa, 27 on the West Indies and North American station, and 15 on the coasts of South America. Most were small sloops and brigs which cost comparatively little to build or man. Behind them as the very visible manifestation of power to contain the ambitions of the French or Russians there was the main battlefleet including 25 ships in the Mediterranean. Nevertheless, the total bill for the Navy in 1837 was under £5 millions – less than the Army vote – and the total number of men serving was little over 30,000 against over 100,000 soldiers; it was a trifling price to pay for world-wide supremacy.

It was living to a large extent on the fat of the war years, the *legend* of invincibility; it was only possible because the other powers accepted it. They accepted it not only from war weariness and because they had pressing internal problems, which distracted their energies from overseas adventure, but also – and here was the masterstroke of British policy – because Britain did not use the power as it would have been used in the colonising days before the Free Trade economists. After the wars she had returned much of the colonial territory she had won, keeping for herself only the vital spots like the Cape of Good Hope or Mauritius which could be used by others as bases from which to prey on her trade routes. She had abandoned the customary tariffs designed to protect her own and her colonies' trade against rivals, and was in the process of dismantling the Navigation Laws which protected her merchant shipping from foreign competition. US merchant shipping especially benefited; the celebrated Baltimore brigs and schooners with their fine underwater lines and rakish stems were capturing the cream of Atlantic and Indian Ocean trade from the traditional tubby, deep-drafted English merchant ships.

This enlightened trade policy literally disarmed Britain's rivals – just as Free Trade economists had argued. They did not quite lead

Burma War; squadron up the Irrawaddy

to the 'harmonisation of mankind's general desires and ideals' which they also predicted, but they did ensure that there was never sufficient resentment against the 'mistress of the seas' to place her in the only position which could seriously imperil her, with Russia, France and America allied against her. It was quite the reverse; as mixed European trading communities grew up in isolated regions they naturally co-operated against local harrassments, and there were many cases of joint naval action against pirates or natives.

Added to enlightened trade and colonial policies, British statesmen played the balance of power game in Europe with a fine touch, now siding with one of the chief rivals against the other, now switching sides to curb the former ally. And outside Europe, British power was maintained by balancing alliances with local rulers; in the vital area flanking the western approaches to India her constant friend in these early years was Sayyid Said, Sultan of Muscat, an Arab potentate with a squadron of European-style warships headed by a 74-gun ship of the line! Said co-operated in putting down piracy in the Persian Gulf and preserving the status quo among rival sheiks in the area, in return for which he had the prestige of being allied to the foremost naval and imperial power, and the assurance that his extensive territories would not be annexed by other European powers – or by his own rebellious subjects.

The explanation for the minute annual premium the British paid on their Empire of the Seas was that it was not maintained by physical power so much as by diplomacy and prestige and liberal commercial policies. Even so, there were never enough ships on the overseas stations. Commanders-in-Chief were always hard-pressed, and the campaigns against both piracy and the slave trade were ineffective for lack of ships – although they took up about one third of the naval force available. All the Admiralty's pleas for more funds for these purposes and applications to renew the rotting hulks in reserve at home met an unresponsive Treasury and Cabinet. The comfortable orthodoxy of the time was to build up national strength by rigid economy and investment in commerce, and far from getting more the Admiralty was constantly fighting proposals for retrenchment. Here is an account of the machinations necessary to obtain approval for one small Dover packet – the Admiralty was then responsible for carrying the overseas mails.

> The Political Secretary had to take up the Navy List and say he wanted two more line-of-battle ships to replace some scarcely fit for service. It was thought that frigates were more wanted. It then became a question whether corvettes would not answer the purpose equally well. A discussion then took place with regard to sloops and gunboats, when having saved so much money, it was thought possible they might accede to my request for a Dover Packet, which was all I really wanted.[1]

The passion for economy went strangely with the dynamic commercial expansion of the empire, and with the foreign policy of that combative, liberal, Free Trade, slavery-hating, commonsensical John Bull of a statesman, Lord Palmerston. The late 1830s and early 1840s, when he was Foreign Secretary, provide illuminating demonstrations of how the circle was squared, and how with the aid of alliances, confidence, luck, fighting spirit and the weakness of rivals or opponents the Empire of the Seas grew stronger and wider.

By then the French had regained much of their former ardour. They had occupied Algeria and there was concern in London about their intentions towards Tunisia and their support for Mehemet Ali, Pasha of Egypt. Mehemet had broken away from his imperial master, the Sultan of Turkey, created an efficient army, and was

expanding northwards through Syria towards Turkey and east-
wards across the Arabian peninsula towards the Trucial coast of
the Persian Gulf. Britain had an interest in Syria because of the
overland route to India down the valley of the Euphrates and so
into the Persian Gulf, and an even more vital interest in a healthy
Turkey to act as a buffer to stop Russian expansion southwards
through Syria to the Persian Gulf and the northwest border areas
of India and through the Dardanelles into the Mediterranean.

The specific danger, as Palmerston saw it, was that Russia would
pose as the protector of the Sultan of Turkey against Mehemet Ali,
and afterwards stay and take over the Ottoman Empire. To forestall
such a move he tried to gain agreement with all the European
powers for joint action to limit Mehemet's advance. France, with
expansionary ideas of her own, and anxious to gain influence in
Egypt, refused to take part. Instead, she reinforced her Mediterranean fleet until it was larger than the British fleet. Palmerston
retaliated by signing an agreement with the other three powers,
Russia, Prussia, Austria, to help the Sultan, if necessary with force.
France, seething with indignation at the obvious rebuff, hinted that
if force were used she might come in on Mehemet's side, and she

A mess in an ironclad's battery in the 1880s

continued to raise more men and add to her Mediterranean fleet, bringing its strength up to fifteen of the line against twelve British.

By this time, 1840, Mehemet's forces had reached the Persian Gulf and occupied two ports on the Trucial coast. The Sheikh of Bahrein had made submission and the British Resident in the area could do nothing as the whole of the East Indies squadron was engaged in a war which had broken out in China. Mehemet's Syrian campaign was enjoying similar success, and practically the whole of the Turkish fleet had deserted to his side. Everything appeared to be going the French-Egyptian way, and the British Cabinet, many of whose members had been doubtful about Palmerston's policy from the beginning, seemed about to split apart; the possibility of a general European war – with the French fleet in the Mediterranean superior to the British – unnerved even those who had supported the policy originally.

Palmerston refused to take the French threat seriously; he doubted if France would hazard a war for the sake of Mehemet Ali, and asked where they would find the ships to contend with the British reserves, much less the Russian fleet which would join the British.

> What would become of Algiers if they were at war with a power superior at sea? Could they help Mehemet Ali by marching to the Rhine? Is the interior so tranquil and united that Louis Philippe would like to see the three military powers of the Continent armed against him?

The Prime Minister, Melbourne, doubted if nations always took such a rational view of their chances, but felt it was too late to back down without serious loss of prestige and, staving off the threatened Cabinet resignations, allowed Palmerston to do his worst. Consequently, when Mehemet Ali refused to accept terms restricting him to the southern part of Syria, the Mediterranean fleet – still inferior to the French fleet which had been keeping it under observation with much panache during the mounting crisis – was ordered to blockade Mehemet's ships in Alexandria and seize the Egyptian supply bases along the Syrian coast.

Meanwhile Palmerston instructed the British chargé d'affaires in Paris to warn the French government 'in the most friendly and inoffensive manner possible' against the temptation to make use of her temporary naval superiority in the Mediterranean,

> and that if she begins a war, she will certainly lose her ships,

colonies and commerce before she sees the end of it; that her army of Algiers will cease to give her anxiety, and that Mehemet Ali will just be chucked into the Nile.

The Commander-in-Chief of the British Mediterranean fleet was Sir Robert Stopford; he was seventy-two years old and had flown his flag first in 1808 during the great wars, since when his powers of decision had deteriorated. He was in any case reluctant to divide his forces in the presence of the jaunty French fleet of fifteen of the line evidently spoiling for a fight. The second-in-command, Commodore Charles Napier, was eighteen years younger though and had a Nelsonic contempt for odds and orders combined with a genius for the kind of cutting-out operations necessary. When in September 1840 he was given a small squadron, including Austrian frigates, a Turkish corvette and some steam vessels, he made short work of the Egyptian garrisons in Sidon, Tyre and Beirut, the chief supply port for the Egyptian army.

This left the fortress of St Jean d'Acre as the key to the campaign to oust Mehemet from Syria since it commanded the only practical land supply route along the coast road. Mehemet's son, Ibrahim, was holding this strongpoint with his army and 200 guns. Sir Robert, doubtful about the Turkish troops with his force, uncertain of the strength of Ibrahim's defences, and very aware that his own orders directed him not to make the attempt unless the prospects of success justified it, hesitated to risk his ships. Fortunately for Palmerston, Napier was by his side. He planned the assault and by sheer confidence and strength of personality overruled his superior's caution. On 1 November he sent frigates in to take soundings and buoy a passage for the larger vessels, and two days later the squadron of seven of the line, frigates and sloops sailed in – the last British line of battle ever to sail into action – coming to anchor inside the marker buoys close under the sheer walls of the fort. The Egyptian guns had been laid to the range of the buoys and most of their shot passed over the British hulls, but the ships, which had been exercised relentlessly by Napier during the crisis, poured in rapid and well-directed fire.

The decisive point of the action was reached after only three hours, when a lucky shot detonated the main magazine of the fortress. It went up with an awe-inspiring roar, devastating the interior and cracking the morale of the survivors, who crept away during the night leaving the British, Austrian and Turkish Brigades to take over unopposed the following day.

'This is of course nuts to us and a great lift to Palmerston,' wrote

The attack on Sidon, 1840

Lady Palmerston. It was the end of Mehemet's career as the new Alexander; he could not hope to continue his Syrian adventure, let alone his march on Constantinople, and such was the moral effect of the brief and brilliantly successful intervention that he also surrendered his Arabian conquests by agreements signed at the end of the year.

It is interesting that this demonstration of British naval power in defence of essentially British interests was achieved by diplomacy and force of character, not by superior – let alone overwhelming – strength, and that it could not have been achieved by Britain alone – not unless Parliament had been asked to vote a war establishment and the ships in ordinary had all been commissioned and – somehow – manned. This would have taken months and would have led to severe internal strains, even if the government had been granted the funds, which is improbable. Even with one of the major rivals so brilliantly isolated, and the other European powers persuaded that it was not in their interests to have a single Moslem state ruling over the whole of the Middle East, it had still been too much for the nerves of the average Cabinet Minister. The British Admiralty had also taken a pessimistic view of the Mediterranean fleet's chances if it came to war, as Sir Robert Stopford himself had done. And without the random factor of a brilliantly insubordinate second-in-command Acre would never have been attempted, let alone taken, that year. It is scarcely too much to say that Mehemet

Ali was cut down by Palmerston and Napier, not by the naval system which employed superannuated Admirals, or the political system which skimped on funds and establishments – although the establishment of the *Excellent* is believed to have been responsible for the superb gunnery displayed at Acre.

The other vital factor in the campaign had been geography; it had been fortunate that Mehemet's main route northwards hugged the coast, that the bulk of his supplies went by sea, and that he was consequently vulnerable to blockade and assault from the sea. But the point about naval power outside Europe in those days before widespread railways, when land transport was slow and small-scale and most produce went by water, was that the centres of trade and influence usually were accessible by sea and river.

This was particularly true of Britain's most important possession, India. The great chain of the Himalayas and the arid wastes on the northwest borders cut her off from land communications, and her economy was entirely dependent on sea-borne trade with Europe, chiefly around the Cape of Good Hope, and a network of routes across the Indian Ocean stretching up into the China Seas. The protection of India, as of the rest of the Empire of the Oceans, was a matter of locking up the main fleets of the rival powers in European waters so that they could neither mount a sea-borne invasion nor seriously interfere with trade routes. Naturally the land borders had to be garrisoned but unless Russia managed to penetrate southwards, not against a European power. Apart from this, opportunities for the successful use of warships were to be found wherever there was a necessity to protect vital interests.

Aden was such a case. The overland route from the Mediterranean to the Gulf of Suez and down the Red Sea to India had gained in importance as steam ships began to promise shorter passages, independent of the monsoons which governed all sailing traffic. Steamers were unable to make Bombay from Suez without replenishing, though, and by 1837 there was need for a secure coaling base on the route. The island of Socotra off Cape Guardafui at the bottom end of the Red Sea had been the first natural choice but disease and difficulties of negotiation with the owner caused its abandonment and attention turned to the ancient port of Aden which had splendid sheltered anchorages either side of a rocky promontory joined to the mainland only by a strip of low sand, and capable of being made impregnable from attack by land.

Matters were hastened when a Madras ship ran aground near Aden in 1838. The survivors were brutally ill-treated; the Commander of a British naval survey vessel in the area demanded an

Coaling ship

indemnity from the local ruler, the Sultan of Lahej, and seized the opportunity to open negotiations for taking over Aden itself; he had been convinced for some time that it would be an ideal base. All seemed to be going well, and the Sultan appeared willing to cede the promontory to the British for an annual pension when the Commander learnt of a plot to overpower him at the final session. He sailed for Bombay without a treaty, but with a perfect excuse for the forcible seizure of Aden as punishment for treachery.

There were many reasons, apart from the need for a steamer base, which made it almost certain that the opportunity to take Aden cheaply would not be passed up. It was the time of Mehemet Ali's expansion across Arabia, and one prong of his advance was directed down the Red Sea towards Aden. As he was supported by France, and there was every probability that in return for support France would gain influence and come to dominate Egypt, it was vital to deny the partnership such a commanding position across the Suez-India route. It is true that Mehemet already controlled the overland part of the route across Egypt – all the more reason to prevent the possibility of France securing both ends of what was bound to become an increasingly important short-cut to India and the East. It would also have enabled her to contest Britain's paramount influence in the Persian Gulf, an influence which was felt to be vital in order to preserve Persia as a buffer to Russian overland expansion. These suspicions of the designs of France and Russia were more of a spur to immediate action than the simple need for a coaling station and apart from the concern to deny such a commanding base to rivals there was the positive consideration that it would be a perfect advanced outpost for the Indian Empire in a most sensitive area.

The deed was done the following year with even greater economy of force than in the campaign to overthrow Mehemet. One of the smallest class of frigate and two un-rated warships with some eight hundred British and Indian troops silenced and took the Arab fortifications with trifling casualties. The Sultan was granted a pension only slightly less than he had lost by his earlier trickery; the Navy had one more vital link in its chain of strategic bases. It is interesting to compare the Admiralty's lack of enthusiasm for steam itself with the speed and unerring instinct with which the strategic consequences of new steamer routes were met, largely by the men on the spot, just as earlier in the century the need for a base to command and succour the developing China trade routes had led to the acquisition of Singapore.

At the same time as the great power game was being played in the Middle East with the important tricks being taken by Great Britain, a nakedly commercial war was being waged in China. The East India Company's monopoly of trade with that Empire – conducted through the city of Canton, which had the monopoly from the Chinese end – had been terminated in 1834 in accordance with the Free Trade philosophy of the British parliament. Since then great efforts had been made by British merchants to open more of what was seen as a vast potential market for British goods. Their efforts came to nothing, partly due to the contempt with which the Mandarins of the Celestial Empire regarded trade and the barbarians from Europe, chiefly due to problems created by the wholesale smuggling of opium into the country in British Indian and American hulls. This highly-organised and very dangerous trade, carried out in swift 'clippers' officered in the main by younger sons of good family who looked to a quick fortune and early retirement to a respectable life in England, was producing vast profits and milking the country of substantial quantities of silver and other precious articles. Hitherto China had enjoyed a favourable balance of trade with Europe and Anglo-India through the export of tea, silk, lacquer ware and *chinoiserie* for the fashionable, but as imports of opium soared from some 5,000 chests in the first quarter of the century up to 30,000 through the port of Canton alone by 1839, the balance of her trade swung sharply into deficit. Added to this were internal problems associated with drug addiction, and the deterioration of what had been a carefully-controlled and civilised commerce with 'John Company' into a lawless, free-booting anarchy reminiscent of the Elizabethans. The Chinese authorities retaliated by imposing harrassing restrictions on all foreign traders, backing them by seizing hostages – customary under Chinese law, arbitrary by British standards – and naval ships were called in to protect British interests.

By 1839 the situation was so bad that the Superintendent of British trading interests reported, 'trade with China at any point remote from the station of our ships is no longer a possible state of circumstances', and the head of the official Trade Mission wrote to Palmerston;

> The true and most important question to be solved is whether
> this shall be an honourable and extending trade with the
> Empire, or whether the coast shall be delivered over to a state
> of things which will pass rapidly from the worst character of
> illicit trade to plain buccaneering.

To Palmerston the alternatives seemed plain: 'either to give up our China trade and to withdraw our subjects and officers from China', or 'to bring the Chinese government to reason with vigorous measures.' If the market involved had not been so attractive, if there had been no need to find wider outlets for British goods which were being excluded from Europe as the Continental nations built up and protected their own industries, if there had been no eager European rivals ready to fill the vacuum which would be caused by a British withdrawal – if Palmerston had not been Palmerston – it is still inconceivable that the logic of commercial and industrial expansion would have been denied in China.

As it was the conflict of interests and misunderstandings turned into armed war without any prompting from the British Foreign Office. A British sailor committed murder, and the Chinese authorities, unable to find the culprit, demanded that someone – any Englishman – should be turned over to them for punishment; this was normal in China where the community was held responsible for its lawbreakers, but was unacceptable to the British. The first action of the subsequent hostilities, known as the 'Opium Wars', took place in November 1839 when the 28-gun frigate *Volage* and the 18-gun sloop *Hyacinth* routed a fleet of 29 war junks inside half an hour, sinking five, blowing up one and disabling many of the others.

The following year, when a large fleet including three of the line and 20,000 British and Indian troops arrived in Canton River, a blockade was established and the islands of Chusan and Hong Kong seized with equal ease. The Imperial fleet with its ancient brass cannon was no match for a European Navy, the Imperial soldiery had no answer to the fire power of the British: as one naval officer noted; 'It takes three Chinese to serve a musket. One carries a crutch, another loads, a third takes aim and fires.' After bombarding and capturing the forts commanding the Canton River, destroying war junks, taking over the city of Macao and forcing a resumption of trade with Canton on British terms, the fleet sailed north and dealt in similar fashion with Amoy and other ports on the way to the Yangtse River. There Shanghai and Woosung were taken, after which the steamers with the British force were sent up-river to survey the channel. On 6 July 1841 the rest of the fleet, now grown to 73 sail, weighed and moved after them through the flat landscape towards Nanking: 'It was a beautiful sight. On a signal from the flagship to weigh, in a few minutes you could see a white cloud three miles in extent, moving up the river.'

At home the brutal demonstration of power, which went far beyond the restoration of British rights, was denounced by Gladstone as aggression on behalf of British traders and manufacturers of opium grown in India; 'We, the enlightened and civilised Christians, are pursuing objects at variance both with justice and religion.' Palmerston, in reply, asked whether anyone seriously believed that the motives of the Chinese government had been to promote moral habits; or why did they not prohibit opium-growing in their own country? 'The fact is that this is an exportation of bullion question, an agricultural interest-protection question.' It was also a question of industrial expansionary forces meeting a stagnant and uncomprehending bureaucracy.

In 1842, with the chief trading centres in British hands, the humiliated Chinese agreed to peace terms which opened the ports of Amoy, Foochow, Ningpo and Shanghai as well as Canton to trade, and which ceded Hong Kong to Great Britain. Hong Kong, a hilly island, eleven miles long at the mouth of the Canton River, with a splendid harbour protected by the hills of the mainland from the north-east monsoons and the summer typhoons, was another inspired choice for a colony. From the first it was declared a duty-free port, and it grew, like Singapore, at a prodigious rate as the thriving emporium of trade with China, as well as a coaling station and the main naval base for the East Indies station; later in the century the area became a separate command, the China station.

[96]

The acquisition of Aden and Hong Kong and the operations against Mehemet Ali which stabilised Turkey and the Middle East and denied France or Russia any gains in this vital area were the most spectacular fruits of British naval and naval-diplomatic power in the early years of Victoria's reign. It would be tedious to detail the other campaigns in which the Navy was employed – they read like a guide to empire. Transporting troops to put down expected risings in Burma which threatened the north-east frontier of India; bombarding and taking Karachi to gain access to the River Indus – and a splendid commercial harbour – feeding troops and supplies up this river road to the troubled north-west frontier of India for long-forgotten campaigns against Afghans and Sikhs. Landing naval Brigades to fight Maoris who were disputing the claims of land-hungry settlers in New Zealand; establishing bases in the Northern Territory of Australia to keep out the Dutch and French, avenging native insults to isolated European communities, keeping watch on French squadrons suspected of seeking colonial bases and territory, hunting pirates, slave ships. It is only astonishing how it was all accomplished with such limited resources; the same ships' names occur again and again in different theatres; the frigate which led at the capture of Aden also scattered the war junks in the first engagement of the China War.

In many of these cases decisions were taken on the spot by colonial Governors, British Residents or naval commanders. Although naval officers did not act under *orders* from colonial authorities, and were within their rights not to take instructions from anyone but their Commander-in-Chief – who received his from London – they usually acted in concert with or 'on the opinion' of the local man. The distinction was often a fine one; it was usually necessary to act immediately to prevent a threat or punish a crime; there was seldom time to wait while despatches made their way to London, where possible responses were analysed, debated, often endlessly delayed before instructions started on their slow journey out again. British influence and trade, and to a large extent colonial territory, developed under its own impetus and the spur of European rivals. Individuals responded to immediate demands or inspiration, and made their own appreciation, confident that the smallest British brig of war was more than a match for local craft, and a naval brigade armed with muskets and cutlasses more than a match for tribesmen.

Nevertheless there were limits to the force that could be exerted by the Navy even outside European waters, and the chief of these was the vast areas to be covered and the few ships provided. Unless

[97]

a vital interest such as a border area of India or the entire China trade were threatened large concentrations were neither necessary nor practical; it was more effective to exercise control by alliances with local chiefs; if one misbehaved there were usually rivals eager to do him down. Diplomacy was as necessary to supplement the shortage of sloops in the Indian Ocean as it was to supplement ships of the line in European waters, and the ideal commander was intelligence officer and statesman as much as fighting man. As an illustration, here is one who lacked some of these qualities; perhaps he was just unlucky.

In June 1845, Captain Kelly of HMS *Conway* was ordered to Tamatave on the east coast of Madagascar, where French and a few British traders had been issued with an ultimatum from the Queen of the Hova tribe who occupied the greater part of the island, that they must either become her subjects and renounce their own nationality, or leave. This was the culmination of years of severe harrassment. On arrival Kelly found a French warship already there also to uphold European rights, and shortly afterwards a larger French corvette arrived. After an audience with the Queen, a formidable woman who refused to reduce her demands, the three commanders decided on joint action to assert European integrity and trade rights by force. Relying on only the sketchiest information about the strength of the main fort, they anchored their ships half a mile off, bombarded and then landed a party to take it by storm. This was conventional punitive action. Unfortunately the fort proved soundly-constructed of massive earth ramparts which were little affected by shot or shell, and a wide ditch all round made it impregnable to such a small force as the ships mustered. After heavy casualties the allies retired, and the following day, after taking aboard traders' property from the beach, the warships left, severely chastened, to return to their bases.

The local British reaction to the loss of face, so different from the usual run of relatively easy conquest over more primitive peoples, was to ask for sufficient reinforcements to exact reprisals. But the issue was not a vital one in the grand strategy of empire and was in any case complicated by the French involvement. The Foreign Office insisted on peaceful negotiation with the Queen, and when this failed Palmerston instructed the Commander-in-Chief at the Cape to open relations with a rival tribe inhabiting the western coast of the island. This was speedily accomplished and a commercial treaty was sealed in return for arms sufficient to maintain the tribe against the Hovas.

A more typical example of naval action and local initiative quite

[98]

The Hon. Henry Keppel in later life, covered in honours and full of the most incredible, true, tales of adventure

untouched by Whitehall is provided by the exploits of Captain The Hon. Henry Keppel, one of the most celebrated of fighting Victorian sailors, against the pirates of Borneo. Piracy, which had been virtually eliminated from the Caribbean and more recently from the Mediterranean, still flourished in the Indian Ocean and China Sea, particularly in the Indonesian archipelago. There the myriad islands and islets, interspersed with channels cut by creeks and rivers sided by sheer jungle, provided ideal cover for ambush or retreat while the political fragmentation of the whole area, often of individual islands, meant that piracy, inter-tribal warfare, slave-raiding and head-hunting were intermixed and part of the normal way of life. The Ilanuns from the Philippines and different varieties of sea Dyaks from Borneo and nearby were pirates by descent and taste.

> They look upon the occupation as the most honourable hereditary pursuit. They are indifferent to blood, fondest of plunder, but fondest of slaves . . . they despise trade though its profits be greater; and as I have said they look upon this as their 'calling' and the noblest occupation of chiefs and free men. . . .[2]

The description is from the private journal of James Brooke, Keppel's partner in the suppression of the Borneo pirates, a merchant adventurer who had become the much revered 'White Rajah' of Sarawak on the north coast of Borneo. He was representative of the best of the individualists who pioneered the Victorian empire; courage and commercial enterprise were inspired with the most visionary idealism:

> If exertion can benefit our race or even our own country; if the sum of human misery can be alleviated; if these suffering people [of Borneo] can be raised in the scale of civilisation and happiness – it is a cause in which I could suffer, it is a cause in which I have suffered and do suffer.[3]

He met Keppel, of the corvette *Dido*, in Singapore in 1841. Keppel had general instructions to protect trade and suppress piracy – which came to the same thing as the Sea Dyaks, roaming in great fleets, would take on and plunder any merchantman insufficiently armed or lying without wind. The two formed an immediate friendship and were soon planning joint action to take the war against piracy right into the pirate strongholds up the rivers of Borneo. When the *Dido* sailed, Brooke was aboard, and they made for Sarawak. There Brooke collected a force of more than 300 loyal natives, and with 80 men from *Dido*, they embarked in boats on the Sarebas River to attack a fortified pirate village seventy miles up-stream. Although the command of forces operating away from a ship was traditionally given to the First Lieutenant, Keppel couldn't resist being present, and he and Brooke went along in his gig in the forefront for most of the time. The First Lieutenant, a young mate, the Assistant Surgeon, a Midshipman, fourteen sailors and five Marines went in the ship's pinnace, armed with a 12-pounder carronade in the bows, and the rest of the men were embarked in two of the ship's cutters, one commanded by the Master, the other by a senior Midshipman. All men were supplied with muskets and cutlasses, and the boats with rations for thirty days. The Malays and loyal Dyaks were embarked in a miscellaneous fleet ranging from large prahus holding 180 men, down to small war canoes, an excitable and undisciplined crew.

They pulled steadily up between the dense jungle of the river banks, stopping for the night and posting sentries. Keppel's gig was tied up some distance from the main body:

I contemplated my novel position – in command of a mixed force of 500 men some 70 miles up a river in the heart of Borneo; on the morrow about to carry all the horrors of war amongst a race of savage pirates whose country no force had ever yet dared to invade, and who had been inflicting with impunity every sort of cruelty on all whom they encountered for more than a century. As the sun went down the scene was beautiful, animated by the variety and picturesque appearance of the native prahus, and the praying of the Musselmann . . . it was a perfect calm and the rich foliage was reflected in the water as in a mirror, while a small cloud of smoke ascended from each boat, to say nothing of that from my cigar, which added much to the charm I then experienced.[4]

The following day the force continued up-river, Keppel's attention soon drawn from increasingly beautiful scenery by sounds of yelling and beating of drums from the jungle on either side. The noises grew louder the farther they went until suddenly, rounding a bend at speed with the tide behind them they came in sight of a jungle clearing with a steep hill rising from it.

The scene was the most exciting I ever experienced. We had no time for delay or consideration; the tide was sweeping us rapidly up. As we hove in sight, several hundred savages rose up and gave one of their war yells – it was the first I had heard. No report of musketry or ordnance could ever make a man's heart feel so *small* as mine did at that horrid yell; but I had no leisure to think. I had only time for a shot at them with my double barrel as they rushed down the steep, whilst I was carried past.[5]

Immediately afterwards Keppel – whose gig was in its usual, leading position – saw a barrier formed of trees across the river; there was a small opening in it about large enough for a canoe, and instinctively putting the gig's head for it, he scraped through.

> On passing through the scene changed, and I had before me three formidable-looking forts (atop a rise), which lost not a moment in opening a discharge of cannon on my unfortunate gig. Luckily their guns were elevated for the range of the barrier; and with the exception of a few straggling grape shot that struck the water around us, the whole went over our heads. For a moment I found myself cut off from my companions and drifting fast upon the enemy. The banks of the river were covered with warriors, yelling and rushing down to possess themselves of my boat and its crew. I had some difficulty in getting my long gig round and paddling up against the stream, but while my friend Brooke steered the boat my coxswain and myself kept up a fire with tolerable aim on the embrasures to prevent if possible their carronade to bear. . . .[6]

Meanwhile the pinnace had brought up against the barrier and the 12-pounder was also firing on the fort, as were the Marine musketeers; men from the leading native prahus had started hacking through the rattans binding the barrier of trees to force a larger opening.

> I was not sorry when I found the *Dido*'s cutter on the same side as myself. The other boats soon followed and while the pinnace kept up a destructive fire on the fort Mr D'Aeth [Midshipman] who was the first to land, jumped on shore with his crew at the foot of the hill on top of which the nearest fort stood, and at once rushed for the summit. This mode of warfare – this dashing at once in the very face of their fort – was so novel and incomprehensible to our enemies that they fled panic-struck into the jungle . . .[7]

The forts and all the houses in the now-deserted village beyond were burned to the ground and the guns and ammunition taken; casualties were light, although one unfortunate sailor wounded in the arm had to have the limb amputated, 'no easy operation in the cramped space of a boat'.

Later a small force led by the First Lieutenant and Brooke in the pinnace pulled up a branch of the river to reconnoitre. They had been gone about an hour when the sound of their 12-pounder shattered the quiet of the evening. Keppel, who was just settling down to an evening meal of ham and poached eggs, jumped into his gig and summoning a bugler to accompany him to give the enemy the impression of reinforcements, made up the river branch towards the sounds of gunfire, now augmented by the war cries of savages. The river narrowed; branches of trees closed overhead from either side, and as they followed the twisting banks in darkness the eerie yelling and bursts of musketry seemed to come from every side. As they approached the scene of action Keppel had the bugler sound 'Rory O'Mory', which was immediately answered with three hearty cheers from the First Lieutenant's party. Afterwards there was a deathly silence; Keppel felt sure that the savages were preparing an ambush as the gig surged on upstream, but presently they came up with the pinnace besieged in a little bay with steep cliffs, at the top of which seven Marines were posted as rearguard. There was not a sign of life in the surrounding jungle, but every now and again spears rained down around the boat. The water was very shallow, and earlier the party had been attacked by warriors wading knee-deep across the stream; they had repulsed them with steady musketry. Keppel's party joined themselves to the defence, standing watch with guns between their knees as rain began to fall.

> The men wore their greatcoats for the purpose of keeping their pieces dry; and several times during that long night I observed the muskets of these steady good men brought up to the shoulder and again lowered without firing, as that part of the jungle whence a spear had been hurled did not show a distinct form of anything living. . . . Few will ever forget that night.[8]

At first light, with some of the men asleep as they sat with their guns, the First Lieutenant fired a signal rocket; this accomplished what the carronade and musketry had not, and the enemy fled precipitately. Afterwards the tide began to rise and the party, joined by the rest of the force, pressed on up-stream, coming presently to an encampment where the pirates had brought their wives and children. They found the warriors utterly dejected and ready to come to any terms the British might impose.

Brooke sent for their chiefs and explained that the invasion of their territory was not for pillage but as punishment for their repeated acts of piracy; they had been warned two years ago that the British would not stand for it. The chiefs appeared humble and submissive, promised to refrain from further piracy and offered hostages for their good behaviour, at which Brooke explained to them the advantages of peaceful trade over plunder and killing, and invited them to Sarawak to witness the benefits of commerce.

The effect of his moral suasion was marred by the behaviour of the loyal natives with the force, who not only helped themselves to the pirates' winter stores of rice and all their livestock, but scoured the surrounding jungle, taking heads, removing the brains with spoon-shaped bamboos and drying the skulls over fires to the accompaniment of triumphant war dances. Preserved heads were the principal decoration in their houses; a young man could not marry without at least one enemy head as proof of his virility.

After burning another pirate stockade and village, whose inhabitants fled without resistance, the expedition returned to Sarawak. Brooke and Keppel were pleased with the results, although well aware that it was only a start, and there were scores more piratical nests to be smoked out before trade in the area could be considered even reasonably safe. Both were more than ever convinced that piracy could only be stamped out by attacking the headquarters and converting the chiefs.

The example made of the Sarebas pirates, far from discouraging others, seemed to spur them to greater efforts; after the *Dido* had left Borneo one tribe in particular, under the leadership of a powerful chief called Seriff Sahib, sailed the coast in huge fleets terrorising native traders and coastal communities, threatening Sarawak itself. Brooke sent Keppel a letter asking him to return.

Keppel did so in company with a light draft steamer, *Phlegethon*, made available by the government at Calcutta. Brooke collected another loyal native force and the mixed expedition led by the *Phlegethon*, in which Keppel, Brooke and officers and men from the *Dido* had embarked, set off for the pirate river. In the meantime Seriff Sahib had been busy constructing five stockaded forts on the banks of the lower reaches to command the approaches to his chief town. Coming upon these the *Phlegethon* steamed in as close as she could before grounding and the British officers, each commanding one of the *Dido*'s or *Phlegethon*'s boats, directed the sailors to pull for the shore while the Marines and those not on the oars replied to the cannon fire from the forts with rapid musketry. Although the officers were under instructions to use the whole assault force to overwhelm the forts one by one, they took no heed and each boat pulled separately for the fort its officers thought likely to make a good fight. As soon as the stems grounded, the men scrambled out and rushed pell mell straight for the fort of their choice, entering by the embrasures while the pirates fled from the rear; in a matter of minutes the whole position was overrun for the loss of one man killed and two severely wounded. Directly afterwards the natives with the expedition stormed into the jungle after the routed pirates, seeking heads.

Sixty-four brass cannon, and several of iron, were found in the forts and either captured or spiked, after which the town beyond was looted and the houses and several hundred pirate prahus and canoes set alight, making a blaze which lasted for three days. The *Phlegethon* weighed and the expedition continued up-river, dividing forces to search out the numerous tributaries, burning more stockaded villages and pirate boats as they went, while Seriff Sahib, whose name had been a byeword for terror, fled before them through the jungle. During an attack on one of these villages Keppel's First Lieutenant was killed leading an impetuous charge far in advance of his men who were still scrambling ashore from the boats. On another sortie to clear the last of the large strongholds up the Sakarran River the whole expedition came near to disaster. Stopping for breakfast one morning during their advance, Keppel had given leave for a division of light native boats which was acting as a scouting force in advance of the main body to go on, but, as they were approaching close to the pirate headquarters, to fall back immediately there was a sign of the enemy. They had scarcely been gone a quarter of an hour when musketry and war cries indicated an attack; the main body immediately cast off and pulled heartily towards the sounds, Keppel's gig as always in the lead.

> It would be difficult to describe the scene as I found it. About twenty boats were jammed together, forming one confused mass; some bottom up; the bows or sterns of others only visible mixed up pell mell with huge rafts, and amongst which were nearly all our advanced division. Headless trunks as well as heads without bodies were lying about in all directions; parties were engaged hand-to-hand spearing and krissing each other; others were striving to swim for their lives, while on both banks thousands of Dyaks were rushing down to join in the slaughter, hurling their spears and stones on the boats below.[9]

Keppel was at a loss to know what to do as the addition of the rest of his force would simply increase the confusion and allow the Dyaks ashore to cross the solid, tangled mass of boats and slaughter his men in close melee. Fortunately one of the rafts ahead was swept by the current against the stump of a tree and caught, breaking the floating bridge and allowing a narrow passage up-river. Through this Keppel passed, assailed by spears and stones and muskets from the banks which were, fortunately, slowly-served. Brooke's shotgun would not go off, so handing him the yoke lines to steer, Keppel kept up a rapid fire with his own piece. Then an officer in one of the boats astern fired a rocket, the roar and phizz of which sent the chanting warriors scurrying in panic for shelter. This proved the turning point in what might have proved a fatal ambush; the force continued up-stream without further resistance and sacked and burned the pirate capital, by then evacuated.

This was a far more widespread and thorough punitive expedition than the first; it broke the hold of the greatest pirate chief of the coast, impressed the Dyaks with the power that Brooke seemed able to summon up at will, and allowed increasing trade. But piracy was too ingrained in the character and culture of the archipelago to be so quickly exterminated. Many more British demonstrations ashore and afloat, and generations of British naval officers were needed to keep it down to tolerable levels. And there was never any systematic drive to wipe it out, only sporadic bursts of individual enthusiasm or official action in the wake of outrages.

Bounty, known as 'head money', had always been paid by the British government for successful operations at the rate of £20 for each pirate killed and £5 for each man present at the action. It was shared out on the same basis as wartime prize money with the Captain receiving a quarter of the total, the Flag Officer of the station a twelfth, the commissioned officers and Master an eighth between them, and the rest of the company taking shares which decreased in size down the ranks and ratings. Although Captains stood to gain huge sums – for instance £42,425 was paid out for the capture of a fleet of 58 pirate junks in 1849 – this stimulus to individual enterprise was no substitute for regularity and system; but because of the shortage of ships and diversity of duties there could never be either, and piracy continued well into the twentieth century.

Before leaving Keppel and the China Seas an anecdote from his next commission illustrates again the wide scope naval commanders enjoyed. The problem on this occasion was the release of a British subject from a Portuguese jail in Macao. He had been locked up, so Keppel was told, for failing to salute the Host during a procession on the Feast of Corpus Christi. When Keppel went to see the Portuguese Governor he was informed this was not correct; the man had been jailed for disobeying an order.

'What order?'

'My order to take his hat off.'

'Do I understand Your Excellency rightly, that you could order any person you chose to take his hat off in the open streets?'

'Exactly so.'

'Then I must ask for his immediate release, for I cannot consider that the alleged offence is any crime at all.'

The Governor replied coldly that Keppel was not acquainted with Portuguese law. Keppel bowed himself out, and returning to his ship wrote a formal complaint. Knowing it would be ignored, he also made plans to release the Englishman by force, first of all ascertaining the layout and routine of the prison with the help of a British military officer who gained an interview with the prisoner by disguising himself as a merchant with a white coat and a basket of fruit. When the Governor replied to Keppel's note negatively, Keppel decided on immediate action. He was officiating as umpire at a regatta that afternoon; while the boats were forming up at the start his own ships' boats, previously manned and armed, started pulling for the shore, and as soon as the race had begun, he excused himself and joined them at the landing place. The army officer who had surveyed the cells also joined them and took an armed party consisting of the First Lieutenant, twelve sailors and six Marines directly to the jail; Keppel despatched a second party after them to secure their retreat, and was waiting for a third boat-load to reach the shore when he heard a burst of musketry; hastening towards the jail he was delighted to find the British party returning arm in arm with the prisoner. The guard at the jail had been caught by surprise, and there had been no resistance after the Marines fired a volley, hitting a Portuguese musketeer in the arm and killing another. The jailer had dropped his keys and fled, and the release had been effected in seconds.

'For this I was reprimanded by the Admiralty, and thanked by Lord Palmerston.'

The same year in the Mediterranean a single British paddle-wheel gunboat was ordered to the Italian coast off Rome to protect British interests against internal disturbances. Her Captain, Cooper Key, wrote:

You cannot imagine the effect of a British man of war. I assure you, people wrote to the Minister at Florence and Naples, and a large number said that my presence at Rome kept the City tranquil, though my ship was 50 miles off![10]

He mused in his Journal:

> English influence still carries the day, and a word of advice
> from us will do anything. How glorious is the title of
> 'Englishman' – and yet we are not loved. How is it? Is it our
> national conceit; or self-confident and supercilious bearing – the
> consciousness of superiority we show? Or is it jealousy? It is
> gratifying to think the latter, but I fear it cannot be that
> altogether. . . .[11]

Key overestimated the influence of British warships and the powers of their commanders. They might take a high hand with decaying empires like China or Portugal, it was otherwise with major
powers. Then punctilious legality was always observed, and no
action taken without authority from the Commander-in-Chief, who
took instructions from the Foreign Office. This was particularly the
case with France, increasingly prickly since her discomfiture in the
Middle East crisis, anxious to reassert herself overseas, and annex-
ing bases wherever she could to make up for the vital strategic
points lost to the British during the great wars. The naval relation-
ship with France overseas was a strange blend of co-operation to
further European interests – and intense rivalry and suspicion of
her expansionary aims. In the early 1840s suspicion was uppermost;
after she had occupied several Indian Ocean islands, well-placed for
the trade routes from the Cape of Good Hope, the Admiralty became
so alarmed that watching and reporting on French squadrons, 'but
without running the risk of allowing your motives to become apparent or your movements to give offence', became the principal function of the East African division of the Cape Station.

An example of the caution which naval officers displayed when
French interests were concerned is provided by the rivalry in the
Pacific. On 9 September 1842 the French Admiral, Du Petit
Thouars, prevailed on Queen Pomare of Tahiti to sign a treaty
ceding the island to France. On 30 September Her Britannic Majesty's Ship *Dublin* (Captain Tucker) arrived at Papeete 'to protect
British interests and give assistance and advice to Her Majesty
Queen Pomare', who claimed that the French Treaty had been
forced on her under threat of bombardment. In such a delicate
situation Tucker could do nothing without orders, yet there could
be no orders until his own appreciation had been sent to the
Commander-in-Chief of the station, from thence to London and back
– all by slow ship. So when Du Petit Thouars objected to Queen
Pomare's habit of flying the national Tahitian flag from her Palace,

and the indignant Queen appealed to Tucker, he could only advise her not to oppose the decree by force, and stand idly by while a party of three-hundred armed *matelots* marched on the Palace, hauled down the offending flag and hoisted the French; he despatched a note of protest to Du Petit Thouars, but it was a formality.

The following year, when a French naval officer imprisoned the British Consul on the island, Tucker was there again, but again could only 'await further instructions from Her Britannic Majesty's Government'. Indeed by this time it was imperative that he do so as French anger at British attitudes over the whole Tahitian question was boiling up, and the following year it actually threatened war. When the troubled Queen wrote to Tucker asking for protection from the French, beseeching him not merely to 'look upon me with your eyes, but really act that it may be well with me', he could only reply, 'From the circumstances of Your Majesty having signed that Treaty I can advise no active measures being taken in opposition to the same.'[12] The annexation of the island was eventually rescinded by the French government, who nevertheless maintained a protectorate over it.

Nowhere was the concern for the susceptibilities of other powers more apparent, nowhere more difficult to observe than in the Royal Navy's fight against the slave trade. In contrast to the lack of system and the sporadic nature of the struggle against piracy, this crusade was maintained continuously along the slaving coasts and Captains were constantly faced with problems over rights of search and capture of suspected ships flying the colours of foreign nations – indeed there were no British-flag ships in the trade. Officers were obliged to play for safety: here is Commander Bosanquet of HM Brig-of-War *Alert* off the west coast of Africa in 1844.

> I yesterday fell in with the brigantine *Uncar* under American colours and as the wind was light at the time I sent the 2nd Lieutenant in the Gig to visit her without obliging her to heave-to, but on her seeing the Gig she backed her main topsail; the Lieutenant after remaining on board a few minutes returned and reported that there were several suspicious circumstances about the brigantine, that she was from the Havannah and that the Captain refused to show any clearance from that or other ports. . . .[13]

Commander Bosanquet decided to board her himself, and as she had filled her sails and drawn ahead by this time, he made all sail in chase and fired a blank gun, causing her to heave-to.

I found both by her log and the declaration of her Captain she had left the coast of Africa last September for the Havannah, at which port she arrived in *ballast*, having only touched at Key West in *ballast* to get a Bill of Health . . . she had again sailed for the Havannah last December with little more than a half Cargo for the Gallinas, a notorious slave place and was to return again to the Havannah in ballast. There was a Spaniard on board, a cabin passenger, of whom the Captain could give no account further than that he was going to the coast of Africa. It appeared to me so highly improbable that any vessel should have come to the coast of Africa to trade with a half cargo and return each time in ballast, and her carrying on a direct trade between the Havannah and the slave ports on the coast of Africa had caused her to lose her national character and subjected her to be treated as a Spanish vessel. I examined her holds and found her fitted with a set of spare open gratings for her hatchways and some very heavy casks of tobacco which by recoopering might be made to hold water, but not finding any other articles prohibited by the Spanish Treaty, and feeling some doubt how far she could claim the protection of the American flag I considered it advisable to let her proceed, fearing it might cause an unpleasant correspondence between HM Government and the United States.[14]

The episode illustrates exactly the position that had been reached in the early 1840s in the battle of wits and resources between on the one side the British government and the Royal Navy, on the other the big business interests behind the slave trade. Britain had first abolished the trade under her own flag in 1807; after the war successive governments, pushed along by a surge of humanitarian sentiment against the evils of the trade, had undertaken to stamp it out altogether throughout the world, a colossal task quite beyond any nation, however powerful at sea, without the co-operation of all governments concerned.

This proved unexpectedly difficult to obtain; the French paid eloquent lip service to the idea but, sensitive to any appearance of servility to the British, would not allow British boarding parties to search vessels flying the French flag. Nor would the Americans, who were in any case too dependent on slave labour to join the campaign with any enthusiasm. The Spanish, Portuguese and Brazilians were easier game for the Foreign Office to bully, but their colonial economies were again so bound up with slave labour that they had neither the will nor the power to act effectively. Interna-

The East African coast; a Royal Navy corvette chases a dhow suspected of carrying slaves

tional courts were set up to try suspected slave ships captured by the Navy, but to secure a conviction it was necessary to catch the ship with slaves aboard – a provision which led to negroes being thrown overboard in some cases when it appeared that a British cruiser would overhaul the slaver, and to many more cases of slaves being confined ashore while ships waited until the coast was clear.

It appeared to me that while cruisers are not allowed by treaty with Spain and Portugal to capture vessels fitted for slaves without the slaves on board, we did more harm than good. Along the coast negroes are brought from the interior and confined in pens, and when closely watched by our cruisers, are frequently starved to death. If a slaver is captured with slaves on board, the price rises on the other side of the Atlantic, which is immediately followed by an increase in the number of vessels that come out.[15]

That was in the late 1830s; by the early 1840s Palmerston, whose views on slavery were so strong that he was said in Cabinet to be not quite accountable for his actions in that regard – had achieved ratification by all governments except France of an 'Equipment

An incident in the battle against the East African slave trade.
Lieutenant Fegen boards a slaving dhow

clause' providing that if sufficient items of equipment necessary for carrying slaves were found aboard a ship, it would be evidence that she was engaged in the trade, without the necessity of finding the slaves themselves. 'Equipment' included the open gratings Commander Bosanquet found aboard the *Uncar*; they were to allow ventilation in the holds where the slaves were packed in tiers one above the other on boards fitted like enormous shelves. These boards and the manacles for fastening the slaves were regarded as 'equipment', as were extra water casks, supplies of food and water in excess of the quantities required for the crew, or extra cooking and feeding facilities.

The French not only refused to ratify this clause, but only granted rights of search in a limited area 10° each side of the Equator on the west coast, and within sixty miles of Madagascar to the east, and then only to ships whose commanders held a special warrant. The Americans were just as touchy, partly because of their own slave-owning interests in the South, and ship-owning interests in the north making vast profits from the trade; partly from recent memories of British naval arrogance in boarding and impressing sailors from American ships during the great wars. Instead of ratifying the Equipment clause they provided a small squadron of US warships for the slave coast of West Africa. As a result a great part of the Atlantic trade in the 1840s was being carried on by ships

[112]

provided with US papers, flying US colours and having a US master, in addition perhaps to a Spanish Master and a spare set of Spanish papers in case they should meet one of the US warships.

Palmerston, not to be outfaced by flags of convenience, instructed the Admiralty that if a commanding officer had reason to believe that a ship hoisting US or French colours did not genuinely belong to that nation, he might board her to ascertain her true nationality. If her papers were irregular or if she had more than one set she might be searched and sent for trial; however, if she seemed genuine she was to be left immediately. This placed extraordinary difficulties of interpretation on British officers, and like Commander Bosanquet they usually took the safe course, not simply because of international repercussions, but because if a suspected ship were found not guilty by a Court, the Captain of the warship which had made the capture was held responsible for the costs of the case and any damages brought by the owners; the Admiralty accepted no responsibility. Commander Bosanquet, who had no doubt in his own mind that the *Uncar* had been slaving, went on:

> But if vessels under these circumstances can carry on the slave trade with impunity then all the efforts of Her Majesty's Government to suppress the slave trade must be futile, and the trade can only be suppressed by the American and not by the English government.[16]

This was the nub of the matter: Palmerston could and did bully the Dutch, Spanish, Portuguese and Brazilians but he could not take a high hand with the Americans, and it was not until 1862, when President Lincoln signed a Right of Search Treaty, that the Atlantic slave trade received its death blow.

In the meantime the British government maintained its own campaign with stubborn determination in the face of all evidence that it could neither stamp the trade out unilaterally, nor even liberate more than 5 per cent of perhaps 150,000 Africans being exported annually from the West Coast, and for this the Navy paid a high price in lives lost and men permanently ruined in health. The fever-ridden mangrove swamps and inlets at the mouths of the Niger and other West African rivers, where the boats' crews of patrolling warships played hide and seek with the slave dealers and the fast clippers that lay waiting for their human cargo, took an enormous toll. The average mortality in the home and Mediterranean fleets was under 10 per 1,000 men, on the West African coast it was nearly 55. In the five years 1839 to 1844, 385 officers and men died from fever or were killed in action with slavers and nearly 500 more were invalided out of the service, a total loss equivalent to five sloops; 128 more died in 1845.

Apart from the inshore work much of the disease was contracted by prize crews sailing captured slavers to Freetown in Sierra Leone, where one Mixed Court sat. Descriptions of the state of the slaves battened down below the decks of small clippers during the Atlantic passage leave no doubts about why this should have been so; here is a description from one captured near the end of her voyage:

> In my life I have never witnessed anything so shocking. About 450 people were packed into that small vessel as you would pack bales of goods; and disease of all sorts became rife with them. One hundred had died before she was taken, and they were and are still dying daily. Some were carried up the side in a state of emaciation such as I would not have imagined it possible to exist with life; others with raw sores, their bones all but through them, and some dreadful cases of smallpox, covered from head to foot. Some children were in the last stages of emaciation and sores. It was dreadful, and so distressing I could have cried.[17]

It was always possible to tell a slave ship by the appalling stench of excrement and diseased flesh, and this clung to ships for weeks after the cargo had been discharged. 'One night the Captain gave orders to put out every light in the ship as he could smell a slaver.' The epidemics contracted from slaves sometimes swept through entire prize crews, leaving only one or two weakened men to manage the craft. Keppel tells of the brig *Harpy*, which had such a sickly complement after a prize crew had re-embarked in her that the officers themselves went aloft to assist loosing sails when she left the coast.

Surgeons, having a wrong conception of the causes of the different fevers, were powerless to cure them. Quinine was often administered to boats' crews on inshore work, but was seldom used as a cure until after mid-century. Blood-letting, blistering, purging were the more usual – and fatally weakening – treatments. Once an epidemic took hold of a ship, she would make with all speed from the coast to the clean breezes and hospital facilities of the British base on the island of Ascension in the Atlantic.

The climate on the West Coast was so unsuitable for work as well as health that on arrival on the station all cruisers took aboard some two dozen natives known as Kroomen from the coast of what is now Liberia. These were solid, dependable sailors and were used for much of the arduous labour like heaving aboard water casks under a torrid sun.

> The native names of these Kroomen were so incomprehensible that on their first joining a ship of war the Captain had to find names for the ship's books. Thus among those left with me were Dr Inman, Seabreeaze, No grog, Prince of Wales, Bishop of London. They were good-tempered, willing fellows, thoroughly acquainted with the coast.[18]

By the 1840s the average number of warships on the coast had risen from less than a dozen to almost thirty, including a number of steamers which proved ideal for the fluky winds and strong currents of the area. Each cruiser was given a stretch of coast to patrol, perhaps 100 to 150 miles in a major river area, far more along the sandy stretches where the high Atlantic surf prevented embarkation. A rendezvous for all cruisers was fixed for a certain date by the senior officer, often only a Commander, who would inspect the vessels and their crews with all the pomp of an Admiral, afterwards probably inviting the commanders to dine with him. Otherwise each ship was left on its own to hunt the quarry from information sold by native traders, to send armed boats' crews up the maze of creeks in search of anchored slave ships or the 'baracoons' where natives were penned awaiting shipment, or simply to cruise offshore to intercept slave ships at sea.

> Lookout men are stationed at each masthead, one of the crew, the other a Krooman, with the reward of a doubloon for the one who should first see a sail that proved a prize; we showed no lights at night; a small hole in the binnacle was all that was allowed the helmsman. . . .[19]

> In our minds for the present all questions of philanthropy, all sympathy with the misfortunes of the negro, all anger towards his oppressor were merged in the single idea of pursuit of game. The ordinary sportsman may on the moor or in the cover experience all the sensations of a slave catcher when he has been a little time at the work. True, the feeling is wider and more absorbing in the slave catcher, but it is not deeper or different in source.[20]

There is nothing so exciting as a chase, especially at night,

[115]

when you cannot make out what you are in chase of. Even the men of the watch below turn out to look on as soon as you are within range.[21]

At daylight the slaver was out of range and the crew asked the Captain to capture her with the boats, but he wouldn't as so many had been killed lately on such operations. We crowded on sail and wetted the sails with the fire engine. Every time the breeze freshened we would gain on her and the slaver would start heaving niggers overboard, some very close as they passed. The third evening we lost her. . . .[22]

The rewards for liberating slaves or capturing slave ships had been decreased by the government as they increased the number of ships on patrol. By the 1830s the bounty paid for each slave released was £5 – it had once been £60 for a male slave – and £1.10s. per ton of slave ship; if the ship were empty but fitted for slaves £4 per ton was paid. Each cruiser appointed an agent to represent her claims to the Treasury for a commission of 2½ per cent and costs; a further 10 per cent went to naval charity, and a Prize balance account, and one-thirtieth of what was left to the Commander-in-Chief of the station. The Captain of the cruiser took 10 per cent and the remainder was divided into shares in the same way as 'head money' for pirates, with commissioned officers getting from 45 to 20 shares, Warrant and Petty Officers 20 to about 7, Able Seamen 4 and boys 1. In money terms this meant that from £2,000 prize money an ordinary seaman might expect £3.10s. and the Captain about £200. There were few fortunes to be made except by the Commander-in-Chief of the station, and it is probably correct that 'the money value of the rewards would never of themselves induce any naval officer to undertake the arduous and unpleasant duty'. Nor were there prospects of accelerated promotion as in normal action. Nevertheless there was the spice of the hunt to compensate for the torrid climate, and detestation of the slave dealers to give purpose to months of weary cruising during commissions lasting some three years. For the men there was the comparative freedom of open boat work besides a good deal of incident.

As well as capturing slave ships at sea, destroying slave baracoons ashore and bringing diplomatic pressure to bear on the governments of powers whose subjects took part in the noxious trade, the British government in the early 1840s started a campaign to win over the native chiefs of the West African coast by Treaties; in return for taking no part in the slave trade they were to be rewarded with bounties:

Her Majesty's Steam Vessel Kite *off the Cameroons, 6th June 1843*

. . . I have the honor to report to you on the arrival of HM steam vessel under my command at King George Town, Cameroons River on the 5th inst; the Certificate having been signed by the traders frequenting that river that no Slave Trade had been carried on there during the preceding year – the Presents were distributed in strict accordance with the instructions contained in the letters herewith returned, to King Angua and King Bell, who signed the Declaration herewith enclosed, and requested that the accompanying List might be forwarded of Articles they would wish for their next year's presents . . .

[*Enclosure*]

We, the undersigned Chiefs of the Cameroons River herein solemnly declare that during the year previous to the date hereof no Slave Trade has been carried on through or from our Territories. And we further engage that no Slave Trade shall be carried on; and that on these conditions only we have received the Presents undermentioned, sent out by the British government, viz. . . .

Calico, East Indian blue	3,000 yards in 3 bales
Flints, Musket	2,000 in 2 casks
Muskets with bayonets and rammers	720 in 6 cases
Coats, scarlet	2
Swords with velvet scabbards	2
Epaulettes, gold	4
Belts, sword crimson leather	2
Case tin	1
Rum, barrels of	8
Powder, barrels of	4

his

Signed King   Bell

mark

his

King   Angua

mark

I have the Honor to be, Sir, Your most obedient humble Servant

J. Pasco Lt. & Commander

[Enclosure]

List of articles which the chiefs of the Cameroons River requested might be sent for next year's presents.

For King Angua

1 frame house, 2 bedsteads and beds, 2 easy chairs, 2 glass chandeliers, 2 mirrors, 2 hand organs, 2 blue frock coats, VR on buttons, 2 hats, gold band and binding, 4 pairs trousers, 6 shirts, 2 pairs red boots, 2 large umbrellas, 2 British ensigns marked 'King Angua', 6 small kegs of different coloured paints. . . .[23]

King Bell's requests were more orthodox; they included muskets, bayonets, gunpowder, rum, but also a British ensign marked 'Queen Victoria-King Bell', a blue coat with red facings and a cocked hat and sword. The Lieutenant commanding the *Kite* suggested that these requests be attended to as he had every reason to believe that the Kings had given up dealing in slaves in favour of legal trade.

On occasions the native chiefs were invited to dine with the 'White Chief of the fire ship' which brought the presents, and at all times they were received with full ceremonial.

Sometimes we would have three or four black Kings on board a day, signing treaties; we would dress ship with flags and give them all a gun salute. The Captain used to send a message to the officers messes and messdecks that a black King was coming aboard and they should lock up all their valuables. They would come off in their State canoes, some with more than forty paddles, with tom-toms beating. Each was given a Purser's No 2 jacket with a Crown and Anchor badge sewn on the left breast. They were served with a bottle of rum and biscuits.[24]

These treaties and the Navy's obligations to the legal traders in palm oil, who were encouraged by the British government to take the place of the slave dealers, involved the Navy in an increasing number of operations ashore. Among them were the duty to protect 'Treaty' tribes against slave-hunting rivals, preserve the peace along a trader's river torn by tribal warfare, sometimes even to take part in secession struggles by supporting friendly claimants in bids to topple Kings who refused to make treaties outlawing the slave trade. Naval support ensured success despite the heavy armaments often mounted by European slave dealers in defence of their own man. In such a way the King of the important slaving centre of Lagos was deposed in 1851 by the combined assault of a rival claimants' forces and 400 officers and men from a British squadron collected for the purpose.

Many of these operations were conducted hundreds of miles up-river by parties embarked in ships' boats.

At night the boat was sometimes a very trying place to live in. Anchored up a creek, with a rain awning over the top, no fresh air could get in or foul air out, and the total of 70 occupants inside, including 30 black men, worked out at about 10 cubic feet per man – a condition which is, I understand, impossible for a human being to live in. We managed to live but it was not pleasant, and I was always glad when the morning came. We should have liked to bathe, but as a crocodile rose to everything that was thrown overboard bathing was not permissible. The hippopotami during the night were a source of annoyance; they breathe so noisily through their wide-open mouths.[25]

The most effective weapon on these expeditions when the British were always outnumbered by enemies who knew every inch of the territory, was the Congreve rocket, a terrifying if erratic thunder-bolt. It came in two sizes, 12- or 24-pounder; warheads were filled with an explosive, incendiary composition of sulphur, saltpetre, resin, antimony and turpentine. They were fired by flintlock from a tube mounted on a boat's gunwale on an arm which could be raised to give elevation. Short tubes were 15 feet, the more effective long tubes 25 feet in length; an elevation of only 15° gave a range of 2,000 yards, while at full elevation of 45° the rocket would travel two miles. In a wind they had to be aimed to leeward, in a strong wind they might describe extraordinary aerobatics, but great ac-curacy was never necessary as the roaring sound they made in flight was sufficiently awe-inspiring to persuade natives that they were agents of the supernatural powers they feared.

At this attack I saw one of these great roaring rockets pass clean through the trunk of a large cotton tree and, swerving widely to the left, enter and pass under a mud bank for some distance, to rise out of it again, and pursue its flight for some yards further before exploding.[26]

As in the Indian Ocean and China Seas, the demands of local traders and Consuls for efficient administration to secure protection for commerce and European property led step by step – despite

A RN officer questions the Nakhoda (master) of an East African dhow about his 'passengers'

government reluctance to spend money on colonies – to protectorates and formal rule taking the place of the Navy's informal influence, a process that was accelerated by the activities of other European powers.

Suppression of the East African slave trade presented even more problems than the West Coast trade. Much of the traffic, and after the 1850s when Palmerston succeeded in closing the Brazilian market nearly all, went to Arabian, Persian, Turkish destinations, where slavery was a part of the culture and economy. Harems were stocked with high-priced concubines from Abyssinia; domestic slaves were a normal part of a merchant's household; vineyards and plantations were worked by slaves. Added to this, the principal slave market on Zanzibar island and many of the mainland ports through which the trade from inland Africa was conducted belonged to the Sultan of Muscat, Great Britain's faithful ally in the Persian Gulf area. The Sultan's revenues were dependent on customs receipts from the trade. Further south on the coast other slave routes from the interior, notably the Zambesi River, reached the sea in Mozambique, nominally Portuguese territory, but not under effective Portuguese control because of impoverished administration and inadequate forces. In any case the colony relied on the slave trade for even such a low level of existence; when the Brazilian market closed in the 1850s slaves from Mozambique were sent in Arab dhows to the market at Zanzibar, and from thence to the Red Sea and Persian Gulf ports which served Arabia and the Middle East.

Apart from the diplomatic problems, catching slave dhows was a harder game than catching Atlantic slavers. For one thing they used no 'equipment' such as West Coast officers were accustomed to look for, but took human cargoes much as they might take any other goods. When chased by a cruiser's boat they would dress up some of the slaves as passengers, some as crew and the females as their wives; unless the boarding officer had an interpreter with him, or was very experienced, it was a difficult situation.

> 'What dem nigger der?' They point to the sails, and make a
> motion with the hand like hoisting it. 'Oh, dem crew men. Who
> dese?' Another wave of the hands from south to north and a
> good deal of jargon in which the words Mozambique and
> Zanzibar occur. 'Oh, suppose dem passengers. Where am
> papers?' This we make them understand by writing with the
> forefinger of the right hand on the palm of the left. The papers
> are produced. They might have been, for all we knew, bills of
> sale for the niggers on board. . . .[27]

In the larger dhows with a full slave cargo there could be no mistake; the conditions were quite as bad as in the Atlantic slavers, in some cases worse as the Arabs were too indolent to organise sufficient food or water even for themselves and their crew.

> On the bottom of the dhow was a pile of stones as ballast, and
> on these stones without even a mat were 23 women huddled
> together – one or two with infants in their arms – these women
> were literally doubled up, there being no room to sit erect; on a
> bamboo deck about three feet above the keel were 48 men
> crowded together in the same way, and on another deck above
> this were 53 children. Some of the slaves were in the last stages
> of starvation and dysentery. . . .[28]

These larger dhows sometimes carried a small cannon, which they used to little effect against chasing cruisers or cruiser's boats. All dhows of whatever size carried muskets – usually loaded with such enormous charges of powder that it was dangerous to fire them – long double-edged swords and round shields of boiled hippo hide, also spears of light cane with iron lance heads. Their favourite trick to deal with inexperienced boarding parties coming alongside to leeward was suddenly to let go the huge sail, which would fall and envelop the boat and its crew, then stab down through the flailing cotton with their swords. To counter this, some cruisers' boats towed a canvas punt and when they neared the dhow the boarding officer went to inspect her in the punt while the boats crew kept the Arabs covered.

An additional difficulty for boarding officers in the late 1840s was the use of free negroes or *engagés* by the French in their Indian Ocean possessions. These were bought and sold by dealers from Mozambique in the same way as slaves and were treated in the same way 'with cruelties which cause an Englishman's flesh to creep at their bare mention, and all this rendered still more revolting by the falsehood and sarcasm contained in the name given the poor wretches – free negroes!' They were taught the right responses to make to boarding officers' questions before embarkation. Just as the US flag was widely used for immunity on the West Coast so the French flag was flown by dhows in the Indian Ocean, a ruse which in the 1870s cost the senior officer of the Cape Station his life. 'It's only a French trader,' he said to his Coxswain, 'we'll run alongside and see if he's got anything to sell.' The Arabs, seeing his boat nearing and the crew carrying no arms, rose as one and poured in a murderous volley at point blank. The Captain was the only man left not wounded and seizing a gun that hung ready across an awning framework in the sternsheets fired, then used it as a club as the Arabs swarmed down into the boat, 'but a sweeping downward cut from a double-edged sword severed all his fingers from the barrel, and another clove his head in two, after which his body was mutilated'.

While there were many running battles with the swift and weatherly dhows and not a few officers and men lost their lives, most dhow-catching was a matter of endless cruising or lying in wait in ship's boats, followed by a chase and for the more scrupulous officers a long interrogation to decide whether 'crew' and 'passengers' were as represented. Boats were away from their parent ship for weeks at a time, but as conditions were a good deal pleasanter than up the West Coast rivers, it is probable that most men enjoyed the freedom from routine.

> From a bluejacket's point of view it was perfect. Directly after leaving the ship, the uniform dress would be thrown aside for a pair of loose blue jean or serge nickers, reaching just below the knee, a flannel shirt, and close-fitting cap; boots were never thought of.[29]

Salt rations for thirty days were carried, but every opportunity

Captured Arab slave traders aboard a British corvette note the
Armstrong breechloader

was taken to fish, shoot wildfowl or barter empty beer bottles or
nicknacks with the coastal natives for eggs, fruit, roots and other
delicacies. Meals would be cooked aboard, the officer taking his in
solitary state in the stern, the men forward. As dusk came on the
rain awning would be spread over the boat and a single 'purser's
dip' lit to serve as a timekeeper for the lookout man who kept his
head above the awning. Evening grog would be served out, or wine
of quinine, and the men might have a sing-song or play quiet games
of nap or euchre before lying down to sleep on the bottom boards;
unlike the boats' complements for operations ashore they were not
too crowded. In the morning they could usually bathe in the crystal
clear water; 'one could look down into limpid depths where fish
coloured every tint sported; on the bottom great sea slugs, sponges
and other marine growths swaying gently to and fro.' Sometimes
they would land and induce a party of natives to sing and dance for
them.

Once, when the Captain was due to visit Pemba Island, the
cutter's crew, the merriest set of reprobates, taught the chief,
Bin Juma, a speech of address to the great white chief
consisting of the choicest swear words in the sailor's
vocabulary. When the Captain paid the visit, Bin Juma . . .
with that stately and graceful air, which seems a natural
characteristic of the Arab, shot forth a torrent of invective that

[123]

would have shocked the ears of a Billingsgate porter. The Captain was much too well up in the ways of the sailormen not to guess what had been done, so accepted the address with a genial bow and congratulated Bin Juma on his flow of English, then turned to his Coxswain with a twinkle and said, 'I wonder who were the damned scamps who fixed up that little job.'[30]

When a slave dhow was caught, slaves and crew were generally taken aboard the cruiser and the dhow burned or used for target practice with the great guns. The dhows were generally small and the distances to the Courts at Aden or the Cape were great, consequently the waste of time and manpower too great to permit prize crews to sail them. With slaves aboard, the character of the sailors showed up to advantage. Here is an officer's view.

The bluejacket is *very* gentle to the negro slave newly liberated; there is no amount of inconvenience he does not cheerfully submit to in their behalf . . . I do not expect to see a prettier sight than I was witness of for several days in succession when witnessing the conduct of the bluejackets towards the negroes. Some of them who had been captured on shore after landing were sadly cut about the feet – especially women and children. It was an established habit of the men to carry them about in their arms when it was necessary to move them from one part of the ship to another to save them from putting their wounded feet on the deck. Then the doctoring that went on, the care with which cooling poultices were applied, and the careful bandaging would have done credit to a village hospital; and that it was a spontaneous piece of charity made it all the more engaging to observe. I should say the poor creatures never had before, and certainly never will have again such gentle treatment as they received at the hands of our English seamen.[31]

The sailors looked on the slave trade with quite as much loathing and disgust as their officers, and the slave markets ashore where the Arabs examined the negroes 'discussing their points and estimating their value just as farmers examine and value cattle at an English market' and where the slave children, 'looking old already . . . had no inclination to play, sat in silence, or rose when required' enraged them.

It is as a rule dangerous to allow British seamen to land at Zanzibar, on account of the slave market; the bluejacket is impelled to make a clearance of the place, which he has done more than once on the spur of the moment. . . .[32]

However, the sailors were never averse to availing themselves of the better-looking female slaves carried aboard, while the scenes of promiscuity in some open boats returning to the parent ship after the capture and burning of a dhow rivalled those on the lower deck in a home port.

It is an unfortunate fact that the effort to extinguish the slave trades in the Indian Ocean and Persian Gulf was even less successful than in the Atlantic. Despite great efforts by senior officers and individual commanders of the East African division of the Cape Station – created in 1844 – and by the Persian Gulf division of the East Indies station, the lack of sufficient vessels and their frequent diversion to more compelling duties meant that the Navy never liberated more than perhaps 6 per cent of the estimated total traffic from the east coast; in the opinion of several officers and men the patrols actually made conditions for the slaves worse, just as the Navy's activities on the west coast had probably increased suffering. In any case the human traffic continued long after the suppression of the Atlantic trade, well into the final decades of the century.

Similar, more exacting boat work was a feature of the other fine, liberal task on which the Navy was engaged, surveying the coasts of the world and printing charts for the benefit of any navigator who cared to buy them from the network of agents supplied by the Hydrographic Office of the Admiralty. Hitherto charts had been few and random, and despite vast inaccuracies generally withheld from rivals. After the great wars the Admiralty, in keeping with the Free Trade sentiment of the country set in motion a methodical effort to bring what had been one of the mysteries of navigation into the full light of scientific knowledge. By 1837 the 'Admiralty chart' was established in much the form familiar today with lines of soundings and standardised abbreviations to denote the nature of the bottom, standardised methods of showing rocks, shoals, particular coastlines, drying heights, compass roses with magnetic North offset, even the system by which navigators updated their own charts by reference to regular issues of *Notices to Mariners*. And at various points around the world small ships with teams of single-minded specialist officers in extraordinarily varied working kit, with musket and pistol handy to beat off native attack, worked their painstaking way along coastlines and up river estuaries to fill in the vast blanks that remained before the sea frontiers of the continents and the myriad islands and reefs which bestrewed the trade routes were thoroughly known.

From very early days, steam vessels had been recognised as ideal for the task, and many were in use by the 1840s. Still, much of the work was done with hand lead and line from ship's boats sailing or pulling along set courses between floating beacons made of casks previously moored in a system of equilateral triangles. Moving from one set of beacons to the next, the boats worked inshore, where an accurate latitude and longitude was obtained by sextant with artificial horizon, then applied to each of the beacons. Soundings were reduced to a common 'datum' level below the lowest tide by observing the rise and fall with marked poles. Points ashore were plotted with theodolites and measuring chains; the distance of visible rocks and other sea marks, including the beacons, by gunfire – timing the difference between the visible eruption of smoke and the sound of the shot. Beautiful results were obtained by sheer dedication to excellence.

> The principle on which surveying is conducted is one of restless energy; even the most unwilling of volunteers finds himself goaded into perpetual activity by the example and precept of his seniors . . . it is a new life entirely different from a man-of-war routine . . . surveying forms the basis of conversation, for it is seldom indeed that any other subject is introduced.[33]

The quest for knowledge of undiscovered parts of the world off the trade routes went forward more spasmodically, the result of individual enthusiasm rather than sustained planning. The most consistent effort went into the search for a Northwest Passage around the top of Canada into the Pacific. It was this centuries-old exploration, now carried on by the Admiralty largely for the sake of bringing the Navy before a disinterested public and perhaps to prevent Americans or Russians gaining the prestige of discovery, which led to the greatest sustained drama of the time, the disappearance of the Franklin expedition.

Sir John Franklin was one of those many veterans of the great wars still on the Captain's list. As a young Lieutenant after the wars he had commanded a vessel on an expedition to Spitzbergen, and had followed this by taking part in an overland expedition to North Canada, experience which appeared to fit him for leadership of an expedition planned in 1844 to push through the known channels north of the islands fringing northern Canada, thence south-westwards towards the Bering Strait and the open Pacific. His age was against him, but when the First Lord tackled him on it, pointing out that he was sixty, he would not have it; 'My Lord, you have been misinformed. I am only fifty-nine.'

He was given two vessels, *Erebus* and *Terror*, which had already been fitted and used for exploration in the Antarctic between 1839 and 1843. Both were immensely broad and stoutly constructed; originally 'bomb' vessels built to withstand the recoil of mortars mounted on deck, they now had massive extra timbers and iron sheathing around the bows. They were also fitted with engines.

The expedition composed of volunteers sailed under Franklin's leadership in May 1845, entering the Arctic Circle in late June; there they took on extra provisions from an accompanying supply ship, which then returned home, and continued up the Greenland coast towards Melville Bay, where they were sighted by a whaler at the end of July. They were not seen again – unless two ships answering to their description seen briefly perched up an ice flow by the Newfoundland Banks six years later were the *Erebus* and *Terror*.

After two years without news, relief expeditions were sent out, and it was one of these under Commander McClure of HMS *Investigator* that discovered the long-sought North-West passage. He came to it from the Pacific side, but his ship was beset in the ice, and he was unable to complete the transit. In fact no ship did complete it either way until the next century.

The following year, 1854, brought news that Eskimos had seen two ships beset by ice with corpses aboard, and a party of white men dragging a boat and sledges southwards. Admiralty attention was drawn to the Crimean War by this time and it was left to Lady Franklin and well-wishers to fit out an expedition to follow up the reports. She was fortunate in engaging an experienced and tenacious Arctic explorer, Captain Leopold McClintock, RN, as leader. The first Autumn, he found himself beset in the ice.

> Sept. 18, 1857. . . . We are doomed to spend a long winter of absolute inutility, if not of idleness, in comparative peril and privation; nevertheless the men seem very happy – thoughtless of course as true sailors always are. . . .[34]

The following summer he forced his way through lanes of ice and when beset again, led sledge parties in the direction indicated by the Eskimo's stories, coming upon the remains of some of Franklin's men in 1859 – skeletons face down, heads to the south, a boat with two skeletons inside enveloped in furs, and by a cairn, two messages from which he learned that the *Erebus* and *Terror* had been beset by ice and abandoned in April, 1848, after Franklin himself had died the previous year; a postscript said the survivors were making overland for the Fish River.

[127]

Many years later, after he had returned home and been rewarded with a knighthood for the success of his investigations, McClintock came to the conclusion that Franklin's men had been defeated by scurvy. Despite the copious anti-scorbutics such as lemon juice, onions, cranberries and malt provided, he suggested that those men who had left the ships to strike overland had been so weakened by scurvy that the sudden change from relative inactivity and warmth to the hard labour of pulling sledges in extremes of cold had brought on the full effects of the disease.

Even without the special rigours of the Arctic, scurvy was attacking some ships' companies and not others in a way that baffled the medical profession, and so it continued until the best opinion at the end of the century held that there was *no* effective anti-scorbutic; food was either tainted, or it was not. This position, which moved the debate several centuries backwards, was probably reached because of the confusion between lemon juice which was most effective, and lime juice which contained only half the ascorbic acid of the lemon, and the gradual replacement of lemons by limes, which the Navy could obtain plentifully in the West Indies. There was even an 'Inspector of Lime Juice', and British sailors became known as 'Limeys' because of the regulation dose they were required to drink. Yet by 1863 half the patients at the Seamen's Hospital in Greenwich were suffering to a greater or lesser extent with scurvy. The disease continued to haunt Arctic and Antarctic explorations. As late as 1912 Captain Scott, making a bid for the South Pole, met with tragedy brought on like Franklin's by scurvy and exposure. The specific anti-scorbutic Vitamin C was not isolated until 1917.

While the Admiralty supported occasional voyages of exploration in the polar regions or up great African rivers to discover their source, it took no official interest in the contours, currents and life of the deep oceans until 1872. Then, at the instigation of the Royal Society and Edinburgh University, the corvette *Challenger* was fitted out as a floating laboratory and sent around the world with a team of scientists headed by Professor Charles Thomson. The *Challenger*'s voyage of nearly 70,000 miles during which oceanic soundings were taken with 1 inch lines 6,000 fathoms long paid out through blocks secured with giant rubber bands to damp out the ship's motion, each sounding backed up by detailed observations of water temperature at different depths, and current flow, together with samples of the bottom and flora and fauna marked the beginning of the science of oceanography. It did not greatly interest the Lords of Admiralty, however, for it had no practical application. The introduction to an account of another voyage of discovery at this time lamented the fact that Great Britain, while doing more than any other nation in scientific and geographical exploration, did less than her position and resources warranted.

> Hundreds of her national ships plough the ocean in time of peace, their almost sole occupation the training and preparation for war, and in the very nature of things, so far as scientific research is concerned, they leave no deeper mark than the track which the sea obliterates behind them, while the few – too few – grudgingly appropriated from the largest Navy in the world place their ineffaceable stamp on works of usefulness which last for ever.[35]

This is criticism more of the government and prevailing attitudes towards economy and research than of the Admiralty; in matters like the investigation of magnetism which had a practical navigational use they were not slow, while the Hydrographic Department and generations of survey-ship officers have left behind a comprehensive and ineffaceably stylish contribution to knowledge of the coasts of the world.

CHAPTER FIVE

WIDER YET AND WIDER . . .

The only war against a European power which the Navy fought between 1815 and the First World War was the Crimean War of 1854–5. By that time the battle fleet had undergone a subtle change; it looked much the same as the fleet of 1837, but the latest and far larger ships of the line had auxiliary engines driving screw propellers. There were seventeen of these either in commission or nearing completion, twice as many as the French, while neither the Russians nor the Americans had any in commission. As their power of movement in any direction gave them a decisive advantage in action with pure sailing ships the Royal Navy was in a more commanding position against any combination of enemies than she had been in 1837.

It was a surprising situation; the country had not demanded it. Interest in the Navy was at its lowest ebb; many people had come to believe from the Free Trade economists that the millenium was at hand; it only needed further reductions in spending on armies and navies to banish international mistrust completely and establish permanent peace based on interlinked commercial relationships. 'Arbitration, the skill of modern diplomats, finance, philanthropy, nineteenth-century civilisation' had made war unthinkable. Boards of Admiralty took a very different view and had argued the Estimates upwards on mistrust of French intentions under their new Emperor, Napoleon III, and especially French building programmes; yet the annual sum spent on the Navy around mid-century was only £7 millions. Then again, few members of any Board had been keen on the idea of steam power for capital units; there were reasoned objections concerned with weakened offensive powers, poor steaming endurance and technical factors like non-watertight stern glands; there was also prejudice and assertion.

'We know the worst that can happen,' one First Lord, Auckland, remarked wryly before a Board meeting in the late 1840s: 'Look fierce, talk loud, and thump the table – which is fortunately between them!'[1]

Going into another meeting, he found one Admiral kneeling on a chair, pencil in hand, altering the lines of the bows on a design for a new ship of the line on the table for discussion. Another Admiral was in a similar position marking alterations to the stern, while the two other Lords were improving the rig and the armament. Auckland called for a rubber and after removing the alterations, turned to the Surveyor – responsible for warship design – and remarked, 'I really do not feel justified in introducing so many *improvements* into a single ship.' The design was then approved by the chastened sea-dogs, and signed.

Somehow or other the Navy had emerged in a stronger position relative to any rivals than at any time since the run-down after the great wars. One reason was the instinctive realisation by all Prime Ministers that the strength and very safety of the realm were bound up with the health of the Navy. They had generally appointed sound and able men to guide the often wayward veterans appointed from the Service, and to represent the Navy's case in Cabinet. One of these, Sir James Graham, had reformed the administration during the 1830s, shaking out a ramshackle confusion of overlapping responsibilities, unaccountable finances, perquisites and sinecures which had baffled former First Lords, and produced a sound system based on five separate departments whose 'Principal Officers' each reported to one of the five Lords of Admiralty – the civilian First Lord and four professional sailors – who collectively decided policy and were responsible to Parliament for expenditure. The five Principal Officers were the Surveyor, responsible for *materiel*, the Accountant General, the Storekeeper General, the Superintendent of Victualling and the Physician of the Navy.

Matters of ship design and engines were therefore under the Surveyor and his departments; the vital factor that enabled him to outdistance foreign competition was the existence of a vast reservoir of private marine engineering skill in the country, exceeding anything elsewhere, so allowing him to tap far greater expertise than his opposite numbers in France, Russia or America. This expertise was in part due to the country's overall industrial lead, chiefly perhaps to a system whereby the Admiralty had handed over the carriage of overseas mails to private steam-shipping companies in the late 1830s and 1840s. The shipowners received annual subsidies from the government for maintaining regular sailings, and these proved sufficient to convert loss-making ocean steamship voyages – because of the inefficiency of the contemporary steam engine and the cargo space taken up by its vast fuel requirements and engines – into profitable passages. No ocean steamship company without a subsidy survived; as no foreign government adopted the idea for some years the subsidised British companies like P & O in the Mediterranean-overland-Suez route to India, Cunard to North America, Royal Mail to South America, and others gained a decisive lead; the British companies who engined them thrived.

That the Surveyors' department tapped these private sources of skill during the 1840s was due chiefly to a series of panics caused by the vulnerability of the British Isles to invasion because of the new freedom of movement enjoyed by steam ships. The panics were heightened by warlike statements from French naval officers and politicians, more seriously by French steam-ship building programmes. It was an elaborate comparison of British and French strength in naval steamers in the mid-1840s that provoked the first British programme for fitting engines to old ships of the line for coast defence. This occurred during a heated debate about the merits of screw propellers versus paddles, which led to trials between two similar sloops, *Rattler* and *Alecto*, one fitted with a screw and the other with paddle wheels. The 'screw' *Rattler* won the speed trials and went on to win the more famous tug-of-war trial. The paddlers remained unconvinced. As there were serious constructional problems with screws still to be overcome, and as few officers

had any conception that steam power could be more than an aid to small ships, or used for towing becalmed great ships into action (there were even proposals for each line ship to have a steamer lashed to her off side to take her into action) it is evident that the impetus to experiment with steam for battleships came directly from France. And it was the French 90-gun screw ship of the line, *Napoléon*, which achieved the extraordinary speed of 14 knots on trials in 1848 which provoked the Admiralty to lay down its first *new* screw ships of the line.

First was the 91-gun *Agamemnon*, completed in 1852. She was followed before the end of 1853 by seven other two-deckers mounting between 70 and 100 guns, and the huge 3-decker, 131-gun, *Duke of Wellington*. These and 51-gun screw frigates of the same programmes had hinged or retractable funnels and had screws which could be disconnected and lifted out of the water. This was accomplished by having two separated stern posts between which was a square shaft like a lift shaft rising to the poop and fitted with guides in which a metal frame – known as the 'banjo' – which contained the propeller was free to run. A flange on the boss of the screw fitted into a slot in a coupling at the end of the propeller shaft. To hoist the screw it was necessary to turn the engine until the slot and flange were vertical, reeve a purchase through pulleys in the 'banjo' up to a timber construction on the poop, and have the after-guard tail on and haul. This apparatus made it impossible to fit a tiller; consequently a yoke (or cross beam) was fitted to the rudder head, from either end of which hide and leather ropes led to the

Mounting a field gun

[133]

drum of the traditional double steering wheel. The yoke could not be long because of the narrowing of the ship at the stern, consequently purchases were necessary on the wheel ropes; even so these ships were bad steerers. It is interesting that no changes could be made to the wheel to improve performance because wheels and drums of just such a size had been used for as long as anyone could remember; four men had always been able to put the rudder over 40° with three turns of the wheel.

The liners carried some 500 tons of coal, but as boiler pressures were scarcely 25 lbs to the square inch and the engines consequently inefficient, this did not give them much steaming range, and power was regarded strictly as an auxiliary for emergencies and battle. There were deeper reasons.

> There was a very strong and universal feeling that it was unseamanlike to use steam, except perhaps in a flat calm, and that a Captain who could not take his ship in or out of harbour under sail with a commanding breeze was 'no seaman'; it was scarcely possible to make a more scathing and derogatory remark against a Captain.[2]

The engines were not sufficiently powerful to work a ship off a lee shore nor were they suitable for sudden emergencies as it took some time to get steam up and screw down. When Captain Keppel was given command of the magnificent new 101-gun two-decker *St Jean d'Acre* in 1853 and sailed her to join the Channel Fleet, he

Hauling a field gun in the 1840s

arrived at slack water and found the ships lying at anchor across the tide in all directions. His screw was up; 'There was nothing for it but to sheet home top and topgallant sails and run the gauntlet between the lines', which he did with such narrow scrapes that he gained extraordinary kudos and the feat was discussed in London Clubs.

By this time war with Russia was looming, due chiefly to the old suspicion that the Tsar aimed at a break-up of the Ottoman Empire to gain access to the Mediterranean. He had built up a powerful Black Sea Fleet and was conducting a bizarre quarrel with Turkey over the custody of Christian shrines in Jerusalem. British and French fleets – now joined together against the apparent threat to the balance in the Mediterranean and the whole of the Middle East – staged demonstrations in Bezika Bay just outside the Dardanelles; Russia responded with troop movements towards the Ottoman principalities on the western shores of the Black Sea. The British and French fleets weighed and sailed through the Dardanelles into the Sea of Marmara. Unimpressed, Russia declared war on Turkey, and after a pause to agree allied action in support of Turkey, the British and French fleets sailed into the Black Sea; by March 1854 the two countries were formally at war with Russia. As the Allied fleet numbered 19 sail of the line, built up gradually to 28, including eight auxiliary steamers against only 14 Russian *sail* of the line the Black Sea passed into Allied hands. The Russian Commander-in-Chief naturally refused to come out of Sebastopol and later scuttled his battlefleet to block the harbour and provide cannon and gunners for the port defences. Meanwhile the Russian Army withdrew from Ottoman territory under the combined threat of troop landings from the Allied fleet and the mobilisation of the Austrian Army.

The chief purpose of the war now seemed accomplished, but in order to employ the hugh Allied force that had been collected it was decided to lay siege to Sebastopol; the subsequent operations by troops already thinned by cholera and quite unequipped for the Crimean winter have become a byeword for administrative chaos and needless suffering. That the operations were eventually successful, despite it all and despite the immense distances from home, was nevertheless a striking testimony to the advantages derived from total control of the sea. Troops were landed almost at will and supplied – when supplies became available – while the Russians were denied similar flexibility. Their supply lines to Sebastopol were cut, and their great waterways flowing into the Black Sea stopped up by commercial blockade.

Meanwhile another Allied fleet operated on Russia's northern flank in the Baltic. The Commander-in-Chief here was Sir Charles Napier, now a Vice-Admiral of sixty-eight flying his flag in the great *Duke of Wellington*. The other contenders for command had been Admiral the Earl of Dundonald – better known as the audacious frigate Captain, Cochrane – now seventy-nine, and Admiral Sir William Parker, seventy-two. The Commander-in-Chief in the Black Sea was Sir William Dundas, sixty-eight.

'Charlie' Napier was not the man he had been at Acre. Doubts about risking his great ships in enemy waters and against stone forts assailed him, doubts too about the new mode of warfare: 'great consideration is required to ascertain how it is best to manage a fleet urged by steam. The system of warfare is entirely different now to what it was formerly; but we will do our best'. This hesitance was in contrast to the Admiralty's confidence in the new type of auxiliary-powered ship of the line which was believed to provide a perfect balance between powers of offence, endurance under sail and free and rapid movement in action; it seemed destined to render the pure sailing ship obsolete for the line of battle. The Russian Commander-in-Chief believed that it had; although considerably superior in numbers and with a fleet whose crews had been well trained, he declined to emerge from his stronghold at Kronstadt to dispute command of the Baltic, which like the Black Sea passed immediately into Allied control.

Yet Napier's doubts about the effect of steam power were representative of most officers who had not made a special study of the

Shipping at Balaclava harbour, Crimean War

question. There had been no opportunity to carry out steam manoeuvres, as the greater part of all squadrons, until 1853, had been
pure sailing ships with a handful of clumsy paddlers; even then
pure sailors, paddlers, screw liners and frigates were mixed in both
Mediterranean and Baltic fleets. Above all, officers were not yet
conditioned to change; neither training nor experience had given
them any expectation that the introduction of novelties like engines, or shell guns, would necessarily alter the fundamentals of
sea warfare, and the idea that they themselves should seek technical change to gain advantage was actually repugnant. Shell guns
had been viewed with horror and had been adopted – as few as
possible – only after the French had done so. Intellectual French-
men instigated change; it was the policy of the British service not
to let them get ahead, and meanwhile to use the novelties forced
upon them in the best way possible. Here is Admiral Philip Colomb:

> Without doubt it was to the naval officers present the most
> natural and appropriate thing in the world that a fleet should
> be composed of sailing ships, screw ships and paddle ships. The
> belief that sailing ships were to go and that paddles were
> almost gone would have been impossible to inculcate. All minds
> would have turned away from that form of reflection to consider
> how the heterogenous elements could best be combined . . . the
> idea was to maintain intact the line-of-battle-ship, frigate and
> sloop of the old days, only more perfect . . .[3]

Napier started his campaign with panache, decorating the
yardarms and mastheads of the *Duke of Wellington* with a splendid
signal:

> Lads! War is declared with a bold and numerous enemy to
> meet. Should they offer us battle you know how to dispose of
> them. Should they remain in port we must try and get at them.
> Success depends on the quickness and precision of your firing.
> Lads! Sharpen your cutlasses and the day is your own![4]

By June 1854 he had changed his mind about the likelihood of
the Russian fleet emerging from Kronstadt to offer battle, and about
the feasibility of getting 'at them' through the narrow and shallow
approach channels commanded by powerful batteries. He had established an effective blockade of the Gulfs of Finland and Bothnia,
but suggested to the Cabinet that the only feasible offensive operation would be an attack on Bomarsund in the Aaland Islands at

the mouth of the Gulf of Bosnia. The Cabinet

'of opinion that the presence of the Allied Fleet in the Baltic must be marked by some result' instructed him to 'begin with Bomarsund . . . success there may be reduced to certainty, and it will be the first hard blow in the battle.'

This proved to be the case. Surveys had been made of the tortuous approaches to the forts at Bomarsund and of suitable landing beaches by a skilled and daring specialist navigation officer, Captain Sulivan, who had learned his craft in Surveying ships. In July he guided the fleet in, 'sometimes almost rubbing our sides against the bushes' to place them 2,000 yards from the forts. In August, when 6,000 French troops arrived to reinforce 5,000 already with the fleet, they were put ashore to the west of the forts while 700 British sailors and Marines landed to the north and east, and the ships' companies of one squadron landed six 32-pounders to form a breaching battery. The guns weighed over two tons each; they were taken ashore slung between boats, then lifted by sheer legs erected on the beach and secured to timber sledges specially prepared for them. Two hundred sailors tailed on to the lines from each sledge and to the rousing accompaniment of the ships' bands towed them four and a half miles 'over execrable ground, the greatest portion of steep rocky hills and ploughed fields'.

The exertions and goodwill of the officers and seamen created much astonishment in the encampment of the French troops, who cheered them in passing, and on some of the most difficult ascents went in voluntarily and most cheerfully to the drag ropes and gave their assistance.[5]

Ringed by batteries from east and west and with the fleet bombarding from the bay, the small Russian garrison in Bomarsund forts surrendered with scarcely a fight; there were less than twenty casualties all told and the British lost only one killed, one wounded. To many, the elaborate preparations and troop reinforcements from France seemed unnecessary, and the British public, for whom the whole thing had been staged, was little more impressed than the naval officers on the spot, who had been urging Napier to attack Kronstadt or the naval anchorage at Sveaborg. Brought up in the heroic tradition of the great wars, they wanted nothing less than the Russian fleet.

The following year both Napier and the Commander-in-Chief in the Black Sea were replaced by new men who were expected to do more than their predecessors. More important, they were provided with vessels of a new type more suitable for operations in the coastal shallows of the Baltic and Black Seas than huge floating castles like the *Duke of Wellington*; they were called gunboats.

The first class had been ordered the previous summer when the need for a shallow-draft bombarding vessel had become apparent, and more had been ordered in the autumn. They were very shallow, flat-bottomed, square-bilged, blunt-ended timber vessels little over 100 feet in length with a draft of 6½ feet. One 68-pounder and one 32-pounder gun were mounted on traversing wooden slides on a flush upper deck at bow and stern to command either broadside, and between was a tall, thin hinged funnel, over engines which could push the craft along at 6½–8 knots. They had three masts, originally intended for small fore and aft sails, but in the event they were rigged with a distinctive combination of square topsails and topgallants on fore and main with fore and aft sails below. As their usefulness in bombardment and cutting-out raids against enemy positions ashore became marked, scores more were ordered during 1855. Their success was, once again, due to the fact that road transport was difficult, railways non-existent, and all bulk supplies had to go by river, coast and open sea.

The first major operation in the Crimean campaign of 1855 was

'How Jack made the Turk useful at Balaclava'

HOW JACK MADE THE TURK USEFUL AT BALACLAVA.

British Officer. "HOLLOA, JACK! WHAT ARE YOU ABOUT NOW?"
Jack. "WHY, YER HONOUR—YOU SEE RIDING'S A DEAL PLEASANTER THAN WALKING ABOUT HERE, AND WHEN THIS CHAP'S TIRED—I MOUNTS T'OTHER COVE!"

the capture of Kertch, on the eastern point of the peninsula, by Allied forces landed nearby. This cut the chief Russian supply line by pontoon bridge across the Strait from the mainland opposite. As gunboats were able to roam at will in the Sea of Azov beyond, destroying shipping, creating havoc ashore with lightning raids on granaries and supply dumps, cutting the subsidiary supply routes as well, the fate of Sebastopol was sealed.

Meanwhile a naval brigade of over 1,000 sailors and Marines from the battle fleet which had no enemy to fight was ashore with the Army, laying siege to the naval base. Sailors had manhandled most of the siege guns up from the Allied supply base established at Balaclava the previous year, and were manning batteries established behind the trenches opposite the great Redan and Malakoff towers. Their health record had been far better than the Army's during the terrible winter of 1854, largely due to the efforts of the commanding officer, Captain William Peel, who had insisted on strict standards of hygiene, regular periods of duty and rest, hot food and shelter as well as a return to the comparative 'comforts' of their ships every four days. But the sailor's own remarkable adaptability and hardihood had been an important factor.

> Find our Jacks queer fellows; they deal in horses or anything else, and as soon as they come out of the trenches they are all over the soldiers' camps, doing work for the officers, repairing tents and that sort of thing receiving part payment in grog, and then share it with the first 'soger' they meet.[6]

They exhibited all the extraordinary recklessness which had fascinated commentators at least from Nelson's time. An Official Medical Report stated:

> There is no class of men so regardless of their lives as the thoroughbred seamen of Her Majesty's Navy; and it is difficult to make them believe that there is not something discreditable in crouching behind stone walls in the presence of the enemy. . . .[7]

This was as true of their officers; Peel, who won a Victoria Cross for picking up a live shell with the fuse burning and hurling it from his battery, led at the storming of the great Redan carrying a scaling ladder himself. When he was wounded Henry Keppel took over as commanding officer, exhibiting as one witness recorded, 'a cool courage which even among courageous men was remarkable.

A perhaps too reckless exposure of himself was redeemed by the inspiring audacity of his presence at all times and in all places.'[8]

Sebastopol was evacuated by the Russians in early September. There was no similar triumph in the Baltic campaign, but Sveaborg had been bombarded the previous month and the chief buildings, arsenal and dockyard largely destroyed. The many fortifications which had been thrown up by the Russians to command the difficult approaches to the anchorage prevented any attempt at taking the place, but within the limits set the attack was considered a triumph. Like the copy-book operations at Bomarsund the previous year, the plan and preliminary survey had been the work of Captain Sulivan: in the face of fire from the enemy batteries he had made a detailed chart of the approaches, showing reefs, rocks, channels and soundings as well as distances obtained by triangulation to the chief targets to be attacked, and when the channels had been swept of 'explosive machines recently introduced by the enemy' – primitive mines – had positioned all the mortar vessels of both British and French fleets in an arc so that each was exactly 3,300 yards from her target. To draw the fire of the enemy batteries he had all the gunboats steam up and down inside the mortar vessels along tracks previously buoyed, also three steam frigates in deep water. Later, rocket boats were sent from the fleet to increase the incendiary effect of the mortar bombs.

> We opened fire on Thursday morning – entirely along the line; by noon two enormous explosions had taken place and the buildings were on fire in several places. The fire continued with scarcely any interruption until Saturday morning, when our mortars were nearly all split or unfit for service. By this time the entire works inside the fortress except the larger buildings were destroyed. These are the works which the fortress was built to protect. . . . Now listen to the wonderful part of this attack. All this has been done without the loss of a life; a few wounded but none dangerously. . . . On Monday morning we left Sveaborg in ashes. . . . You have seen our chief and can judge how undemonstrative he is. Well! After the affair was over, and Sulivan went to congratulate him, he shook him warmly by the hand, and said, almost choking – 'I owe you a debt of gratitude I can never repay. Everyone in the fleet knows that our success is due to you.' – and tears dropped from his eyes.[9]

The last sizeable operation of the war, and from its consequences for warship design, the most momentous of all, took place in the Black Sea in October. Five sand and stone works comprising Fort Kinburn, which commanded the mouth of the rivers Bug and Dnieper were bombarded, and forced to surrender in under six hours. What impressed naval observers was the performance of three French armoured floating batteries which opened the assault from close range and proved impervious to anything the forts could hit them with. They had been designed the previous year to the instructions of the French Emperor Napoleon III, who appreciated, like Napier and the Board of Admiralty, that neither Kronstadt nor Sebastopol could be attacked successfully by deep-draft unarmoured ships. Plans of the proposed batteries had been sent to England, but three vessels ordered by the Admiralty to the design arrived too late to take part in the action at Kinburn. It was left to the French to demonstrate that 4½ inches of iron bolted over 17 inch thick timbers could keep out all existing shot and shell.

Napoleon III instructed his *Directeur du Matériel* to carry this action proof to its logical conclusion with a fleet of armoured, ocean-going, auxiliary-screw vessels which would be the master of all existing unarmoured ships, however powerful. The Surveyor of the British Navy took a similar step by designing an armoured, ocean-going auxiliary screw corvette but the Admiralty preferred not to commit itself to such a fundamental change, and continued to build magnificent screw liners and frigates in the usual way.

The campaigning season of 1855 was the last in the Crimean War. With the success of the armoured batteries and gunboats, which both British and French continued to amass by the score, and the probability that Kronstadt would fall when the Allies transferred their main effort to the Baltic in 1856, the Tsar agreed peace terms which confirmed Turkish suzerainty over the principalities on the western shores of the Black Sea and declared that sea a neutral zone forbidden to warships.

A triumphant conclusion, apparently, to the policy of supporting Turkey as a buffer to Russian expansion, the long-term effects were perhaps to hasten the decay of the Ottoman Empire by importing western industrial and liberal values. And it was not long before Russia started rebuilding her Black Sea Fleet. Once again, while British naval strength had been a major factor leading to Russian discomfiture, Britain had not acted alone. The successes achieved had been distressing and costly for Russia, but naval power could never have starved her into submission, for she was a net exporter of food, nor harmed any vital interest without the support of considerable land armies. The *appearance* was different. On 23 April

1856, shortly after the Peace Treaty had been signed, there was collected at Spithead for a review by the Queen a fleet of 22 steam line of battleships, 3 steam frigates, 16 steam corvettes and 160 gunboats – 218 steam warships in all, 'a force numerically large beyond comparison, marvellous at a time when steam was, as it were, only just springing into being'. Behind them were the paddlers, and lying in ordinary or serving on foreign stations squadrons of sailing vessels. Unlike the procedure at later reviews when ships were anchored in lines down which the Royal Yacht passed, for this first real *steam* review, the whole fleet weighed and steamed in two lines around pivot ships placed near the Nab Light vessel, then back again past the Royal Yacht.

The gunboats amassed for a campaign that never materialised had scarcely been laid up when other pressing uses for them arose. Disputes between the Chinese authorities and European trading communities, endemic since the Treaty forced on the Chinese by the Opium War, flared up at Canton, and the small British and French naval forces were not sufficiently strong to hold the river against a guerrilla campaign conducted with floating explosive and incendiary devices. The Admiralty hurried a squadron of gunboats and similar but larger types known as Gunvessels around the Cape to Hong Kong. When they arrived in the early summer of 1857 the senior naval officer, Rear-Admiral Sir Michael Seymour, led them and a miscellaneous assortment of shallow draft paddle steamers upriver to attack a fleet of imperial war junks gathered near Canton. Second-in-command of the expedition was the ubiquitous Harry Keppel.

As ever, his journey to Hong Kong had been exciting; his frigate had struck an uncharted rock amidst the islands of the South China Sea, driving over it at 7 knots and ripping part of the bottom out. He had sailed her on, sinking slowly while all hands turned to the pumps, and reached just short of Macao before grounding in shoal water close by a French frigate; he had given her a gun salute just before his deck disappeared beneath the water and his keel took the ground.

Now, having hoisted a broad pennant as Commodore in a paddle steamer called *Hong Kong*, he led a division of gunboats to attack the main squadron of twenty imperial junks moored high up a creek off the Fatshan branch of the Canton River, while Seymour dealt with a fort which commanded the approaches. The gunboats grounded one by one as they neared the creek; the *Hong Kong*, which drew less water, last of all. As each came to a halt, boats manned and armed steered out from behind them and pulled towards the junks, Keppel soon leading in a six-oared galley. They met a storm of fire, 'shot richochetted down the river as thick as hail' from the Chinese cannon, musketry and gingals – large-mouthed blunderbusses firing scrap metal – sweeping away whole sides of oars, stoving in boats, whose crews swam to others. Keppel's own galley was sunk beneath him, five out of his six crew either killed or wounded; he scrambled aboard another boat and called a retreat, then waited, standing on the paddle box of the *Hong Kong* as the tide rose and enabled the deeper vessels to work up towards him with more armed boats. As this second wave reached him Keppel noticed some of the junks letting go their moorings.

'The rascals are making off!' he called, shaking his fist at them. 'You beggars! I'll pay you off for this! Man the boats, boys!' and he went over the side into a cutter with his Coxswain bringing a piece of blue bunting to represent the Commodore's pennant, his dog Mike leaping in with him.

At this moment there arose from the boats as if every man took it up at the same instant, one of those British cheers so full of meaning that I knew at once it was all up with John Chinaman. They might sink thirty boats but there were thirty others which would go ahead all the faster.[10]

The battle of Fatshan creek

Then began an extraordinary, wild chase as the junks, picturesque in red and green paint, streaming with flags from every mast
and swathed with smoke clouds from their own cannon and gingals,
whose reports punctuated a hideous continuous dinning of gongs,
let go one by one and moved off up-stream with the British boats'
crews pulling all they were worth to catch up, sailors and Marines
in the stern sheets keeping up a steady fire. As they came up with
each junk it pulled in towards the bank, and the Chinese leaped
out and made off across the fields while the British crews entered
and set it alight. For Keppel, in a white pith hat with blue trousers
tucked into Russian boots, it was like an unusually exciting and
dangerous regatta, and he followed the junks over six miles around
the bends in the stream, capturing or burning all but three before
leaving off. At the end 'he stood up in the stern sheets of his boat
and shook his fist good-humouredly, saying "You rascals, I'll come
back again to you soon!" And these extraordinary Chinese, they too
laughed.'

Seymour could not follow up the rout with an attack on the
imperial forces in Canton itself as he had received news of the
outbreak of the Indian Mutiny, and many of the troops and Marines
he had been sent had to be re-directed to Calcutta. Among them
was the gallant William Peel, now Captain of the *Shannon*. He
formed a Naval Brigade from the ships' companies in the Hooghli
river, and with ten 8-inch guns manhandled by bluejackets per-
formed prodigies at the siege of Lucknow, where he was wounded
again. He died in India.

It was not until December, after the crisis of the Mutiny had
passed, that Seymour was able to complete preparations for the
occupation of Canton; the Chinese authorities were still refusing to
negotiate seriously on the points at issue. It was planned to land
5,500 men to assault the walled city, a French division of nearly
1,000 amongst them, and the inevitable Naval Brigade. This was
composed of 1,500 sailors organised in three divisions to haul 12-
pounder guns as field pieces. Each of the divisions was instructed
to dress differently, the 1st with blue frocks and white trousers, the
2nd all in blue, the 3rd with white frocks and blue trousers. Each
man was to carry three days' provisions, and each division four
100-pound bags of powder for use, if necessary, against the gates of
the city. The two first companies of each division were to carry
scaling ladders. The orders were made out in great detail, allotting
particular tasks to each body of men to be landed, and targets for
each of the gunboats lined up along the river walls of the city. It
was no impetuous assault of the kind sometimes adopted against
primitive peoples.

All passed off largely according to plan. The landings were begun to the east of the city soon after the gunboats had started a deliberate bombardment and were completed before nightfall, when the detachments moved into their positions for the following morning's assault. This was made in the face of heavy musketry from walls some thirty feet high and an attack from a body of imperial troops who sallied out from one of the gates in an outflanking movement. They were driven back after fierce skirmishing, and the parapets were cleared by the 12-pounder batteries, at which the scaling-ladder parties rushed forward into the ditch surrounding the walls and planted the ladders, and the assaulting parties behind scrambled up. Once on top they swarmed along the walls to the forts and batteries which commanded the city, taking some at the point of the bayonet or cutlass, occupying others as the defenders fled. Once in command of the walls, which formed a continuous communication all round the city, and the various strong-points built in it, the battle was over. It had taken about four hours.

The following day the governor, Yeh, whose unyielding negotiations had led to the show of force, was seized by a party of British sailors while preparing to escape from the palace, after which a division of the Naval Brigade was used to preserve order. Still the Chinese government refused to concede the trading terms which the British mission headed by Lord Elgin, joined by Russian, US and French delegations, was attempting to have ratified. Seymour was, therefore asked for another demonstration, this time up the Peiho River to threaten the celestial city of Peking. Once again gunboat bombardment, accompanied by landings, knocked out the forts at the mouth of the Peiho, and the British squadron in line ahead proceeded up to Tientsin where, at the end of the Grand Canal, they commanded Peking's commercial outlet. Within days a Chinese delegation met the European plenipotentiaries and signed a trading charter known as the Treaty of Tientsin. One of its terms was that it should be ratified within a year.

It soon became apparent that the Chinese had no intention of doing this, and in 1859 Lord Elgin called for yet another show of force. In anticipation of something of the kind, the Chinese had strengthened the Peiho forts, and this second attempt to silence them carried out by Seymour's successor, Sir James Hope, provided the Navy with its most serious, indeed its only sizeable defeat in the hundred years between the great wars of the nineteenth and twentieth centuries. The plan was overconfident and less meticulous than Seymour's, and instead of the forts succumbing to the fire of surrounding gunboats, the gunboats found themselves trapped by

Volage and *Hyacinth* against Imperial Chinese war junks

strong barriers in a narrow space swept by the guns of the forts.
Some went aground and became sitting targets while assault parties sent ashore to retrieve a desperate situation slithered and sank
in mud and provided equally easy targets for Chinese small arms
fire.

> They had horrid fire balls firing at us when we landed. I saw
> one poor fellow with his eye and part of his face burnt right
> out. If a piece struck you, it stuck to you and generally burnt
> you away till it was all gone . . . The Chinamen fought like
> anything.[11]

The survivors were forced to discard the equipment and retreat,
after which Hope, who had part of his leg and thigh shot away and
was visiting the scenes of action and encouraging his men from a
cot slung from a pole in a boat, abandoned the operation. There
were 434 British casualties, 89 of whom died; 'abaft the mainmast
it was nothing but blood and men rolling about with arms and legs
off, nearly all round shot wounds'. Four holed gunboats were left
behind, only one of which was subsequently recovered.

It was unthinkable that such loss of face could stand unavenged
and in the summer a larger operation was mounted with French
support and careful planning. The offending forts were over-

The gunboat *Cockatrice*, 1896. Note the rig

whelmed and the fleet of gunboats proceeded up-river to Tientsin in parallel with a strong Allied Brigade ashore which – after yet another round of talks had foundered – pushed on to the celestial city and committed the ultimate sacrilege, destroying the Emperors' exquisitely beautiful Summer Palace. So the commercial pressures which had been forcing China open against an unwilling and supercilious bureaucracy since the 1830s were consummated in an act of extraordinary vandalism. Again, the brutal success carried within it the seeds of the collapse of an oriental empire, and the task of the British gunboats soon changed to one of co-operation with local authorities to put down uprisings and piracy, and warn off rival nations who sought territory as well as trade from the decaying carcass.

Japan was opened to trade by a US squadron of warships in 1854 which was soon followed by British merchants and gunboats. Although no extraordinary demonstrations of force were used, the same kind of strains on traditional values, the same kind of hostility between the Daimos or Feudal Lords and foreign traders led to numerous incidents. The most serious of these started with the murder by Samurai of a British merchant who unknowingly violated etiquette during a Daimo's procession. British demands for an indemnity and punishment of the leading Samurai failed to produce satisfaction, and finally a British squadron of screw frigates, corvettes and gunboats bombarded Kagoshima, the headquarters of the Daimo concerned. The ships were opposed to shore batteries which caused considerable damage and casualties and after they had been silenced and parts of the town beyond set ablaze, the squadron withdrew. The following year, 1864, a combined British and Dutch squadron conducted a more successful demonstration against another Daimo, bombarding, and then landing assault parties which stormed and took forts guarding the Straits of Shimonoseki.

So, in the brief space since Victoria's accession, China, Japan, the Ottoman Empire, had fallen prey to western merchant ventures, chiefly British and American, backed by warships. In India, too, the suppression of the Mutiny marked the beginning of the end of co-existence between traditional and Western ideas; power was transferred formally from the East India Company to the British Crown in 1858; informally more Indians began to think in Western terms. Elsewhere in Africa, Australasia, the Pacific, less powerful cultures, Maori, Ashantee, Zulu, Dyak had been and continued to be chastised by the superior fire power of British troops and Naval Brigades whenever they defied the traders' terms or the Western law. And as commercial steamships became economic with the adoption of high-pressure compound engines in the late 1860s and 1870s, shortening and regularising trade routes, and steam railways were pushed inland opening up vast new markets, demanding huge new resources, as telegraph cables were laid across continents and under oceans, linking Europe and America with their new dependencies, the whole world became a 'Western' province.

For policing ever-widening interests, the shallow-draft gunboat, born in the Russian War, and proved up Chinese rivers, was ideal; it combined sufficient heavy gun-power with far greater mobility than the traditional deeper-draft warship. And it was cheap. Class after class was laid down, some under 250 tons, carrying 30–40 officers and men, armed with a 68-pounder forward, a 32-pounder aft and perhaps two smaller howitzers or the latest breech-loading guns. Larger classes, termed gunvessels, were from 500 to over 800 tons, carrying 60 to 100 men and as many as three heavy guns. Speeds under steam varied from 7 knots up to 11 as boiler pressures rose to 70 pounds to the square inch during the 1870s. The officers berthed in the after quarter-length of the hull under the flush upper deck, the Captain's single cabin right aft over the screw or screws; his doors led out into a diminutive wardroom forward of the mizen mast with a skylight over. In a larger gunvessel there would be bunk-length cabins either side for a Lieutenant, two Sub-lieuten-

ants, an Engineer-in-charge, assistant Surgeon, and Paymaster –
an up-graded Purser. In the smaller classes, gunboats, there would
be only one Lieutenant commanding, one other Lieutenant and an
Engineer. They were of course very low between decks: 'I could not
stand upright in spite of my comparatively short stature, and when
I wanted to do so I had to put my head through the skylight!' The
whole of the mid-length hull was occupied by boilers and engines
and all the men berthed in the forward quarter-length around the
foremast. Despite their small size they seem to have been wonderful
sea boats, rising 'like a duck over all the big lumps of water'.

Cheap as they were to build and man, ideal as they were for
hunting pirates, investigating murders, outrages, isolated incidents
in distant dependencies, the mid-Victorian Navy was scarcely better
provided than the early Victorian Navy in numbers for the overseas
stations. In 1880, high noon of the 'Gunboat era', there were only
28 gunvessels and 18 gunboats out of a total of 105 vessels of all
types in commission on eight overseas stations:

Mediterranean	21
North America and the West Indies	14
South America, East coast	4
Pacific	10
Cape of Good Hope and West Coast of Africa	11
East Indies	12
China	24
Australia	9

The swing, since 1837, from the West Indies and American stations to China, now split off from the East Indies with its own base
at Hong Kong is striking. It is numerically the largest overseas
fleet with one battleship, four corvettes, three sloops, nine gunvessels, five gunboats and a despatch vessel.

At home successive Boards of Admiralty grappled with baffling
problems thrown up by advanced industrial technology applied to
naval warfare. Up until 1858 they had been able to brush them
aside, and had done so for very good reasons and sound prejudice.
But in March that year the first of the armour-clad, ocean-going
warships ordered by Napoleon III as a result of the lessons of the
Crimean War were laid down, and it became a matter of the utmost
urgency to respond to the challenge they posed. Reports indicated
that although the vessels were technically frigates, with only one
main gun deck, they had the scantlings of a three-decker and were

[150]

expected by the French to replace conventional ships of the line.

> So convinced do naval men seem to be in France of the
> irresistible qualities of these ships, that they are of opinion that
> no more ships of the line will be laid down, and that in ten
> years that class of vessel will have become obsolete.[12]

The Admiralty of the day could not go so far: 'no prudent man would at present consider it safe to risk upon ships of this novel character the naval superiority of Great Britain', and they continued to lay down wooden two and three-deckers and frigates. At the same time they came up with specifications for a type of armoured frigate which would be able to catch and overmatch the French 'iron-sided' ships. It was to have a speed of 15 knots, full ship rig, a battery of 68-pounder guns – the heaviest in service – and be plated with 4½ inches of solid wrought iron armour; firing tests had proved this impervious to any existing gun. Finally the decision was reached to use iron instead of timber for construction. This was partly for longitudinal strength in a vessel which would have to be very long to achieve a high speed without filling the hull with engines, partly because iron would resist the incendiary effect of shell-fire. It would, therefore, be possible to limit the armour-plating to the vitals of the ship, leaving the ends unarmoured and saving weight.

The specifications and construction of this type, which emerged as superior to the French iron-sided frigates as they were superior to conventional ships of the line, was a triumphant vindication of the 'wait-and-see' attitude of previous Boards. Iron construction had been urged long before the Crimean War and had actually been used in one class designed as frigates but employed as transports after firing trials against iron plates had suggested that the showers of splinters accompanying penetration, and the difficulty of stopping up jagged holes below the waterline made them unsuitable for action. Armour had been urged at the same time, but again the thickest plates available had been shattered by shot on the proving ground.

Meanwhile, a number of inventors in various countries had been perfecting rifled shell guns throwing pointed projectiles which spun in flight; these were not only vastly more accurate over greater distances than spherical shells but carried a larger bursting charge, and they reinforced Napoleon III's conviction that unarmoured fighting ships were doomed. His decision to build armoured first-line warships was accompanied by a decision to equip his fleet with rifled shell guns; the system he chose employed projectiles with protruding studs which fitted into spirally twisted grooves in the bore of the piece.

It was not to be expected that the British Admiralty would show similar enthusiasm for change, in any case they were handicapped after the Crimean War by losing control over the guns supplied to the fleet. All ordnance manufacture was put under the Ordnance Committee of the War Office, and the Admiralty had no department dealing specifically with guns, ammunition, or mountings. Any experimental work was undertaken by the Captain of the *Excellent*, who shared with the Surveyor the informal task of advising the Naval Lord responsible for the final decision on all gunnery matters. In the background was a mass of conflicting advice from the War Office which controlled and had to account for expenditure through the Army vote, and from the Royal Gun Foundry, the Royal Carriage Department – responsible for gun-mountings – the Royal Laboratory Department of Woolwich Arsenal, and a number of private manufacturers like Armstrong, Whitworth and Lancaster – whose oval-bored guns throwing oval section shells had actually been mounted aboard some ships during the Russian War.

In the period immediately after the war the most persuasive arguments were supplied by the private manufacturers, especially

Firing an early Armstrong breechloader in the 1860s

Sir William Armstrong. His revolutionary guns were constructed of spirally-wound ribbands of wrought iron, welded at white heat and shrunk around a steel tube to form the barrel. The shells were loaded through the breech end, which was closed after the cartridge by a massive breech block held firm by a great, hollow screw, and they were coated with lead to engage in shallow, spiral grooves cut into the bore to impart spin. The astonishing accuracy and lightness of these pieces in comparison with the clumsy cast iron cannon of traditional pattern aroused the enthusiasm of the military and despite naval tests which showed 200-pounders to be inferior in piercing power to the existing 68-pounder service gun – because a smaller powder charge was used – it was decided to arm the fleet with them. Heavier versions were ordered for the new class of armoured frigate.

So it was that the British Admiralty was pushed into taking the lead in breech-loading rifled ordnance at the same time as it was pushed into building the first iron warship – and that also was due to private firms. British shipbuilders led the world in iron merchant ships, and without such a background it is certain that the Surveyor's department would have designed iron-clad timber ships of traditional dimensions as the French had. The final designs were only arrived at 'after consultation' with one of the leading merchant

The Royal Navy soon returned to muzzle loaders; here is the battery deck of the cruiser *Nelson* in the 1880s

ship designers; the vessels were built in private yards and private marine engineering works provided the engines. Nevertheless the Board of Admiralty, which reacted with such speed and boldness to the French challenge, together with all the previous Boards which had encouraged sufficient experiment to allow the swift response, deserve credit for taking the right decisions at the right time.

The first of the new class, HMS *Warrior*, was laid down at Black-wall on the Thames in 1859 and completed at the end of 1861. She marked a distinct break with warship design evolved over the last three centuries – long and graceful as a huge clipper with a yacht-like bow and a sweet run to the single, lifting propeller, 'a stately and noble vessel whose beauty was a delight to behold'. She was rigged to the scale of an 80-gun ship of the line, with two telescopic funnels between the fore and main masts; on her steam trials she did nearly 14½ knots, making her the fastest warship afloat, and nearly 1½ knots faster than the first French armour-clad, *Gloire*. As she had a larger spread of canvas and carried heavier guns higher out of the water behind thicker iron she was evidently superior to the French ship.

In fact she was superior to anything afloat. Her battery of 68-pounders and the new 110-pounder Armstrong breech-loaders was protected from any existing shot or shell by 4½ inch wrought-iron bolted to 18 inch thick teak extending from five feet below the waterline to the upper deck. As she was faster than any existing warship and had an unlimited radius of action under sail she was evidently the prototype of the new capital ship. Before the end of 1861 the Admiralty had ordered 13 others of varying sizes, the largest 400 feet long with a displacement of 10,600 tons, five iron masts and armour covering the entire length from stem to stern. By 1865 Britain had thirty ironclads afloat against eighteen French, most of which had timber hulls; industrial and marine engineering supremacy had transferred easily into naval superiority under the new conditions.

Something else had happened. It was only dimly perceived at first but soon became unmistakable: industrial technology and invention had taken over from fighting men and sailors and started a competitive process outside their control – indeed outside its own control. The *Gloire* and *Warrior* were not heirs of the great ships of the line – 'O, the navies old and oaken, O, the *Temeraire* no more' – but the beginning of a cannibalistic progression of mutants swallowed up by their own progeny. There could never be certainty again. More, the new conditions encouraged a new kind of officer, one who was excited by technical challenge, grasped eagerly at new possibilities – played up to and so intensified the competition. When these officers came to power towards the end of the century they had little patience with the old men, or even with contemporaries who differed with their own concept of progress; rifts and schisms appeared and deepened the faster the pace of change.

The process could be seen at work most obviously among the warship designers themselves. Each one of a succession of outstanding men first overturned the concepts of his immediate predecessor, and when his own turn was up quarrelled intemperately and usually very publicly with the successor who upset his own creations.

The signs were visible as early as 1862. An Armstrong gun designed to throw a 300-pound shell threw a solid shot through a mock-up of the *Warrior's* side on the proving ground at Shoeburyness. In 1864 the French Navy introduced guns capable of piercing anything less than 8 inches of solid iron. The first generation of ironclads was obsolescent, and the problems for naval architects had begun. And each time they responded to a more powerful gun by applying thicker armour, necessarily reducing the armoured area so that it would not render the ship immobile, a yet heavier gun went into service somewhere. Ships became obsolescent before they were completed; many were altered while building to take successively heavier guns. The design problems posed were made virtually insoluble by a requirement for second and subsequent generations of ironclads to be of the smallest possible displacement, chiefly to present as small a target area as possible, also on the grounds of manoeuvrability and cost and, as ramming tactics began to exercise naval officers, to hazard less to one fatal blow.

The ship, it was argued by ramming enthusiasts, had a thousand times the momentum of the heaviest projectile, and its underwater ram would pierce below the armour in the most vulnerable section of the enemy. Again, it is typical of an era of mingled enthusiasm, total uncertainty, and administration as yet unequipped to cope with technology, that no systematic trials were carried out to see whether a ship *could* ram another which took appropriate avoiding or ramming action herself. A few individual officers satisfied themselves that it could not be done if the enemy was under command, and they were right. But official doctrine in all navies was that the ram would be the major factor in future naval warfare. However, this posed yet another problem for designers; they were required to produce maximum ahead-fire from the guns so that an enemy might be battered with shell during a ramming approach. Again, the most elementary trial would have shown that unless two vessels were approaching end on, the best way to miss an opponent would be to steer straight for her, unless of course she was stationary.

Designers were trapped between an impossible number of absolutely conflicting requirements: heavy armour and guns, but small displacement; high speed, but a short hull for manoeuvrability and to provide the smallest area to protect; for the same reason, and to present a difficult target, a low hull, yet with great guns mounted high enough to be worked in a seaway; a steady ship as a gun platform, yet hull form and stability suitable for worldwide cruising under sail; clear arcs of fire, especially ahead, yet a cat's cradle of standing and running rigging for the masts and sails interfering in every direction. Out of it all came a bewildering succession of different solutions. The earliest second-generation ironclads had a belt of armour right around the waterline, usually thinning at the extremities with a central box of armour six to eight inches thick rising to the upper deck and enclosing a battery of a few heavy guns firing through broadside ports.

Next, British designers sought to have the central battery projecting out either side of the ship by setting the main and upper decks in, thus allowing ahead-fire through forward gun ports as well as broadside fire. By this time the iron was 12 inches thick around the waterline, 8 to 10 inches thick on the battery. The extreme example of this type was the *Alexandra* of 1877: she mounted two 11 inch guns capable of piercing 13½ inches of wrought iron at 1,000 yards, and ten 10 inch guns of piercing 12 inches of iron, mounted on two decks, so giving her an ahead fire of four pieces and a broadside of six.

Long before the *Alexandra* was designed the Service had given up its advanced breech-loading guns because of structural faults resulting in breech blocks blowing out and barrels splitting or even departing with the projectile towards the target. The pieces had been christened 'them two-muzzled guns'. In their place a muzzle-loading rifled system had been adopted very similar to the French with protruding zinc studs and a copper 'gas check' on the shells engaging in deep spiral grooves in the bore. This was in 1864; at the same date the French introduced a new breech-loading system employing a breech block with a screw thread cut away in channels parallel to the axis so that the block could be thrust straight in, then given a fraction of a turn to lock it. However, at this stage the type of loading was less important than the armour-piercing power of the gun, and here it was the weight of metal around the breech end where the explosion took place which counted; the thicker the breech could be made, the larger the explosion that could be con-

tained and the more the 'muzzle velocity' given to the projectile. So
it was that guns became hugely thick and stubby and were referred
to by their weight rather than the diameter of the bore; the heaviest
in the *Alexandra* weighed twenty-five tons. Naturally the old timber
carriages had long since departed; in their place were wrought iron
mountings which recoiled along slides pivoted at the gun ports so
that they could be trained around brass 'racers' laid in arcs in the
deck; recoil momentum was checked by friction between a series of
plates known as compressors fixed to carriage and slide. The great
pieces were elevated by means of toothed gear wheels and their
shells were loaded with the aid of endless chain purchases rove
from the deckhead on sliding pulleys.

As the guns grew in size, the advantages of mounting them in
centre-line 'turrets', which could be revolved to command arcs all

An early Coles type turret in the battleship *Inflexible*

round the ship instead of just on one side, became marked. The idea had been pioneered by the Swedish engineer, Ericsson, and the British naval Captain Cowper Coles, whose inspiration had come after experience in bombarding shore targets in the Sea of Azov during the Crimean war.

He had developed ideas for a fleet of shallow draft vessels mounting a few heavy guns on the centreline, free to command either broadside, each protected behind its own hemispherical shield. After the war, with the help of the engineer Marc Brunel, these shields developed into revolving cupolas or turrets, which the Admiralty, with admirable open-mindedness, built, tested and found very suitable for coastal defence craft.

This did not satisfy Coles; he had convinced himself that a low profile turret ship needing only a small amount of armour to protect minimal freeboard, and mounting the heaviest guns afloat, each commanding almost 360° of arc was the answer to all the conflicting problems besetting designers of *ocean-going* warships. He pressed his view on the Admiralty with such fanatical persistence and with the backing of *The Times* and other newspapers, high-ranking naval officers, even the Prince Consort, that the Admiralty was forced into the extraordinary step of allowing him to design and have such a ship built.

It says much for the new scientific attitude to ship design in the Surveyor's department that they resisted to the utmost. The Chief Constructor, Edward Reed, knew from stability calculations that low freeboard with the full rig needed for an ocean-going ship was a recipe for disaster. But in that innocent dawn of service technology Coles and his enthusiastic supporters, whose minds were filled with the enormous advantages of the scheme, were quite unwilling – as well as unable – to examine the practicability of the design. Coles's ship, HMS *Captain*, was built in a private yard to his own plans with the Admiralty's express denial of all responsibility. She was lost in September 1870 only six months after her trials. As Reed had warned, the side of her main hull, rising less than seven feet above water, provided no extra stability after 21° of heel. When she was struck by a squall in the Bay of Biscay she went right over in a smooth roll, carrying all but eighteen of her officers and crew with her – and Coles himself.

Coles paid the ultimate penalty for his supporters' scientific incomprehension and his own contempt for 'theories'. At the same time the impetus he gave to turret design was already pointing towards the true line of warship evolution. Reed, who had constructed a sea-going turret ship, similar to the *Captain* in size, armament and rig, but with a conventional high freeboard, had also designed three coast defence vessels which embodied all Coles's ideas except the fatal full rig. This design was shortly up-graded into a 'mastless' capital ship for service with the battle fleet in European waters, and the first of the type, HMS *Devastation*, was completed in 1873. She is usually regarded as the first modern battleship.

The *Devastation* was 285 feet long by 62 feet, with a displacement of 9,330 tons, only 100 tons less than the pride of the masted ships, *Alexandra*, but with a far greater proportion taken up by armour – totalling over 3,000 tons. Her hull, subdivided into several watertight compartments, rose only 4 feet above the water and was protected with 12-inch wrought iron on 18 inches of teak outside the hull plates, decked over with 3-inch wrought iron covered with

Cleared for action and firing to starboard, a battleship's forward turret in the 1880s

teak planking. A similarly armoured and decked citadel 7 feet high
was raised from the middle of this 'raft hull' with unarmoured
structures either side and forward to give the vessel flush sides
rising 11 feet out of the water. The drum-shaped turrets, constructed of layers of 6-inch teak, 6-inch wrought iron, 6-inch teak,
8-inch wrought iron, rose through the armoured deck at each end
of the citadel, each mounting two 12-inch 35 ton guns capable of
penetrating 15 inches of wrought iron at 1,000 yards. Between the
turrets rose funnel uptakes and a small superstructure supporting
a flying deck. Below, two pairs of engines drove two four-bladed
propellers. Steam was supplied by eight box-shaped boilers at a
working pressure of 30 pounds to the square inch – this was just
before the introduction of compound engines. On trials nearly 14
knots was achieved, and she proved a good sea vessel, pitching
rather less than conventional ships in heavy seas – it was supposed
because of the weight of water falling on her decks, damping out
motion.

> The foremost turret makes a most perfect breakwater; it
> receives with impunity the force of the water, which after
> spending itself against it, glances off overboard. There was one
> sea which rose in front of the vessel some ten or twelve feet
> above the forecastle, and broke on deck with great force, for the
> moment completely swamping the fore end of the vessel. A
> mass of broken water swept up over the fore turret, and heavy
> volumes of spray extended the whole length of the flying deck,
> some small portion of it even finding its way down the funnel
> hatchway.[13]

The *Devastation* was a floating, armoured castle invulnerable to
any foreign guns – for a while – whereas her own projectiles could
break through any foreign warship's armour, at least in theory. As
her coal capacity of 1600 tons gave a steaming radius of 9,200 miles
at 5 knots – the average for cruising ships of the line – she was the
most powerful and effective capital unit of the day. She was also
the best engineered; Reed had broken away from timber shipbuilding structures with the second generation ironclads and pioneered
a 'bracket-frame' system, virtually forming the bottom of longitudinal box girders. The *Devastation* was followed by the similar
Thunderer, then by a scaled-up version, *Dreadnought*; she was
10,800 tons with 14-inch armour and mounted four 38-ton guns.
These were elevated and loaded by hydraulic pistons operated by
steam-driven pumps. The recoil energy of the guns was also

absorbed by hydraulic pistons, a system devised by Armstrongs and first tried in the *Thunderer*. Here is an account of the *Dreadnought's* firing trials:

> Before the firing the ship was stripped as if for action. The armour covers were placed over the coaling scuttles, the bow bulwarks were let down, the guard rails and davits lowered, the sashes removed and hatchways battened down and lamps lighted below. The anchors and other impedimenta on deck were also doubly secured. The experiments began with the two guns in the forward turret. . . . The last test was a salvo, the two guns being fired simultaneously with maximum charges of 160 lbs. The concussion of the discharge was tremendous, the whole ship heeling over to port 2°. The whistles jumped out of the voice tubes, the glass from the sashes fell in showers, and

Open barbette mounting for heavy battleship's guns in the 1890s

Forward 18-inch gun turret, bridge and twin funnels of the battleship *Sans Pareil*, sister ship to the ill-fated *Victoria*

the faces of the tell-tales and engine room telegraphs were also fractured. No indications of distress were observed in the structure of the ship itself, nor signs of weakness in the hoist gear . . . although on the trials of the *Thunderer*'s gun under less stringent conditions several knees and angle irons on the breastwork deck were found to have been fractured and torn from their attachments.[14]

For loading, the fore turrets were trained aft, the after turrets forward, and the guns depressed until their bores formed contin-uations of loading tubes beneath the armoured deck. A hydraulic combined sponge rammer-waterspray was entered to cool and clean the bore, then cartridge and projectile were pushed home with the same combined rammer.

The *Dreadnought*, completed in 1879, was closer to the developed battleship in armament and armour positioning and in the relative weights devoted to them than any other ship of the transitional '60s and '70s. Her two compound engines offered striking economies in fuel consumption, giving her twice the radius of the *Devastation*, and with a top speed of 14½ knots she was undoubtedly the most formidable and impregnable ship in the world. Yet she suffered, like her prototypes, from lack of habitability below decks, particularly by comparison with the light and airy quarters of the large sailing ironclads, and her low freeboard of 10 feet, while making her an elusive, frequently submarine target, and a steady platform for the guns, raised doubts about her effectiveness for action in a seaway.

> In the morning the wind sprang up fresh and strong, and by the time St Catherines was passed, had risen to a gale, blowing right astern. The seas now swept the whole length of her upper deck as they rolled on from behind yet the motion of the ship was very slight indeed, dipping and rising easily and slowly. As the east end of the island was rounded, the wind was blowing very hard on the port beam and the spray at times completely shrouded the ship as the seas broke against her side . . .[15]

Before she was completed Armstrongs had produced 100-ton guns firing 16 cwt projectiles capable of shattering 36 inches of wrought iron, and Reed's successor as Chief Constructor, Nathaniel Barnaby, was forced up new design paths – this time by the Italians, who mounted these monster guns in two vessels designed to be the masters of anything afloat. In his reply, HMS *Inflexible*, Barnaby was unable to spread the immense thickness of armour required very far, and he confined it to a central citadel occupying a third of the length, rising ten feet out of the water from a submerged armoured deck extending over the whole of a lower hull subdivided into numerous watertight compartments. Protruding from diagonally opposite corners of the citadel were two 34-feet diameter turrets each weighing 750 tons when complete with a pair of 80-ton guns with a theoretical penetration of 23 inches of wrought iron at 1,000 yards. The eccentric positioning was to achieve right ahead and right astern fire from all guns. Below, two compound engines, 12 cylindrical boilers, 39 auxiliary engines for pumps, fire mains, ventilating fans, ammunition hoists and hydraulic machinery for the guns, together with magazines and shell rooms were all contained within the citadel, whose armour was made up in four layers: 6 inches of teak reinforced with horizontal angle irons, 12 inches of solid wrought iron, 11 inches of teak reinforced with vertical angle irons, 12 inches of wrought iron – a total thickness of two feet of iron. Forward and aft of this, along the unarmoured sides about the waterline, were a series of 4-foot watertight compartments filled with cork to preserve flotation if the side were punctured. Inboard were 2 foot-wide compartments stuffed with layers of canvas and oakum. Farther inboard were coal bunkers, and then storage compartments. The accommodation was above and in two long centreline deckhouses narrow enough to permit the guns to fire right ahead past their sides, at least in theory. Over all were two iron masts spreading a reduced area of sail.

Reed was publicly scornful of the design, considering the cork chambers liable to speedy destruction in action; 'the ship will then be left without stability'. A Committee of Inquiry was set up which rejected his argument chiefly on the evidence of naval officers who knew the difficulties of naval gunnery and considered it impossible that both unarmoured ends would be demolished, especially as any ships engaging the *Inflexible* would need heavy, thus few and slow-firing guns.

'Imagine a floating castle', Barnaby wrote, worried all the same about the design 'which the progress of invention in artillery has finally driven us to resort to . . .' Imagine the keel, a steel girder 40 inches deep; skin plating almost an inch thick, main deck beams 14 inches deep supported on wrought iron tube pillars. Imagine rivets in double, quadruple rows, bolts 4 inches in diameter to clench the massive slabs of armour to the frames. Imagine in the engine rooms a temperature of 110° despite two upcast shafts with fans sucking air out, black-faced engineers, coats buttoned to their throats feeling for over-heated bearings, playing hoses to cool them, the hiss of rising steam inaudible in the shattering din as the pistons hammer back and forth inside cylinders connected by staybolts to the bulkheads, lest the concussion should unseat them. Imagine 120 stokers breathing thick black coal dust in the far bunkers shovelling coals into barrows, wheeling them to the stokeholes at either end of the engine rooms. Imagine the oven heat about the boilers, each fourteen feet high, the livid glare from the open furnace doors as Welsh nuggets are scattered in by greyskinned men, their faces and arms chased with rivulets of black sweat.

In less than twenty years the timber 'liner' with auxiliary lifting screw had given way to the most advanced creations of industrial skill. Sails, which had been clung to for more elemental prejudice than the reasons usually advanced were now redundant for first class ships. The constraints they imposed on designers, the interference of their rigging with the arcs of fire of the great guns, and the danger of their wreck and obstruction in action outweighed any advantages they might have possessed. Even if one of the *Inflexible*'s main engines were to fail or be damaged in action there was another

[164]

in a separate watertight compartment driving a separate screw; all the auxiliary engines were similarly duplicated. At last, with great reluctance, the decision was taken to do away with sails for the *Inflexible*'s successors.

At the same time as sails went for 'battle' ships, a new form of breech-loading gun with the French interrupted screw thread breech block was adopted. The chief reason for the change was the discovery that the speed of burning of gunpowder could be controlled by manufacturing it in small moulded blocks which burned slowly compared with the sudden explosion of loose grains, and produced a continuous build-up of gas whilst the projectile was travelling up the bore – hence greater velocity could now be achieved by having a long barrel instead of a massive breech to contain sudden explosion. Longer barrels increased the problems of loading through the muzzle, which were complicated enough in any case. The first experimental breech-loader of the new type was ordered from Armstrongs in 1878; weight for weight the long breech-loader with slow-burning powder was a far more powerful piece than the dumpy muzzle-loader.

Simultaneously the manufacture of armour was transformed by the development of steel armour, first as a hard face 'cemented' to

Quarterdeck of a battleship in the 1890s showing the after barbette turret

a wrought iron backing to provide flexibility – as steel had hitherto been too brittle and had simply shattered when struck – and towards the end of the 1880s by all-steel plates which were two and a half times more resistant than wrought iron. Steel freed designers from the necessity to have such a massive thickness of armour, and together with the elimination of sails and the introduction of breech-loading guns, led the way from the central citadel idea of the *Inflexible* and her successors, back towards a higher freeboard version of the *Dreadnought* with a pair of great guns at either end of a mid-length superstructure; such were the 'Admirals' of the early 1880s. They were built entirely of steel, which freed more displacement for armour and armament, hence it is possible to see the *Inflexible* with her composite iron/steel construction, vestigial brig rig, eccentric turret placing, slab-like armour and cork flotation chambers as the last of the transitional types. It is significant that the term 'battleship' came into use with the 'Admirals' in place of 'ironclad' of the 1st, 2nd or 3rd class.

This was not appreciated at the time. The startling visual impact of the varieties of experimental types of the 1860s and 1870s which made up the British battlefleet, and their very different armament, protection, speed and manoeuvrability, tended to confuse discussion of how they would be used in action – in fact it had become accepted that tactics were obsolete as each individual Captain did the best he could in the indescribable confusion of a close-range ramming mêlée. There was an equally wide variety of 'cruising' ironclads: many were as large as the 1st class ironclads, but sacrificed extent of armour and weight of guns for steaming endurance. There were also 'protected' ironclads with a small belt of armour and a submerged armoured deck similarly designed for commerce protection, totally unarmoured frigates designed for maximum speed to catch enemy commerce raiders – and unarmoured corvettes, sloops and gunboats, all of which classes, types and diminutives of types carried full suits of sails and continued to do so for many years.

Besides the visual confusion there was the threatening apparition of the torpedo to drive out whatever theories survived. There were three types of torpedo in use in the British Service, all duplicated in foreign navies. The 'spar' or 'outrigger' type was a guncotton charge held out before the bows, or away to one side, of a small boat at the end of a long pole, pivoted to allow the charge to be dipped and exploded under water by the side of the enemy ship. It was fired with electricity by the officer in charge. There was the 'towing' type with its charge encased in copper inside a timber and iron vessel some 5 feet by 1 foot 9 inches by 6 inches, which was designed

[166]

'Spar' or 'outrigger' torpedo rigged for action in a ship's steam picket boat

like a Scottish poacher's 'otter' – or modern paravane – to diverge out 30° from the wake of a towing ship. It was buoyed to keep it at the required depth, under the enemy armour, and had an 'exploding bolt' at the forward end, which was driven in by contact with the enemy hull. If in the fearful confusion of action it seemed set to strike a friend the buoys could be released, when it was supposed to sink harmlessly beneath! In exercises it proved impossible to strike anything, but it was provided for all large ships, together with steam cutters for 'spar' torpedoes.

Far more formidable, at least in theory, was the 'locomotive' or 'fish' torpedo, known in the British Service after the inventor of the most successful type as the 'Whitehead'. This was a steel cylinder, the longest 16 feet by 16 inches diameter, pointed at both ends, with two contra-rotating propellers at the rear driven by compressed air contained within the casing. The guncotton charge was in the forward end with a percussion pin projecting from the nose; at mid-length was an ingenious depth-regulating device working on a combination of water pressure and angle of travel, known as the 'Whitehead secret'. All governments buying or manufacturing the weapons under licence were pledged not to reveal its workings. Needless to say the 'secret' was very open. By the beginning of the 1880s the British 'Whitehead' could travel a mile at 8 knots or lesser distances at greater speeds; at 25 knots its range was 200 yards.

It was launched either from an above-water 'impulse' tube employing a compressed air piston to drive it out, or from a similar submerged tube fitted with watertight valves at both ends. In that case the tube was opened to the sea after the torpedo had been placed in position and charged with air from a compressor. Both above- and below-water tubes could be aimed by traversing them around brass racers set in the deck, and in both cases a projection on the inside of the tube operated a lever on the torpedo as it was

JOINING UP THE FIUMÈ.

The Whitehead or locomotive torpedo

forced out, starting the motor. Whiteheads were also 'run' from slings over the side of steam cutters or 2nd class torpedo boats, which were 60 foot long, very slim steam boats carried aboard ironclads.

However, it was the sea-going or 1st-class torpedo boats which were of greatest concern to the Admiralty. Thorneycrofts of Chiswick, pioneers of fast steam boats from the early 1870s, had gained foreign orders for high-speed torpedo boats and by the 1880s had been joined by another British firm, Yarrow of Millwall. Both were now producing 70–80 foot boats of very thin steel with high pressure compound engines capable of driving them at 22 knots. Private firms in France and Germany were building similar types, and in France a group of officers, soon to become known as the *Jeune École* had seized on them as a counter to British battlefleet superiority, which seemed even more assured with the products of the technological revolution than in the days of the timber ship of the line. The *Jeune École* imagined fast torpedo boats making the traditional British strategy of blockade off their coasts impossible; in an offensive light they saw them as commerce destroyers which could sever Britain's trade and starve her of raw materials. Besides this, they were cheap; whole flotillas could be built and manned for the cost of a single ironclad.

A British Admiralty Torpedo Committee reported in 1876 that 'none of our large vessels could remain for any length of time during war off an enemy's coast . . .' The defences recommended were pa-

trols of 'guard' or picket boats around the fleet, electric lights concentrated in beams by dioptric projectors which could be pointed in
any direction, nets of galvanised iron hung around each battleship
from projecting 40-foot spars, and a machine gun armament. All
these were adopted, together with greater internal watertight sub-
division of ships, also recommended by the Committee.

The machine guns used were all multi-barrel weapons and were
carried on the upper or flying decks of ironclads. There was the
light Gatling with ten barrels, each 18 inches long with its own
lock, which revolved past a vertical feed case and was capable of
more than ten rounds a second, and the heavier Nordenfelt with a
similar vertical feed case, but only two or four barrels placed side
by side and fired by working a lever rapidly to and fro.

> The Nordenfelt provided a little excitement on one occasion at
> General Quarters. The Commander was in charge of the bridge
> and thought he would investigate them as they were new to
> him. He therefore drew back the firing lever with the result
> that the charges dropped into place. He then advanced the
> lever, firing all four barrels and actually hitting the flagship.[16]

The Nordenfelt's chief rival was the Hotchkiss revolving cannon,
a five-barrelled weapon fired by turning a crank to circulate the
barrels past a solid breech block fed with cartridges from a trough;
a rate of a round a second could be achieved with shells which in
the heaviest version weighed 4 pounds. Both these, and the Maxim
gun which was developed to fire similar projectiles in the early
1880s, were able to pierce the thin steel of torpedo boats at over a
mile, well outside effective range. But in 1881 as larger boats came
into service in foreign navies, the Admiralty advertised for a heavier gun to stop them, able to fire at least twelve aimed rounds a
minute. In responding to this challenge both Nordenfelt and Hotchkiss developed a single-barrel 'quick-firing', or QF, gun which had
charge and projectile combined in a brass case, removed after each
shot, thus eliminating the need to clean the bore of smouldering
remnants of powder between rounds. They proved so successful that
they were soon enlarged and copied by the major ordnance manufacturers, Armstrongs, and Krupp in Germany, who took them up
to 4.7, then 6-inch calibre, when they became useful for attacking
the unarmoured portions of the largest ships. Thus the response to
the torpedo boat threat led to a new factor in battleship design – a
secondary battery of medium-calibre QF guns ranged along each
broadside, able to fire at the extraordinarily rapid rate of six rounds
a minute.

The Nordenfelt machine gun for repelling torpedo boat attack

The ligher machine guns, meanwhile, added a new dimension to punitive expeditions and naval brigades overseas, increasing their superiority in fire power over primitive peoples, already augmented by the adoption of Enfield rifles in the place of the old muskets during the mid-sixties. Strangely, only the Marines were issued with bayonets; bluejackets fitted old-style cutlasses to the muzzles of their rifles. Such was the background to the European 'scramble' for territory in the undeveloped parts of the world, particularly Africa, during the last decades of the century. This was the final, accelerated stage of the rivalry for trade and influence played out around the coasts of the world since the beginning of the Victorian era, the former participants now joined by other industrialising powers.

The frenzied period began in Egypt, whose importance had been hugely increased by the Suez Canal when it opened in 1869. Although the Canal had been inspired by France and cut against a background of British opposition, it had been almost taken over by British steamships since; 80 per cent of traffic flew the Red Ensign. British finance had become as deeply involved, and the two Services even more so; both saw the Canal in the hands of either France or Russia as the most dangerous threat to India and the whole British position in the East. 'My belief is that if a war broke out with France, their first step would be to seize Egypt,' a War Department spokesman said in evidence in 1881 during an Inquiry into the defence of British trade and possessions. He believed it would be a race for Egypt; France was advantageously based in Toulon, Algiers and Bizerta; 'we ought to be prepared for such a race and have men and material ready to enable us to take possession of Alexandria and Port Said immediately on outbreak of war.'[17]

When the threat to the Canal came in the following year, it was not from any European rival but from a nationalist revolt led by Colonel Arabi of the Egyptian Army, largely in response to the Europeanisation of Egypt. Both British and French warships steamed to Alexandria ready to protect their nationals' interests in the usual manner; for Britain it was the *national* interest that seemed at risk: 'At the Admiralty our immense stake in the safety of the Canal was the governing factor . . .'[18] The Prime Minister, Gladstone, champion of independent peoples and opponent of all forms of colonial involvement, was determined that the affair should be solved in concert with the European powers, and there was constant negotiation with the French by telegraph. They, however, had preoccupations in Europe and recalled their ships, leaving the British Mediterranean fleet the only powerful force in the area just as anti-Christian rioting, massacre and looting seemed to demand intervention. For the Admiralty it was still the Canal that was paramount, and preparations were made for Naval Brigades and Marines from both Mediterranean and East Indies fleets and reinforcements from home to occupy Port Said, Ismailia and Suez. Sufficient ships were collected to patrol the whole length of the waterway and orders made out in detail which extended to the despatch from Malta of a water-distillation plant, and specially made rifle-proof shields for machine gun crews of patrolling warships.

The excuse to go in was provided when the Egyptians began strengthening lines of forts commanding Alexandria harbour, where the British fleet lay. Gladstone's cabinet was persuaded to allow the British Commander-in-Chief to issue an ultimatum that the work be stopped or the fleet would open fire on the forts. The ultimatum expired on 11 July 1882, and the first – and last – British ironclad squadron to go into action opened the bombard-

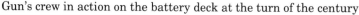

Gun's crew in action on the battery deck at the turn of the century

[172]

ment. It was a miscellaneous selection of ships. The most modern was the *Inflexible*; most were 'belt and battery' vessels, including Reed's fully-masted turret ship, and one more than usually unique vessel armed with 'disappearing' guns that sank in recoil into a well below the barbettes. Soon their masts and spars were shrouded by great clouds of smoke; officers stationed aloft to 'spot' the fall of shot watched the shells rise towards the shore – over a mile away in most cases, then made use of their powerful voices to pass observations to the officers of the quarters. Guns' crews, stripped to the waist with neckerchiefs bound around their ears went through the loading drill they had rehearsed endlessly. Every now and again, above the 'full-toned bellow' of the stubby pieces, there was a roar from one of the *Inflexible*'s 80-ton turret guns, followed by a rumble as the studded shell 'wobbled in the air with a noise like that of a distant train.'

These guns took so long to load that they could be fired only once in five minutes, and for a long time after they had been fired the whole ship would be enveloped in a yellow fog, while the projectile could be seen soaring away in the distance like a huge bird.[19]

Although the forts' reply was ineffective, and conditions were ideal with bright sun and the gentlest offshore breeze, the organisation for controlling the aim of the great guns proved deficient; there were no range-finders or fire control telegraphs, and messages passed by voice-pipe were frequently inaudible in the din. Meanwhile, the flat calm created problems for gunlayers trained to take aim as the ship rolled the sights on target; in at least one vessel the whole ship's company not employed at the guns was marshalled to move back and forth across the battery deck to create a roll; in others, guns' crews had no sooner laid their piece to the required elevation with the slow gear wheels than another gun or turret fired, affecting the heel and the whole process had to be repeated. The ships making the best practice were the *Inflexible* and one other with hydraulic control; even there it was evident that the gigantic pieces had outrun aiming mechanisms and organisation.

Nevertheless the increasing volume of fire from the fleet, the occasional direct hit on a gun or its embrasure, and mounting casualties eventually broke the defenders' morale, and the forts were abandoned after two days. There were only fifty-three British casualties in the action, and none of the ships suffered materially from very indifferent Egyptian fire. The report made out by two

[173]

senior Captains pointed out that it would have been a different story had the enemy possessed torpedo boats, mines, machine guns or even trained gunlayers.

The capture of the forts was only a beginning; Egyptian nationalism was further inflamed. More rioting in Alexandria, Colonel Arabi's threats to block the Suez Canal, the Admiralty's pre-thought plans to safeguard it, fresh troops and military commanders arriving from England all ensured that the campaign slipped from cabinet control to the local commanders just as it had in the days before telegraph cables; this had been certain from the moment Gladstone allowed the fatal ultimatum precipitating the bombardment. Naval Brigades were active in the fighting that followed, maintaining martial law in Alexandria, bringing up heavy guns, mounting them in ingenious, extemporised ways in the sand dunes, armouring a railway engine and trucks in which they mounted a 40 pounder, and Gatling and Nordenfelt machine guns for reconnaissance and sabotage up to the enemy lines. Finally the overwhelming fire power of the troops smashed Colonel Arabi's army at Tel el Kebir.

In the resulting vacuum Britain assumed temporary control of the country. Because of the immense financial and strategic issues this became permanent and drew British troops and Naval Brigades

Bayonet charge of the Royal Marine Light Infantry at Tel el Kebir

into further campaigns up the Nile to maintain stability in the Egyptian dependency of the Soudan. Probably Egypt had to pass into British hands after the Canal and steamships brought new patterns of trade and new vital threats to India and the Eastern Empire, and it is significant that it actually happened under a Prime Minister opposed to the use of force and the acquisition of colonies.

But it was no small island peninsula like previous strategic bases, and the take-over finally upset the delicate balancing act by which British diplomacy had avoided dangerous combinations of European rivals against her. Protestations that the Navy had gone in to restore order and protect life and property made no impression against the fact of unilateral action, evidently planned in advance, carried through with ruthless precision from both ends of the Canal simultaneously, and culminating in control of the most vital strategic hinge between East and West. From beneath liberal, humanitarian trappings the 'Empire of the Oceans' had emerged as a naked threat to the aspirations of rivals; France and Russia came increasingly together to curb overweening power by huge naval building programmes of their own, at the same time seeking territorial compensations wherever they could. Resurgent 'navalism' and the scramble for colonies, in which the new major powers, Germany, and the smaller western European nations joined enthusiastically, meant the end of Britain's low-cost, piecemeal, largely inherited naval superiority; she was forced into mounting expenditure and serious planning.

CHAPTER SIX

HIGH NOON
OF NAVAL POWER

By the mid-1880s, when the British were at last awakened to the fact that their privileged world position rested on the Navy, and governments were persuaded that more money was needed to make up for the economies of more than half a century, the Service had changed sufficiently to allow very swift transition to a modern force. This was not apparent to younger officers, the late Admiral of the Fleet Lord Chatfield, for instance:

> The '80s and early '90s were years in which the older officers were still embedded in sails and all the thought that pertained to them. They hated engines and modern guns; the mine and the torpedo were anathema to them . . . nor had they the technical education that was now being given to younger officers. They were fine and many of them magnificent personalities, these great old seamen. They were the last who in a great ship could call all hands on deck and see every man on deck or aloft.[1]

'In fact the main training of the older officers and men had been in seamanship,' wrote another of the new generation; 'tactics, strategy and the finer arts of gunnery were but dreams of the future.' A more caustic critic wrote that the hard manual work on the sailing ship and the necessity of driving men to a high pitch of physical exertion had developed techniques unsuited to the requirements of the machine age.

> Everything had to be done at the run and the most trivial tasks were carried out in an atmosphere of strain and hurry with the ship's Police shouting at the men who did not move fast enough. In some ships there was a great deal of bullying and

abuse of subordinates, but this was accepted as part of the normal routine. No one thought any the worse of a certain Captain who, during general drill, shouted at the Quartermaster to bring him a bucket because the Commander made him sick![2]

The bizarre collection of fully-rigged ironclads and cruising ships accentuated the impression, especially as mast and sail work formed the basis of all drills during the 1880s. In many ways the outward show was misleading. A start had been made at providing higher education for officers with the establishment of the Royal Naval College at Greenwich in 1873. The courses included pure and ap- plied mathematics, nautical sciences, fortification, naval history and tactics, international and maritime law as well as physics, chemistry, metallurgy and modern languages amongst many other subjects. Naval architecture and marine engineering were taught at South Kensington, and in 1880 a Royal Naval Engineering Col- lege was established at Keyham, Plymouth. The *Excellent* mean- while had developed a mining, torpedo and electricity branch which in 1873 was accommodated in a second vessel, HMS *Vernon*, moored nearby; within three years the *Vernon* was independent.

At the Admiralty itself the technological revolution had been recognised by raising the former office of 'Surveyor', now Controller,

Divisions

COMMANDING OFFICER, WHAT'S ALL THIS

A.B. FLESH, SIR

[177]

to the Board as 3rd Naval Lord in 1882 with proper departmental staff, including a Director of Naval Ordnance, a post established sixteen years earlier. The principle of Admiralty payment, hence control of ordnance, was accepted in 1882 although full control was not recovered for some time. Also in that year the nucleus of an intelligence department was formed at the Admiralty as the Foreign Intelligence Committee under a brilliant officer, Captain W. H. Hall. This department collected information and issued reports on foreign ports, anchorages, naval bases and coast defences, naval strengths and building programmes, training and standards of foreign personnel and the results of foreign naval manoeuvres. Within five years it had been expanded into a Naval Intelligence Department with a Director of Naval Intelligence also responsible for mobilisation and reserves.

This problem of a reserve of men, to expand the peace establishment of under 40,000 to the 100,000 or so needed in a major conflict, had been tackled after the Crimean War exposed the acute dangers of the old lack of system; whole squadrons had been delayed for want of men or had sailed short-handed. By 1861 a scheme had been worked out whereby active merchant seamen who had reached AB standard could volunteer for a Royal Naval Reserve. They received a retaining fee of £6 per year and a pension of double that at the end of the time, and had to serve four weeks a year in a Royal Navy ship or shore station. By 1865, 17,000 men had enrolled, and the numbers increased steadily.

Changes in manning the active fleet were as significant. These had started just before the Crimean War; now the old method of signing a crew for one commission from a pool of sailormen had been replaced by a long-service system, whereby a boy received training in an old timber 'liner' moored at one of the home ports. Then, at the age of eighteen, he signed on for ten years' continuous service. To make the career more attractive and encourage him to sign for a further term, an AB's pay was raised to 1s 4d. a day and a new rating of Leading Seaman created at 1s. 10d. a day – plus 50 per cent in the tropics with steam up! A new rating of Chief Petty Officer had also been created.

In the early part of 1872 I saw on some recruiting posters for the Royal Navy that the lowest standard height for boys was 4 feet 10 inches. I ran home and measured myself against the door and thought I was over the height required and begged my Aunt to see a Magistrate whom she knew personally, and ask him for a recommendation for me to take on board HMS

Impregnable, the training ship at Devonport. My Aunt called on the Magistrate and he gave her a very good recommendation. I walked to Devonport. . . . Several watermen were standing about on the quay-side. I told one of them I wanted to join the Navy and asked him if he would take me aboard the *Impregnable*. I have often remembered his words in after life. He told me he had served his time as a man-of-war's man, and would do it again if he were a boy. 'It's a fine life,' he said, 'but hard, sometimes very hard.'[3]

The lad was rowed out to the old three-decker *Impregnable*, where he was taken to the Master at Arms, measured and found to be a quarter of an inch below the standard height. 'Try as I would I could not stop the tears coming to my eyes.' The Master at Arms, seeing how keenly he felt, told him to take off his coat and waistcoat and measured his chest; 'That boy will do; with his fine chest he will grow to be a fine man.'

I had to sign a form stating that I would serve for a period of ten years after arriving at the age of 18 years. This I did with

Inspection bags and bedding

much pleasure. Looking back after so many years, the main
thing which comes to my mind was the kindness and
encouragement I received when joining as a sailor boy.[4]

This lad, Patrick Riley, eventually reached Chief Gunnery Instructor, and retired very happily on a Greenwich pension in 1907,
returning briefly to the Service he loved during the First World
War as an Instructor.

In London, the best-known recruiting station was the back par-
lour of the Swan and Horseshoe at Westminster, where a Sergeant
of Marines regaled wide-eyed young aspirants with marvellous tales
of Service adventure 'which will never be surpassed, if they are
equalled, for the Sergeant had cultivated the art of descriptive lying
to an extent that would have put Baron Munchausen to shame'.
The lads were brought up sharply to the realities of naval life when
they joined one of the training ships. The Ship's Police all carried
canes as thick as a man's thumb, and the Instructors stout ropes
with a Mathew Walker knot in the end.

Whenever the Assembly sounded the Police would run around
the decks cutting indiscriminately at the boys as they rushed
up the ladders. . . . It was thought at the time that the proper
way to bring up a boy for the Navy was at the rope's end, and I
must say that the doctrine was run for all it was worth.
Notwithstanding, the corporals and instructors were anything
but brutally inclined. That was the custom of the Service and
they carried it out; outside of that they were uniformly kind
and considerate.[5]

The author of that memoir found the usual bullying and fagging
among the boys and from the Ship's Police ritual birchings and
floggings for petty misdemeanours, but was clear at the end that
the tone and training were 'morally, mentally and physically'
beneficial:

Every boy felt that he had to live up to the traditions of the
Service, which led him carefully to avoid all mean actions and
cultivate exaggerated ideas of what constituted a sailor's
virtues . . . becoming imbued with those numerous little things
which in the aggregate go to form that frank, fearless
disposition which Englishmen look on as a recognisable
characteristic of the Bluejacket's temperament.[6]

The training consisted of mast and sail drill, small boatwork,

Jack ashore – Sally Point, Portsmouth

great gun drill, rifle and cutlass exercise and signalling, together
with the usual sweeping up and scrubbing decks, cleaning paintwork, washing clothes and scrubbing hammocks, varied by swimming in the summer, occasional picnics, a run ashore twice a week
and home leave twice a year.

With the 'long-service' volunteer system came an official uniform.
This followed the lines of the one the men had evolved, although
the number of 'inspection' as opposed to 'working' garments increased, and petty regulations about the exact size of a trouser leg
or collar multiplied and provided Ship's Police or divisional officers
with a taste for regularity yet more opportunities for finding fault.
By 1891, when an officer inspected his division he carried a short
wooden ruler marked with various uniform measurements:

[181]

The men, however, still endeavoured to decorate flannels and black silk handkerchiefs with fancy designs beautifully worked in coloured silk, but they had to conceal these garments from the eyes of the officers of their divisions. . . . Many were the regrets I used to hear for the old days when the men were permitted to dress 'fancy'. . . .[7]

The men still made their own uniforms from material – blue serge or white duck for working gear – obtained from the 'slops' aboard, and the cost was still deducted from their wages; it was not until 1907 that ready-made uniforms were issued. Thursday afternoon was set aside for 'Make and mend', and other special times for washing clothes – to wash them out of routine was a punishable offence, presumably because the wet garments were afterwards

'Make and mend'

hung on lines about the upper decks. A man lived out of a water-proofed canvas bag in which all his clothes, together with his 'housewife' containing needles, thread, buttons, etc. were stowed.

With the more complicated internal arrangements of the iron-clads the single berthing area of the old broadside ships was often not possible and messes were installed wherever space could be found in a corner or passageway. They were collapsible tables and benches which could be hauled to the deckhead to clear decks, with a rack on a bulkhead nearby in which the messes few extra pro-visions and garnishings were stowed, together with personal 'ditty boxes' in which each man kept a few treasured possessions.

Meanwhile, punishment and shore leave had undergone slow change. At the beginning of the 1870s, largely in response to an outcry in the press as much on behalf of soldiers as sailors, the Admiralty had issued a circular which restricted corporal punish-ment to serious summary offences. As a result the number of flog-gings at the gangway dropped from fifty-seven in 1870 – in itself a marked drop from previous years – to an average of seven a year; in 1879 it was abolished altogether. Unofficial floggings by the ship's company probably continued; here is one administered in a gunboat which was nearly run down at night by a ship without lights:

By the laws of the Royal Navy the Captain can only give a very light punishment for such an offence. The Petty Officers took the law into their own hands, made out a warrant and gave one of the lookout men a dozen lashes with the hammock clew. I will be bound to say that the lookouts will keep a much better lookout in future.[8]

A punishment known as '10A' had taken the place of flogging for a host of minor crimes; it meant extra work and no leisure time at all, and was generally awarded for seven, ten or fourteen days at a time.

They [10A men] were ordered out at 4 a.m., and on their knees, not saying their prayers, but holystoning some dirty spot by rubbing wet sand into the deck with large sandstones. All their meals were eaten under a sentry's charge, and they carried their hammock over their shoulders on the quarterdeck until 10 p.m.[9]

Their grog was stopped too! There were a number of other pun-

The water carnival

ishments devised by ingenious officers to fit the crime. Ridicule was popular: one Commander had men who used bad language stand facing a bulkhead on the mess-deck during their off-duty time, calling out the nature of their offence and the words used every half hour after the ship's bell struck. At the other extreme there was shot drill; men had to stoop without bending their knees, pick up a 32-pounder round shot and, holding it out clear of their body, take a number of paces, halt, bend and deposit the shot in a chock – and continue the process for an hour or more. For serious offences, or after a number of spells of '10A', a man would be put in the cells. Disciplinary offences were tried by court martial; for example, in 1876, a sentence of five years penal servitude was awarded one smart hand for striking a Petty Officer who had jerked him out of a sail on which he was lying asleep after a pipe for 'Sweepers and clear up decks!'

Although the number of punishments awarded rose in the wake of the restriction of flogging, reaching a peak of 163 per cent of the total number of men serving in 1874, they steadied and declined again during the 1880s. Disciplinary offences, which reached the highest recorded figure of 10.9 per 1,000 men in 1881, dropped to 5.5 by 1885 and under 3 per 1,000 in the 1890s. Meanwhile Captains were forced to revise their attitudes to shore leave – the more liberal had, long since. Now the men were classified: 'habitual' (leave breakers), in which case they were allowed ashore only once in ninety days, 'general', allowed ashore once a month, 'privilege' allowed ashore on most occasions in harbour, and 'special' on every occasion shore leave was granted. A man could work his way up through the classes by remaining sober and returning on time, or down by breaking his leave – in which case he also had a day's pay stopped for every six hours he was adrift.

These were the outward changes following the introduction of long service. Industrialisation had worked its inward changes: sailors still went barefoot and moved like cats aloft, 'the give and spring as they landed on deck was absolutely cat-like', but in the ironclads especially a mechanical precision drill had been imposed by the great guns. The same went for small arms for a different reason: Naval Brigades were such a feature of the Navy's work that training for shore operations was taken very seriously. The head-quarters of this training, HMS *Excellent*, was notorious throughout the Service for its military style, smartness and immaculate turn-out. Where before in marching Jack had slouched 'apparently to the order "Go as you please!" ', without keeping time or step, he was now drilled by bull-voiced officers and Instructors to high standards of parade ground discipline. *Excellent*-trained Gunnery Officers and Petty Officers transferred this to sea-going ships, where attitudes had been more casual; as late as the 1870s small-arms men had been taken through their aiming and loading drill in bare feet.

Most obvious of the industrial changes were, of course, the new breed of stoker ratings, engineer artificers – skilled fitters and machinists – and engineer officers, who had come up the same way. All had been greeted with a certain derision at first; for a stoker to show himself on deck in his grimed stokehole rig was to court certain punishment, and the officers, who had achieved commissioned status in the early 1850s, were still not accepted in any social sense. This was not so much because they had usurped the executive's sole command of the powers of motion, and threatened to make sailing seamanship, the executive's pride and art and poetry, redundant, but because they came from the entirely different background of a factory bench, usually from one of the great industrial cities. The equivalent 'tarpaulin' executive officers had long since been replaced by rather smoother sons of professional and aristocratic families, and it is not surprising that engineer officers messed separately from the wardroom officers and were generally 'snubbed, subdued, subordinated men' referred to by such unattractive titles as 'greasers' or 'fats'.

Infantry training at the gunnery school HMS *Excellent* at the turn of the century

I must say, however, that though they were emphatically cads, this old class of engineers was composed of thoroughly practical men, who were not above their business, and managed to keep themselves apace in a most commendable manner with the development and progress of steam machinery.[10]

By the mid-1870s when engines had become complex and were essential for the fighting as well as motive power of large ships, the treatment of engineers and their consequent shortage had become potentially dangerous. To improve their status an Engineering College was established at Plymouth as well as a training ship at Portsmouth; engineers were ranked as 'military' officers with a 'military' instead of civilian uniform and their separate messes were abolished so that they became members of the wardroom in the early 1880s. None of this narrowed the social gulf between them and the executive, but they were essential preliminary steps. One superb sailing officer, Captain Heneage, celebrated for his exquisite elegance and shining dark curls, refused to heed the names of any of his Chief Engineers, but referred to them all by the name of the first 'Chief' he had sailed with. When one day after the new dispensation he caught sight of the Marine sentry at the gangway of his ship presenting arms to his Chief, he was cut to the heart. 'That a Chief Engineer should receive the same mark of respect given to

The naval square for repelling a charge

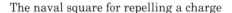

his commanding officer!' he exclaimed to the Major of Marines in the theatrical voice that went with his appearance. 'I haf it! Take away the sentinel's musket!'[11]

The executive officers themselves had not escaped change; shortly after the establishment of training ships for boy ratings it had been decided to send officer entrants, now known as Naval Cadets, to the same ships for practical training before they joined a sea-going vessel. This had proved such a success that in 1858 another three-decker, re-named *Britannia*, was fitted out for officer cadets only. She was moved to the River Dart in Devon where it was thought the open surroundings were morally healthier than a naval dock-yard. The ship was run on the same lines as the ratings' training ships by Ship's Corporals and Petty Officer Instructors, and everything was done on the run, but there was a great deal more theoretical instruction and no ropes' ends. Corporal punishment was awarded comparatively rarely, although this differed with different regimes, and usually for 'very serious offences such as smoking, unparliamentary language and fagging'. It was carried out ritualistically with a cane on the orlop deck in the presence of the Captain, officers and Surgeon, who had previously examined the victim – a process which 'generally gave the inexperienced criminal the impression that he was going to be beaten almost to the point of death'.

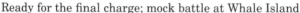

Ready for the final charge; mock battle at Whale Island

By the 1890s the *Britannia*, now joined by a two-decker, *Hindus-tan*, moored ahead of her and connected by a light bridge, was being run like a nautical public school with 'term lieutenants' acting the part of housemaster to each term of cadets. The boys slept in ham-mocks over their sea chests, and the morning routine after a cold plunge was much as aboard a sea-going ship with schoolwork taking the place of drills. The syllabus was heavily weighted with algebra, spherical trigonometry, nautical astronomy, chartwork and theor-etical seamanship, but included French, drawing and steam engi-neering, while two sloops provided a practical introduction to sail-work aloft. Studies or drills continued after the midday meal until 3.30 p.m., when the cadets shifted into flannels and were pulled ashore to enjoy a wide variety of formal sport or informal recreation. There was a photographic dark room, racquets and squash courts, a gymnasium, the *Britannia* beagles, in the summer river bathing and boating and cricket, in winter hockey, rugby, soccer or lacrosse.

> The boating was what I most enjoyed. We had skiff dinghies,
> four-oared gigs, six-oared gigs and several small sailing boats,
> half-decked and rigged with a mainsail and jib.[12]

It was still necessary for a boy's parents to find a senior officer to 'nominate' their son for entry to the Service via the *Britannia*, but a competitive examination weeded out perhaps half the nominees. Memoirs of the time all mention a period at one of the 'crammers' which specialised in getting boys through the exam.

At the same time as entry was thus gently being removed from the control of individual Admirals and ships' Captains, and instruc-tion was systematised and greatly broadened, the Admiralty was bringing order into the chaotic career structure which had left officers unemployed for years at a time, perhaps for ever. The method used was to retire a large proportion in each rank, sugaring the pill by the form of words 'Reserve half pay', and both increasing that 'half pay' and stepping the officer one rank up on retirement. In this way the elderly, incompetent or simply less fortunate were removed from the lists; nevertheless promotion remained slow through the 1870s. The rank of Sub-lieutenant had been introduced in the 1860s, formalising the old path from Midshipman via Mate to Lieutenant, and a young man might remain four or five years as a 'Sub' before becoming a full Lieutenant, another fifteen or more before being promoted Commander, and a further ten years before becoming Captain. Captains reaching the age of fifty-five were re-tired as Rear Admirals without ever flying their flag. For a man

Cutlass drill at HMS *Excellent* at the turn of the century

without 'interest' the best chance of beating these averages was by gaining commendations on active service, although '1st class' marks in the examinations for Lieutenant did gain extra seniority.

The general fighting officer became increasingly specialised; the executive included three specialist lieutenants, 'Gunnery', 'Torpedo' and 'Navigating' all of whom could go on to the highest ranks afloat or at the Admiralty. At the same time the Purser of naval legend had become a much more respectable 'Paymaster', the senior ones with the rank of Commander, handling all the ship's wages as well as provisions, and providing Captains and Commanders-in-Chief with a Secretariat.

In total the changes amounted to revolution; from a haphazard, largely practical seamanship training in sea-going ships and promotion prospects dependant on the whim of individual seniors, the naval officer had gained a systematic theoretical training and a rational career structure. This was accompanied, as on the lower deck, by greater outward uniformity; by the 1890s a diamond tie pin was considered a mark of individuality. More important were profound changes in outlook; the middle and lower ranks had become filled with men well attuned to the machine age; they were its product and they were only waiting their chance to create a Service in their own image. Here is a memorandum for private circulation in 1883:

> Sending steamers which sail badly to make long sea passages under sail is inconsistent with the spirit of the age . . . it is a

Field battery exercise, HMS *Excellent*

waste of time and both officers and men know this and it
disgusts them. The men read much more than they used to and
they know quite well that a high state of efficiency in shifting
topsails will be of no use to them in wartime.[13]

The author was Captain C. C. P. Fitzgerald, described by one
officer who served under him as 'probably the most able seaman in
the Navy as regards the management of sails. He could work the
Inconstant just like a yacht'.[14] Four years later, when Fitzgerald
was continuing his campaign in a lecture at the Royal United
Services Institution, he described the advocates of sails as lumber-
ing up the nautical express with old mail coach paraphernalia and
stage properties to the curtailment of fighting power. But he saw
the real danger as the diversion of enormous effort and resources
from the study of modern naval warfare:

Evolutions aloft are so attractive and so showy; there is so
much swagger about them, our Admirals have always so highly
commended and attached so much value to the smart shifting of
topsails or topgallant sails, and so many lieutenants have
worked their promotions out of the successful cultivation of this
sort of seamanship in their ship's companies, that we seem to
have lost sight of the fact that it has nothing to do with
fighting efficiency in the present day.[15]

The younger officers present agreed, as did Captain Philip Colomb, who added his analysis of the real reason underlying the arguments of the retentionists, 'the poetry and romance of a sailing ship'. Colomb was another brilliant exception to any generalisation about officers whose professional skills extended little further than 'the replacement of broken spars and ropes or split sails.' He and his brother, John, a Marine officer, were among the first to study naval history in an analytical spirit and attempt to worry out lessons applicable to the new weapons and types of ships. In the 1850s and 1860s when it had seemed that steam made invasion possible and all strategic thought had swung towards coast defence ships to protect overseas bases, they had shown up the fallacies and argued that command of the seas around Europe with ocean-going fleets was still the only strategy, and that the British Empire was most vulnerable to an attack on trade. They had likened the trade routes to arteries of empire; once severed, the heart would stop without a single foreign soldier being landed in the country. This view of the Navy as a force primarily to 'protect our merchantmen on the high seas, and perhaps to convey them from point to point' while the main fleets at home and in the Mediterranean marked the enemy main fleets, had gradually won acceptance.

Another pioneer of trade protection, Admiral Alexander Milne, as First Sea Lord in 1875, constantly argued that the strength of the Navy should be based not on the strength of French and Russian fleets, but on the vast trade and colonial possessions it had to defend. His demand for scores of new cruising ships was rejected, but the government set up a commission to inquire into trade and colonial protection. Its findings revealed such dangerous shortages of cruising ships and such vast wealth in terms of imports, exports and merchant shipping at stake that they were kept secret. The final report concluded that Britain's survival in war depended on the protection of her trade; this was the Navy's overriding task.

As in strategy, so in tactics, the Colomb brothers were the first to show up the hopeless confusion into which ramming and torpedo enthusiasts had plunged contemporary thought. While French and Italian theorists, copied by less hard-headed British officers, either dismissed the study as impossible under the new conditions or worked out ingenious formations based on military manoeuvres, impossible in action as well as inappropriate, Philip Colomb pointed out that both ram and torpedo were very close-range weapons and asked why any Admiral should force a close-range mêlée which would hazard his own ships as much as the enemy's while he could by superior gunnery and tactics destroy his opponent outside torpedo range. 'The English mind will require to be shown,' he wrote in a phrase perfectly describing the practical, non-speculative genius of the British officer, 'that every Admiral will determine to use the ram, which will give him no advantage.'[16] It would also need to be shown how an Admiral could force a ramming action against an opponent's will. He put concentration of force, mutual support, and the best formation for bringing maximum gunfire to bear as the prime tactical requirements, thus arriving back at the simple and ancient 'line of battle', each ship following in the wake of her next ahead.

That British tactical thought was moving towards this conclusion, far in advance of Continental navies, is shown by the annual manoeuvres through the 1880s. When the 'Admirals' and later classes of battleships came into service their secondary armament of medium calibre QF guns, ranged along each broadside, made line ahead the only practical formation, and the close-range mêlée appeared even more impossible. Meanwhile other thinking officers like Admiral Phipps Hornby had been testing the defence against torpedo boat attack; it was established that at sea a battle fleet needed to turn 16 points (180°) away from an attacking flotilla to bring the torpedo tracks astern, and Hornby advocated that fleets should be accompanied by a flotilla of sea-going torpedo boats armed 'with an alternative gun armament so as to serve as torpedo boat destroyers when so required'.

So it was that by 1884, when a journalist named W. H. Stead, editor of the *Pall Mall Gazette,* raised the first effective cry of alarm over the strength of the Navy in a sensational series of articles *The Truth about the Navy* – with information supplied by Captain 'Jacky' Fisher, most powerfully aggressive of the new breed of technically-minded officers – the Service was ready for transformation. It had sound organisation, solid strategic and tactical theory, well-trained officers with the will and in positions to sweep away the shibboleths of the old guard. All they lacked was money. As the press agitation increased and the public became affected with a mixture of pride in their vast empire and anxiety lest their fleet was not strong enough to protect it, so the naval estimates grew. The most dramatic increase was marked by the Naval Defence Act of 1889; the 'Two-Power Standard' of parity with the next two naval powers, France and Russia, which had guided the Admiralty since 1815 was pronounced very publicly as the cornerstone of policy, and a building programme was authorised for seventy new vessels costing £21.5 millions over five years.

Heading the programme were the Royal Sovereign class of battleships. These were the tangible expressions of the Colomb theory of battlefleet command by ocean-going ships able to dictate a gun action outside torpedo and ramming range in all seas. They embodied for the first time all the features of the mature battleship, except protection for the heavy guns' crews. In order to carry the guns high enough to be worked in a seaway they were mounted in open barbettes. Otherwise their specification of high speed, high freeboard for sea-keeping, wide steaming range, heavily armoured vitals and waterline belt, main armament carried at either end of a mid-length quick-firing secondary battery remained the essentials of battleship design to the end.

Class after class of larger and larger versions of the type, 'Majestics', 'Canopusses', 'Formidables', 'Londons' followed them, stately and assured symbols of naval power which were individually better balanced and in combination immensely more powerful than any rivals. The open barbettes grew protective shields over the guns revolving with them to form a modern 'barbette turret'. Flexible chain rammers enabled loading to be carried out at any angle of training so that the great pieces could be fired twice a minute. Gunpowder charges were replaced by a more powerful 'smokeless' propellant called cordite, the result of chemical experimentation. By eliminating the dense clouds produced by the old black powder charges, this allowed QF guns to be *aimed* as fast as they could be fired, enhancing the battleship's superiority over torpedo craft.

For world-wide trade protection forty-two 'cruisers' without sails and with speeds over 20 knots, light armour protection to the waterline or submerged armoured decks, replaced the rigged frigates, corvettes and sloops of the transition years. Like the battleships they had one or two guns mounted behind turrets at either end and batteries of QF guns between. Against the threat posed by a French policy of torpedo boat war against trade in the Mediterranean and English Channel, torpedo boat 'catchers' or 'destroyers' were built from 1893; their other role was to protect the battlefleet and this soon became their primary function. Great speed and sea-keeping were the first consideration in design; they were achieved by high turtle-backed forecastles, extremely light steel construction with such thin plating that in the early boats it concertinaed in and out as the bows plunged into heavy seas, and huge engines producing some 20 HP per ton of displacement, as against little over 1 HP per ton for contemporary battleships. Here is a full-speed trial of a '30-knotter':

> . . . observe the chargeman in the stokehold stand with his
> hand on the fan regulator, his eye on the gauges, his foot

among the coals. He inspects the fires through his coloured
glasses and directs the fireman, who visits each furnace with
unceasing regularity, spreading shovel loads evenly over the
fires with a species of sleight of hand . . . In the engine room
the indicators have gradually crept up to 400 revs. The triple
beat of the engines merges into a prolonged roar, occasionally
assuming a distinct period as the two engines get into step; this
is felt throughout the whole ship, the stern in particular
appearing to jump violently up and down; and one cannot
repress a feeling of wonder to observe that the engines remain
on the whole in the same place. In the stokeholds the faces of
all gradually get blacker and blacker and the atmosphere is a
whirlwind of coal dust, occasionally relieved by spray taken in
at the cowls and distributed impartially by the fans. Dust
obscures the gauges and telegraphs; dust gets into the fan
engines, which promptly run hot and require water to cool
them. The water descends on the bare necks and heads of the
firemen . . .[17]

Engineers filled the main bearing oil-boxes with one hand, with
the other directed hoses at red hot gudgeons or bearings, drenched
and breathing in a compound of oil and sea water which formed a
haze throughout the machinery spaces.

These exciting craft offered commands to young Lieutenants and
such a different informal style from the rigid and centralised discipline of 'big ships' that they attracted devotees among officers and
men, despite the bare and cramped accommodation and the violent
motion which upset nearly all stomachs on leaving port.

There are really two navies: Big Ship Navy and Small Ship
Navy. The former is all gold lace and etiquette, the latter junior
and jovial. In the former a Post Captain is *fairly* important, in
the latter a lieutenant is lord of all he surveys.[18]

Navigating early destroyers was as hair-raising as the high-speed
evolutions they were practised in:

The bridge was a circular platform round the 12-pounder gun
which was mounted forward, and a chart box was secured to the
rail. The steering wheel and compass were in a kind of small
box on the starboard side underneath the gun platform. The
Torpedo Coxswain at the wheel could not see what was
happening abaft four points on the port side, and the steering

compass was quite unreliable owing to its being surrounded by
so much steel.[19]

In the Naval Manoeuvres of 1906 one division making home from
the Casquets arrived seventy miles adrift in Cardigan Bay.

As the ships of the Naval Defence Act were completed and commissioned through the 1890s it was apparent that once again Britain's
marine engineering strength had enabled her to shrug off competition. For a brief spell her naval power seemed to allow her to
dispense with traditional alliance diplomacy and rule the seas – as
she had always claimed – in isolation. The unrivalled strength of
the Mediterranean fleet proved decisive time after time in preventing colonial crises from spreading to Europe; it became established
dogma at the Admiralty that 'the best guarantee for the peace of
the world is a supreme British fleet'. The strain was taken up by
the press and public, interested as never before in *their* Navy;
Admirals were subject to the popularity and public scrutiny reserved today for stars of sport and entertainment. Music Halls
echoed to popular pride of Navy and Empire; versifiers exhorted the
people to reckon up their battleships – 'ten, twenty, thirty, there
they go'. Naval memoirs and naval history enjoyed a wider read-
ership than ever before. Most astonishingly successful of all were
the works of the American naval historian Alfred Thayer Mahan,
whose *Influence of Sea Power* books added a new dimension to
historical thought and a great many clichés to naval discussion.
Many of his basic ideas were borrowed from Colomb; his arguments
reinforced the battleship-dominated British strategy, which was
soon aped by all other industrial powers.

The appearance of supreme world power reached its apogee in
Queen Victoria's Diamond Jubilee year, 1897, when 21 battleships,
53 cruisers, 30 destroyers, 24 torpedo boats and small craft, all
drawn from home commands without weakening the premier battlefleet in the Mediterranean or any of the overseas squadrons, were
gathered for a Royal Review at Spithead.

Truly a marvellous pageant and one which Britons may take
pride in knowing to be such as could be exhibited by no other
nation, nor indeed by all of them put together.[20]

That year the Naval Estimates were almost £22 millions – double
the 1884 vote at the beginning of the 'navalist' awakening. They
continued to increase every year as ships grew in size and the fleet

which had to be maintained increased. By the end of the century they reached nearly £29 millions.

More than ever now the strategic fulcrum of the Navy – and the Empire – was the Mediterranean; here a fleet headed by the latest battleships, under the most able Admirals, marked the main French fleet at Toulon and a growing Russian fleet in the Black Sea to prevent their junction, meanwhile protecting the Middle East buffer to India and the main shipping routes through Suez to the East. By the turn of the century there were fifty British warships in the Mediterranean based on Malta. Their smartness was legendary; it was maintained, as in the sailing days, by intense rivalry between ships in various drills and evolutions that had replaced mast and sail drill:

> Outstanding, and indeed above all other excitements was the Monday forenoon's competitive drill. All Sunday evening was spent in preparing for getting in and out torpedo nets, putting wire hawsers into boats and pulling them out again, or at sea towing ship, mooring against time on arrival. Every drill had to be prepared so that it could be completed in a few minutes or even seconds. For the first ship to break the 'I' pendant (completion of drill) was to receive an approval from the C-in-C that was the envy of all.[21]

The appearance of ships was another point of keenest rivalry; they were gaily painted with white topsides, yellow masts and funnels and black hulls with red waterlines, and a Commander's promotion had come to depend much on the prettiness of the ship he ran, both inside and out. Those Commanders with a long purse who could buy enamel paint, gold leaf, brass funnels for their steam boats, emery paper for burnishing the steel fittings, 'Globe' polish were at an advantage over their poorer brethren. 'Hours were spent in burnishing stanchions, davits and steel blocks till they shone in the Mediterranean sun'. Decks were holystoned white, iron ring bolts in the planks burnished and fitted with canvas covers to protect them between inspections; 'the huge armoured doors of the battery were taken off their hinges and the armourers and other ratings were employed filing down their surfaces till they were smooth enough to take a polish'. The watertight doors and all the guns were similarly filed and burnished and fitted with flannel covers, the ready-use shot and shell painted as brightly as the sparkling topsides; 'there is no doubt that on Sunday morning the whole ship presented a blaze of splendour to the Captain as he went his round of inspection'.[22]

[197]

Fleet regatta Mediterranean Station. Before the race: sailing . . .

Perhaps the highest pitch of fleet rivalry was reached during the sailing and pulling regattas that were a major feature of life on the station. Large sums changed hands in wagers on the results, and those hands not taking part lined the sides and shouted themselves hoarse as the boats approached the finish between the ships; near the end an anxious silence descended.

. . . pulling

Every face was set and tense waiting for what they knew was coming. Then it came. Like a pistol shot over the water came a cry from the *Colossus'* coxswain – 'Off!' And with a mighty roar from the assembled onlookers the final spurt commenced. They shouted, cheered, danced and waved their arms in a paroxism of enthusiasm. . . .[23]

There were, besides, sailing races every week and frequently private pulling races between ships' crews. Even when not racing there was an enormous amount of sailing and rowing, as the use of steamboats was forbidden for the ordinary work of the fleet:

they could not even be hoisted out without the permission of the Admiral, and all the communication between ships, and between ship and shore was carried out by boats under oars or sails, for preference sails. The sailor was always in a boat in those days and from the amount of rowing he had to do he should have developed corns both on his hands and on his stern.[24]

On passage from port to port 'showing the flag', the fleet was taken through steam evolutions which, like the quarterly target practice with the great guns, were considered by many of the keen middle and younger officers to be too artificial for the chances of real war – 'quadrille-like movements carried out at equal speed in accordance with geometrical diagrams in the signal book' according to one critic. It was during one such exercise, designed to bring all battleships simultaneously to anchor in their correct order in two lines in the Bay of Tripoli, in 1893, that the Navy suffered one of its worst peace-time disasters.

The Commander-in-Chief, Admiral Sir George Tryon, a formidable autocrat with a reputation for brilliance in fleet manoeuvres, and a penchant for keeping his Captains on their toes with unexpected variations of formation, signalled for his two columns to reverse their course by turning inwards towards each other. His flagship, *Victoria*, was leading the starboard column. It was evident to all the Captains in the fleet that the columns were too close for such a manoeuvre to be carried out, but Tryon evidently had a blind spot about this manoeuvre. He had ordered it some years before, only that time he had heeded warnings. On this occasion he would not; instead he grew impatient when the *Camperdown*, flagship of his second-in-command, leading the port column, failed to acknowledge his flags because the manoeuvre was so obviously dangerous; he signalled, 'What are you waiting for?'

The second-in-command, faced with this public rebuke and the knowledge that the fleet was steaming straight for shoal waters suddenly realised that Tryon intended circling his own column *outside* the port column; the flags ordering the manoeuvre were in two hoists and it flashed upon him that Tryon would have the signal for the port column hauled down before the signal for the starboard column. After a hurried consultation with his Captain he ordered his own flags hoisted close up, signifying he understood; immediately Tryon's two hoists were hauled down *simultaneously*.

The wheels of the two flagships were put over in opposite directions and they began to swing inwards towards collision. The *Camperdown* went to collision stations; the hands began closing the multitude of watertight doors between compartments. Meanwhile the *Victoria*'s flag Captain tried to alert Tryon to danger, but the great man was in his usual position staring aft at the following ships and when eventually he turned and saw the *Camperdown* little over 400 yards away it was too late. Only combined action could save the ships, but neither could ease their own wheel lest the other did the same – and even then it was doubtful if they would pass clear. The flagships' officers and the fleet watched horror-struck as the *Camperdown* continued her turn right into the *Victoria*'s starboard bow, her ram below water slicing a great gash through the unprotected lower hull. As the crew of the flagship rushed to close all doors Tryon, standing on the upper bridge, murmured to himself, 'It was all my fault.'

The hole in the flagship proved fatal as it covered two watertight compartments, and there was not time to close the ventilators and ports which had all been open because of the hot day. She settled by the bows, listing, and after only twelve minutes turned over and dived, taking over half her complement of 700 with her. The orderly scenes at the end and the discipline of the stokehole and engine-room parties, all of whom went down with the ship, were in the finest traditions of the Service. Tryon went down with his ship.

Outside the Mediterranean, the imperial policing Navy of small ships carried on exactly as it had throughout the century. On the Pacific station, where coaling bases were widely scattered, sails were used well into the twentieth century. Here is an episode from the commission of the barque-rigged sloop *Pylades*, called to Tonga in 1903 after some trouble with German traders had resulted in the British Consul being insulted.

The King [of Tonga] was dressed in an off-white uniform

decorated with orders cut out of cigarette tin lids hung on bits of coloured silk, a large pith helmet complete with spike and a cavalry sabre but no shoes.[25]

The British Consul, backed up by the Captain of the *Pylades*, demanded an apology for the insults, stipulating that the British flag should be hoisted at noon the following day and saluted with twenty-one guns from the small brass cannon which formed the Tongan heavy artillery. Hearing of the ceremony, vast crowds of Tongans arrived from all parts in canoes, causing the small British party some concern about the consequences should the King decide not to fire the salute. All passed off smoothly however, and, honour satisfied, the *Pylades* rugger team played a native team: 'the home team won the match as they were naked and covered with grease, so they were quite uncollarable'.

A more important function of the Pacific squadron was the attempt to suppress 'blackbirding', the hiring of virtual slave labour like the French *engagés* for work in the sugar plantations of Queensland and Fiji.

In the Persian Gulf a squadron of similar small ships continued to keep at least the maritime peace among local sheiks.

Visiting the places on the coast was fun but rather scaring. We had to land through surf, and we were always surrounded by fierce-looking villains armed with spears and festooned with huge daggers. The cutter's crew had rifles in the boat and lay off as close to the beach as the surf permitted, ready for action. We tried to look completely unconcerned whilst fierce arguments went on [between Sheiks] with a great deal of screeching and spear-shaking. We settled several arguments and promised all sorts of things through the interpreter; we didn't know what *he* said of course.[26]

Both coasts of Africa provided similar local excitements for ships of the Cape station. The commission of the Cape flagship, the cruiser *St George*, from 1895 to 1898 illustrates the continuous activity. Her first action was in suppression of the Brassmen of the West coast, who had risen and raided one of the trading stations of the Royal Niger Company. 'The fighting consisted chiefly of boat attacks on stockades in the narrow, winding creeks of the Brass River. These stockades were invariably armed with smooth-bore ordnance, from 3-pounder to 9-pounder.' The 1st Lieutenant and two men were killed before the fire power of the British rifles and Maxim

The naval brigade of HMS *St George* encamped on the march to Mwele, East Africa

guns overwhelmed resistance, and the Brass capital, Nimbe, was taken and burned.

The cruiser had scarcely returned to Simonstown in March before news came of a rising in East Africa. Steaming to Zanzibar it was learned that an Arab Sheikh, who had established himself as a powerful ruler in the trading territories of the East African Company, had conspired against the British. Once again a naval brigade was landed, this time to march inland through unknown jungle to the Sheik's capital, Mwele. This proved to be at the top of a steep, tree-clad hill; it was assaulted in three columns, taken and burned. Three months later the Ashantee warriors of what is now Ghana rose in rebellion and the *St George* steamed back to the West to join a force assembled off Cape Coast Castle. She didn't take part in the fighting, however, as the Jameson Raid into the Transvaal caused her to be diverted back to the Cape, where she stayed until the dust had settled. Afterwards, in the summer of 1896, she started a cruise up the East Coast only to discover a *coup d'état* in Zanzibar following the death of the Sultan, a friend of the British. Anchoring off the Royal Palace, the Commander-in-Chief, Admiral Rawson, demanded unconditional surrender from the usurper, failing which he would bombard. The ultimatum was timed to expire at 9 a.m. the next morning. No reply was received and 'scarcely had the hour pealed from the clock in the Palace tower, when the signal "Open Fire!" was struck in the flagship'. After a short, sharp engagement the Palace was reduced to a ruin and one of the aspiring Sultan's ships sunk at her moorings. The usurper was then replaced by the rightful heir.

The cruiser *St George*, flagship of the Cape Station 1895–8

Early the next year, 1897, the West Coast again claimed attention. The British acting Consul for the Niger Coast Protectorate,
together with seven, white companions, was ambushed and killed
while on a journey to discuss trading concessions with the King of
Benin. The King had told the British party it was inopportune to
visit him as he was making Ju-ju for the soul of his father – a
ceremony involving hideous human sacrifices, which he thought
unlikely to please the British. However, Rawson was ordered to
take charge of a massive punitive expedition to be assembled from
ships and gunboats of the Cape Station and two additional cruisers
from the Mediterranean.

It was a maxim of the British after their long experience in Africa
never to despise the enemy, and Rawson's plans, mimeographed in
elaborate detail, included two simultaneous feints to seize native
strongholds to the east and south of Benin while the main assault
force under the Admiral himself marched on the capital. The force
comprised 560 seamen, 120 Marines, 250 African Housa troops, 70
local scouts and some 2,000 native carriers for fresh water, food,
ammunition, hospital chests and poles for carrying sick and
wounded, canvas shelters for the night, officers' tents, officers' field
latrines, hammocks, cooking utensils, billhooks, pickaxes, shovels
and telegraph instruments. The food was packed in biscuit boxes
each containing rations for 24 men for one day – 12 lbs of biscuit,
12 lbs bully beef, 3 lbs sugar, chocolate, tea, coffee, salt, pepper,
curry powder, candles, matches and three pints of rum. The boxes
were given wooden bases for carrying on the head. Water was taken
in 4-gallon paraffin tins similarly fitted with wooden bases; the

ration was a quart a day for combatants, a pint for carriers. In addition lime juice, onions, rice, extra biscuit, sugar and bully beef was packed in bulk loads of 50 lbs. The men wore serge jumpers, trousers and drawers (optional), pith helmets and boots. Spare kits, one waterproof sheet and one blanket per man were packed four in a bag, weighing 56 lbs. Field gun, Maxim and rocket ammunition was also made up into bulk loads, and the combatants carried a rifle each – now the Lee-Metford magazine rifle – 100 rounds of ammunition, a waterbottle and ½ lb of biscuit – total weight 25½ lbs.

Because of the dense jungle the force would advance through, command was decentralised as much as possible, the tactical unit reduced to a half company of 24 men controlled by an officer. The advance had to be made in column along narrow tracks and to prevent straggling, heads of columns were told that the pace was not to be more than 1½ miles an hour. After each march of about 50 minutes a favourable position was to be selected for a ten-minute rest.

The importance of saving ammunition was impressed upon the whole force. When unexpectedly fired at from behind cover, steady volleys by word of command were to be fired in the direction of the attack. Magazines were on no account to be used except to stop an actual rush of the enemy across an open space. Where the leading portion of a force advancing in single file expected an ambush, or discovered the enemy, they were instructed to halt and kneel down, the front rank turning to the right front, the rear rank to the left front. Two volleys were then to be fired in order, searching all the places where the enemy might be, the line advancing again if no fire resulted. Should the enemy open fire in reply, instructions were given to kneel down at once and fire volleys, advancing slowly after each volley to ascertain the enemy's position, extending as far on each side of the track as possible, and then to move rapidly on the enemy, without losing touch of the main body. The general rule for fighting was to be 'rapid fire by volleys, and rapid advance without losing touch'. The importance of advancing against native races, whose fear of the white man makes them unable to stand a charge, was impressed on all ranks. Clearings in the bush were to be turned before advancing across them, and positions once gained were to be resolutely held, no retreat being authorised in this warfare.[27]

Sending a field gun ashore

The expedition put off in ships' boats and established a base camp
some thirty miles up the Benin River. From there the two diver-
sionary forces moved off and the main column started its march for
Benin, through the jungle. The column was headed by native scouts
in skirmishing order; after the scouts came a half company of Housa
troops, then a Maxim gun party, a rocket tube party, another half
company of Housas, a demolition party with explosives, two 7-poun-
der guns on field carriages, a company of Bluejackets and another
Maxim gun party – 200 men all told. Behind this division came the
Commander-in-Chief himself with a reserve division of Marines
together with ammunition and baggage carriers, and bringing up
the rear another division of Bluejackets, Housas, Maxim and rocket
parties and water and baggage carriers. The force found itself under
continual harassment from natives who either climbed trees or
concealed themselves in the dense bush and deliberately picked off
individuals, but the policy of returning fire with volleys, following
up and keeping the snipers on the move allowed a steady advance.
In five days the column emerged from the jungle into a broad
clearing or avenue leading to the capital.

On the first appearance of our column in the open some of the
enemy armed with guns attempted a charge, cheering as they

[205]

came, but were driven back into the bush by volley fire and
Maxims . . . the force then advanced on Benin, the Marine
battalion on the right, the Hausas in the centre and the seamen
company on the left. The enemy occupied the bush on both
sides, and were also up in the trees. The advance having been
sounded the troops charged down the avenue by half companies,
cheering as they went. The heat was terrific – without a breath
of air – and the whole force was exhausted, having been on the
march for seven hours without food. The whole way having
been contested by the enemy it had been impossible to halt for
more than a few minutes at a time.[28]

The 7-pounder guns were brought up in the wake of the charge,
rockets fired into Benin, and a final assault down the clearing
gained the King's compound. The King and his entourage had fled
long since, after a rocket had landed close by them from out of the
sky. 'The heat was terrible in the place, the sights ghastly, and the
stink awful. Human sacrifices and corpses were everywhere.' The
compound was secured against counter attack, and the following
morning a force was sent out to search for water, the reserves being
down to a quart per man. Another force went back to base camp for
provisions; other parties set about burning the capital, finding
everywhere more grisly testimony to the King's Juju; crucified
slaves, bodies cut open, the smell of death hanging in the close heat.

After taking a place, stay in it one or two days. Nothing
demoralises natives more than this. If you find there are other
villages in the neighbourhood destroy these also. In fact you
should not leave the district until you have thoroughly
demoralised the tribe.[29]

Rawson followed this advice from an experienced African hand,
Sir Francis de Winton, and stayed four days, burning everything in
the area before making back for the coast and re-embarking five
days later.

The whole operation was a superb example of retribution, meticulously organised and swiftly delivered. The ships had been concentrated from distances up to 4,000 miles away between 15 January,
when Rawson had received his orders, and 9 February. The force
had been landed on the 11th, Benin taken on the 18th – 34 days
after the Admiralty orders, only 45 days after the original massacre.
This was a far more rapid response than had been the rule earlier
in the century. It was made possible by the spread of telegraph

cables out from London to all parts of the Empire in the 1870s and 1880s. The losses from enemy fire were three officers and ten men; a further thirty-eight officers and men had been wounded, many seriously, but the major casualties came after embarkation from malaria; 2,300 cases were reported in the squadron, and in the *St George* herself only 100 out of 338 men who landed escaped fever.

The outbreak of the Boer War shortly after the *St George*'s return home involved Britain in colonial fighting on a new scale altogether, and Naval Brigades played a subsidiary role to the Army, as they had in the Crimea, chiefly bringing field guns to the front and manning batteries. One Brigade from the armoured cruiser, *Powerful*, arrived in Ladysmith with ship's QF guns on extemporised mountings just before the Boers closed around the town. Their two 4.7s and four 12-pounders were the only ordnance available to the defenders capable of equalling the range of the Boer guns. More naval quick-firers up to 66 inch calibre on extemporised field mountings from the *Powerful*'s sister ship, *Terrible*, were sent with the force which fought its way to relieve Ladysmith. As in the Crimean War, this Naval Brigade and its officers gained a reputation among the military for reckless courage. It was particularly marked at the battle of Graspan, where the Naval Brigade led the assault on a Boer-held *kopje* (hill). They began the assault in open-order line with brief rushes. An army officer wrote,

> In the breathing space between these rushes one conspicuous figure was to be seen standing erect and marking the position taken up by the Naval Brigade. This was the commanding officer, Captain Prothero, a man of great stature and immense physique, who elected to stand thus, leaning on his walking stick while his men lay prone. Eventually the inevitable happened and he was seen to drop, happily only wounded and out of action for a time.[30]

Although out of action, Prothero called out, 'Men of the Naval Brigade, advance at the double! Take that kopje and be hanged to it!' And they did, losing many of their surviving officers in the hail of Mauser fire. 'You fellows are too brave', said another army officer,

> It is utterly useless for you to go on as you do for you will all get killed in this sort of warfare. I saw your officers walking about in front of the men even when the latter were taking cover just as if they were carrying on on board ship.[31]

'Did you watch the Naval Brigade?' said one Colonel to a Staff

[207]

Officer, 'By Heaven, I never saw anything so magnificent in my life!'[32]

Important as these contributions were, and particularly the long-range naval guns on improvised field mountings, the Navy's really vital function was to isolate the conflict from other European powers; it fulfilled this simply by existing on the 'Two-Power Standard' supreme, unchallengeable in the Mediterranean and home waters.

Before the end of the Boer War, yet another nationalist rebellion broke out in China, spearheaded by a fanatical sect of the Heavenly Fist – 'Boxers'. An international force was collected from squadrons of all the industrial nations which had been clustering around the carcass of the Chinese Empire, and once again warships bombarded the forts commanding the Peiho River. This time, when assault parties were landed, British officers racing at the head of their men for the honour of being first in to the forts found themselves in competition with Japanese officers. After the forts had been taken, the squadron steamed up-river to Tientsin, which was captured after sharp fighting. The British Commander-in-Chief, Admiral Sir Edward Seymour, then set out by rail for the relief of Peking, where European nationals were besieged in their legations. The 'Boxers', armed chiefly with spears and swords, tore up the lines, and when they were joined by Imperial Chinese troops deploying cavalry and modern artillery the relief column was forced back to Tientsin with heavy casualties. Reinforcements were hurriedly assembled from all parts of the empire, naval guns landed – including four long 12-pounders from the *Terrible* which had arrived from South Africa, and a second, successful, attempt was made to relieve Peking.

One of the many British casualties of this last campaign of the Victorian era was Captain H. T. R. Lloyd of the Royal Marines.

> We had halted and he and I lay down together and were
> talking about things in general. He told me that now he had
> been through so much, and had hitherto been untouched, he
> would get through all right, but he added, 'Even if one is killed,
> one's people will be proud of one for the rest of their lives.' As
> he spoke he raised himself on one elbow. I heard a bullet whizz
> past my nose and hit him. . . .[33]

CHAPTER SEVEN

WAR NAVY

Few looking on the British Navy of 1900 and reading the orthodox version of British naval strategy contained in the works of Mahan and his many disciples could have imagined that the whole theory and practice on which it was based would, in the course of five years, be changed almost beyond recognition. It was not just a great fleet, without parallel in the world or in history, it was virtually a new fleet. The creation of the Naval Defence Act, 1889, its main units, all alike, gave an impression of stability in design and purpose. Its world-encircling chain of bases, linked by telegraph and capable of swift reinforcement, assured an overall command which appeared permanent. 'Five strategic keys lock up the world,' exulted Admiral Fisher, most influential of all British Admirals: Singapore, the Cape of Good Hope, Alexandria, Gibraltar and Dover; 'these five keys belong to England!'

The fleet was headed by homogenous squadrons of battleships of 14,000 to 15,000 tons displacement, the latest with all-steel armoured vitals and waterline belt. They could make 17½ to 18 knots, had a steaming radius of some 8,000 miles, and were armed with four 12 inch guns in barbette turrets, and five or six 6 inch QF guns on each broadside between, with numerous anti-torpedo boat QF and machine guns. There were ten battleships in the Mediterranean fleet, eight in the Channel fleet, four in the China fleet; while at home the Admiral class and other ships of the 1880s and early 1890s formed a powerful reserve. The largest armoured cruisers were more than 14,000 tons with a 9.2 inch turret gun fore and aft and six 6 inch QF on each broadside. They could make 22½ knots, and were designed to hunt down enemy commerce raiders; their other rôle was with the battlefleet to pierce an enemy cruiser's screen and keep contact with the enemy main fleet, in action even to lengthen the battle line. There were two 1st class cruisers with the Mediterranean fleet, two with the Channel fleet and six in China. Smaller, unprotected cruisers served as scouts for battle squadrons and formed the backbone of the overseas stations, with gunboats still for policing duties. There were also torpedo boats for coast and harbour defence, and torpedo boat destroyers of some 300 to 400 tons with names like *Boxer*, *Bruiser*, *Banshee* for stopping enemy flotilla attack on the battlefleet or trade.

In all there were 580 ships of all types on the Navy List, 160 of which were serving on foreign stations – 50 in the Mediterranean, 39 in China, 13 in the East Indies, 16 at the Cape of Good Hope, 14 on the North America and West Indies station, and smaller squadrons in Australia, the Pacific and the south-east coast of America, a state of affairs which had come to be accepted as a law of nature. £2½ millions was being spent on an extension to Gibraltar dockyard, £1¼ millions at Hong Kong, £1¼ millions at Malta, £2½ millions at Simonstown, over half a million at Bermuda in addition to normal maintenance.

As an essential background to the Navy's presence, the British merchant marine, ship-building and marine engineering industries were still in a class of their own. Over half the world's sea-borne trade was carried in British ships built in British yards; the merchant fleet totalled over nine million tons, much of it in new, high class liners owned by companies whose familiar houseflags seemed

An early torpedo boat destroyer

An early idea for disposing of submarines; a destroyer attacking with a spar torpedo

as enduring as the White Ensign. P & O to India, Alfred Holt's Blue Funnel to the East, Cunard and White Star to North America, Union and Castle Lines to South Africa, Shaw Savill to Australasia, the Allan Line, Orient Line, Pacific Steam Navigation, Ellerman, Elders and a host of others. By contrast the nearest competitor, France, had less than a million tons of merchant shipping.

With such support British engineers had led the development of marine engines and were still doing so. The greatest single advance of recent years had been the turbine invented by Charles Parsons, who had served his apprenticeship with Armstrong's Newcastle works. For the violent, continually reversing piston thrusts of reciprocating engines the turbine substituted a smooth, continuous rotation of moving parts which not only allowed lighter power units but brought fewer stresses and greater efficiency. The Admiralty had reacted quickly and by 1899 had two turbine-fitted destroyers, *Cobra* and *Viper* running trials. They achieved speeds of over 36 knots, surprising even their most enthusiastic supporters.

At the same time the British shipbuilding industry, with support in depth from tiers of specialist sub-contractors, was unmatched anywhere for size and speed and cheapness of building. Its sales of warships to foreign countries vastly exceeded those of any other nation, and in many cases these privately-built cruisers, destroyers and smaller craft pioneered design features which were adopted by the major navies. In addition to the private yards, the Royal Navy had its own yards at Portsmouth, Chatham, Devonport, Sheerness and Pembroke. The largest of these could build battleships – although not cruisers – more cheaply and speedily than the private yards. The 15,000 ton *Magnificent*, for instance, was launched one year after her keel plates were laid at Chatham, and completed and commissioned within twenty months – a phenomenal speed for such a huge and complex vessel. Admiral Sir John Fisher was able to say with confidence, '*Whatever type the French have, we must go one better*, and that is a principle which will always keep us safe, and if we build as quickly as we ought to build, we ought always to commence after they are well advanced and have the more powerful vessel afloat beforehand.'[1]

With such an apparently unassailable position added to the Royal Navy's uniquely triumphant history it was small wonder that British naval officers strode the world with the assurance of demi-gods, and a genuine belief not only that the Anglo-Saxon race was the most fit to bring law and civilisation to the world, but also that 'the British nation owned the world's supply of pluck'. Their assumptions of superiority were quite as impressive as their great ships: 'Tell these ugly bastards,' Captain Pakenham said to his interpreter in the midst of a mob of brigands whom he supposed to have been committing massacres in Armenia, 'that I am not going to tolerate any more of their bestial behaviour!' He was several miles inland, accompanied only by an interpreter and one Midshipman aide. His immaculate white uniform, erect bearing, clipped speech, the gold cigarette case which he flipped open, impressed his audience with the presence of 'a being from another world, such as no one present had ever seen,'[2] and the interview was carried off peacefully. Foreign navies were regarded with equal disdain. Here is Fisher, as Commander-in-Chief Mediterranean in 1900 explaining his view of strategy to the Colonial Secretary:

> What we require for naval fighting is 'splendid isolation', and to use your own famous words 'only a congenital idiot with criminal tendencies' would permit any tampering with the maintenance of our sea supremacy, which is the basis of our system of imperial defence.[3]

Such was the appearance, and for a short while the reality; yet the very factors which went to ensure supremacy also made for vulnerability. A Naval Intelligence Report of 1900 drew attention to the immense wealth at stake on the high seas – £523 millions of imports, £354 millions of exports, excluding the value of the ships themselves and the earnings they brought in to help balance the visible trade deficit. It pointed to Britain's dependence on foreign grain for her bread supply – there was only six week's stock in the country – and her equal dependence on raw materials for her factories from abroad, hence the internal dangers which would follow the cutting of her shipping routes by an enemy. It also mentioned increasing competition in world carrying trades, which would make it impossible for British ship-owners to afford the kind of war risks premiums levied during the great wars. This was something an influential group of French naval officers believed to be Britain's Achilles heel, and French naval policy against England had again shifted decisively towards war against trade. The First Lord argued the need for greater expenditure on cruisers to protect trade as the only true insurance.

> To us, defeat in maritime war would mean a disaster of almost unparalleled magnitude in our history. It would mean the destruction of our mercantile marine, the stoppage of our manufactures, scarcity of food, invasion, disruption of Empire.[4]

It was apparent that the standard of a 'Two-Power' battlefleet was no longer applicable. The French were concentrating on commerce-raiding cruisers and on nests of torpedo boats which would keep a blockading battlefleet at a distance. They had also developed submarine torpedo boats to a point where they seemed an even greater potential threat to a blockading fleet. To seek an answer to the 'submarine' the Royal Navy was forced to order five of a type which had been developed in America. It had always been

One of the great fleet Admirals who trained the pre-War navy, Sir
Arthur Wilson

a maxim at the Admiralty that this form of warfare should not be
encouraged as it threatened the whole basis of British strategy, yet
the French development left no alternative – at least the alternative
offered by one supreme battlefleet tactician, Admiral Sir Arthur
Wilson, that all submarine crews should be treated as pirates and
hanged, was believed to be impractical.

[214]

An equally serious threat to traditional British strategy was the growth of modern navies outside the two chief rivals, France and Russia. None were yet in a position to challenge British supremacy, yet it was evident to those who looked beyond the Royal Navy's immediate crushing superiority that two of the new powers, the United States and Germany, had greater industrial strength than either of the historic rivals, and it would be impossible for Great Britain to build against them all. There was also Japan, whose British-style Navy had been developed with astonishing speed and efficiency, and was now headed by five very British-looking battleships. The Far East was the point of greatest immediate danger, for Russia was also building up a fleet at a newly-acquired base, Port Arthur, which commanded the approaches to northern China; already she had five modern battleships there and six armoured cruisers. The French also had a small squadron headed by one battleship. The Royal Navy's four battleships and two armoured cruisers would have been powerless against a Russo-French-Japanese combination; reinforcements could be sent, but this would have weakened the fleets in the Medterranean and home waters.

Within a year of Fisher's exposition of 'splendid isolation' British diplomats were negotiating an alliance with Japan, and the Treaty was sealed in February 1902. This safeguarded the British stake in China without either weakening command in European waters or necessitating a building programme designed to ensure a 'Three Power standard'. A similar recognition of the Navy's inability to command in every ocean had already resulted in informal co-operation with the US Navy in American waters. The most significant outward demonstration was the British decision to allow the US government unilateral control over the proposed canal through the isthmus of Panama; with the new American drive for overseas expansion and the accompanying ocean-going battlefleet programmes it would have been folly to have antagonised her. British diplomacy was playing its traditional balancing game but on a far wider scale, with modern industrial powers and with more naval counters at stake.

These adjustments to the strategy of world-wide command so soon after its realisation in the mighty fleet of the Naval Defence Act, were symptoms of a profound change in Britain's world position. The full implications were not easy for any but a few visionaries to grasp, but they stemmed from the two complementary facts that the railways which industrial Britain had given the world were capable of knitting larger economic units than sea routes, and that the two nations which had benefited most, the United States and

Germany, had as a consequence narrowed Britain's unique industrial lead and in many areas actually overtaken her. As navies
were advanced creations of industry and invention it was only a
matter of time before Great Britain would have to yield the trident.

This was not so evident in 1900. To Fisher, preparing for the
Battle of Armageddon against a Franco-Russian fleet in the Mediterranean off Port Mahon in Minorca, the growing German Navy
presented a challenge to be met in the traditional way by building
more ships. 'No use the British Empire having two or more battleships than the French and Russians . . . you want a sufficiency left
over, intact, after settling with the first hostile combination, as to
be ready to deal with, say, our German cousin, who has kept neutral
ready to bag the booty.'[5] In 1901, he was calling for a 'Two-and-a-
half Power standard'.

By the middle of the following year the view had changed. The
real purpose of recent German battleship building programmes had
been discerned – not perhaps the full extent of that purpose but
sufficient to sound the alarms. A visit by an Admiralty official to
Kiel and Wilhelmshaven had resulted in 'some very serious reflec-
tions'. A confidential memorandum drew attention to the thorough
and purposeful way in which the German fleet was being expanded
and pointed out that the concentration on battleships could have
no meaning against Germany's Continental rivals; armies were the
only appropriate force on land.

> Against England alone is such a weapon as the modern German
> Navy necessary; against England, unless all available evidence
> and all probability combine to mislead, that weapon is being
> prepared.[6]

The British Foreign Office had already come to this conclusion. The
British press had similarly discovered German ill-will and was
promoting an image of a militarist nation under a warlord Kaiser
preparing to throw an Army across the Channel to march on
London. Fisher, who had been called from the Mediterranean to be
2nd Sea Lord, now believed 'the Germans are our natural enemies
everywhere! We ought to unite with France and Russia!' Preliminary talks with the French Ambassador in 1904 turned into a
formal *Entente* with France, whose common border with Germany
gave her even more urgent reasons to fear that nation's military
and industrial power.

For Britain the changes had come with astonishing speed. From
a position of 'splendid isolation' she had become within four years

partner in a formal naval alliance with Japan, an informal one with the United States, and an understanding with her former chief rival, France. As France was allied to Russia, every naval power of consequence except Germany was either friend or ally. While the government sought to prevent the *Entente* from becoming a formal military compact which would limit Britain's traditional balancing rôle, every increase in German strength, every revelation of her ambition to dominate Europe pushed Britain farther towards France until the once independent 'Mistress of the Seas' became little more than senior naval partner in a defensive coalition

Signallers on the bridge, early twentieth century

Two great reformers who jolted the Navy into the twentieth century –
Admirals 'Jacky' Fisher (extreme right) and Percy Scott (third from right)
against the pretensions of Imperial Germany. This was not appreciated at the time. The Royal Navy was still overwhelmingly larger
and more splendid than any other, its history longer and prouder,
its prestige higher. It still saw its rôle as the arbiter of peace in
Europe, the great deterrent to German aggression; as for its officers
and men it needed more than *Ententes* and alliances to change the
arrogant assumptions of a century.

Changes in tactics and expertise were as fundamental as the shift
in grand strategy. The changes had started in response to the dangerous isolation at the turn of the century long before the German
challenge was recognised; they marked the triumph of the new
breed of technically-minded officer. Most effective and catalytic of
these was 'Jacky' Fisher. Appropriately he was a product of technical departments; he had been an Instructor at the *Excellent*, the
first Instructor in the *Vernon*, Captain of *Excellent* when it was
decided to move the establishment ashore to Whale Island in Portsmouth harbour for better facilities than the old wooden walls could
provide; later Director of Naval Ordnance at the Admiralty during

the debut of QF guns, afterwards 3rd Sea Lord and Controller, responsible for all *materiel* departments when the new battleships, cruisers and destroyers of the Naval Defence Act were filling the building slips. He was a man of volcanic energy, single-mindedly devoted to the Service, ruthless in pursuit of efficiency with a personality that literally terrified those who could not measure up to his standards.

> I have still a vivid recollection of the awe which the great Jack inspired whilst on board. He had such a terrific face and jaw, rather like a tiger, and he prowled around with the steady, rhythmical tread of a panther.[7]

When he came to the Mediterranean fleet he was determined to shake it out of its established routines and prepare it for war, and he set about it with total disregard for peace-bred institutions of seniority and the feelings of senior officers who did not share his views, which gave personal focus to a sharp split which soon grew up between the technical men, 'materialists', and an old guard of traditionalists such as had existed to oppose every change throughout the century. One of his first acts was to call together a Committee of officers distinguished not for their rank, but for their ideas on war strategy, tactics, gunnery, torpedoes; many were young:

> impossible to exaggerate the new ardour, the feeling of relief among younger officers who felt that the day had dawned when mere peace ideas and manoeuvres were about to give way to war preparations.[8]

The fleet was exercised at long-range gunnery, firing in company instead of individually, continuous high-speed steaming such as war must bring, exercises designed to test the strategy of blockade under the new conditions, destroyer protection for the fleet. Captains and officers were confronted with unexpected situations by day and night, their reactions judged; for those who failed the test, 'the saying used to be, "Will he go home on the *Alpha* or the *Beta*?" '

Fisher was not the only Admiral with an interest in war tactics or reform of many traditions that had become out-dated. There were many others and had been from time to time throughout the nineteenth century, but the isolated position of the nation in 1900, the realisation after Boer successes against the Army in South Africa that the Navy might be similarly out of touch with real war, and his own sheer ruthlessness combined with a flair for pithy argument and publicity brought him to the forefront as the leader of the new 'materialists'.

> It is difficult for anyone who had not lived under the previous régime to realise what a change Fisher brought about in the Mediterranean fleet, and by example and reaction throughout the Navy . . .[9]

The writer of this comment, later to become Secretary of the Committee of Imperial Defence, was nevertheless concerned about Fisher's ability to 'keep afloat with the awful millstone of naval prejudice trying to sink him'. In a letter of June 1900 he noted that naval officers generally reviled Fisher 'because he goes on lines of his own – fools, they hate anyone not hidebound by their own ridiculous traditions!' By the time he was called to the Admiralty as 2nd Sea Lord in 1902 the seeds of a rift in the Navy had been sown. The radical reforms he introduced, once there, the system by which he packed all departments with his own favourites, and the ruthlessness with which he discarded anyone opposed to his ideas shocked even some of those who sympathised with his aims. The rift between 'materialists' and 'traditionalists' deepened into a feud which threatened the hitherto unquestioned loyalty of the Service.

First of the reforms was an attempt to bring the officer structure into line with the changes since engines had come to dominate most aspects of the fighting power of a ship, and at the same time bridge the social gap which still existed between the executive officers, now drawn exclusively from the very top social and economic classes, and the less polished engineer officers. Both were to enter what was now the 'Britannia Royal Naval College' in her buildings ashore at Dartmouth as Naval Cadets at the age of twelve or thirteen, and only decide on their specialisation as executive or engineer officers on reaching the rank of Lieutenant. Marine officers were also included in the original scheme but they preferred to retain their connection with the Army. Both engineers and executive would thus have a common background, with engineering and mechanical instruction alongside the traditional 'Britannia' syllabus, and engineers would have equal opportunity to reach flag rank, even to command ships. The scheme did not overcome the prejudice in favour of the executive or 'fighting' branch – not unique to the Navy – and there were practical difficulties arising from the increasing complexity of both engineering and executive specialisations like gunnery, which made it impossible to realise 'equal opportunity' in a command sense. Nevertheless 'common entry'

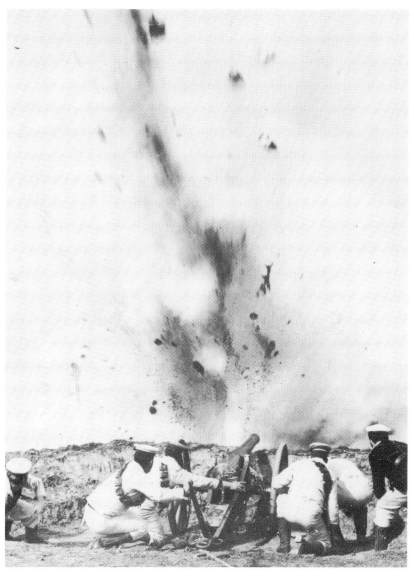

Naval field gun's crew firing

marked a significant evolution in officer training in the machine age.

His next major reforms, carried out when he was made First Sea Lord at the end of 1904, were all essential parts of one pre-thought 'Scheme' designed to move the Service bodily from its preoccupation with imperial policing towards preparedness for the looming European struggle – more correctly in Fisher's mind towards preventing that struggle, by ensuring that no power or combination of powers could contemplate a war with the Royal Navy on the opposite side; he believed fiercely in the Admiralty's favourite maxim that a supreme British Navy was the best guarantee of world peace.

> And the Navy must always so stand! Supreme – unbeaten! So we must have no tinkering! No pandering to sentiment! No regard for susceptibilities! No pity for anyone! We must be ruthless, relentless, remorseless! And we must therefore have the Scheme! The whole Scheme!! And Nothing But The Scheme!!![10]

In a whirlwind of changes, much that had been familiar to generations of officers was pruned away. The independent commands in the Pacific and South America, the ancient bases in the West Indies were abolished; the East Indies, China and Australia commands were made into detachments of a Far Eastern Fleet to be concentrated in war on Singapore; 154 vessels, mostly gunboats and small, slow cruisers were ruthlessly scrapped. New classes of ship designed for European waters were laid down and concentrated at home, and the men released from the host of small ships overseas made it possible to man a reserve fleet with 'nucleus crews' – some two fifths of the total complement of each ship, including all the specialists so that on mobilisation all the key men knew their ships intimately. By 1910 the strategic centre of the Navy had been shifted decisively to the Channel and North Sea. There were still 31 ships in China, but the largest were 4 armoured cruisers and most were shallow draft river gunboats or destroyers. There were another 8 vessels headed by a small cruiser on the East Indies station, 9 cruisers around Australia, 3 small vessels at the Cape and 2 on the west coast of South America. The Mediterranean retained a fleet of 7 battleships supported by 8 cruisers and 11 destroyers, but all the latest battleships and cruisers were in the Home Fleet, organised in two divisions each with 8 battleships, 5 armoured cruisers and 24 destroyers. There was besides a fully-commissioned Atlantic fleet comprising 6 battleships and 4 armoured cruisers, bringing the total available for rapid concentration in home waters to 22 new battleships, 14 armoured cruisers and 48 destroyers. Behind them was the 'nucleus crew' reserve fleet of 22 battleships and 160 cruisers and destroyers distributed between Chatham, Portsmouth and Devonport. It was a formidable armada, fittingly recognised in 1914 as the Grand Fleet.

Most contentious of all Fisher's reforms were the new types of ship he initiated. These stemmed in the main from developments in great gunnery over the past few years. A small and fiery *Excellent*-trained officer, Captain Percy Scott, had spearheaded a revolution in accuracy. Meanwhile the problem of long-range gunnery had been tackled by 'fire-control' enthusiasts spearheaded from outside the service by an inventive genius named Arthur Pollen, who had a brother in the Navy. Aware that the only way to hit a distant, moving ship was to correct the guns for her *future* position, he worked on plotting machines to compute the relative movement of firing and target ships. Long-range firing trials also disclosed the need for better rangefinders and fire control communications from an aloft position, and Percy Scott, appointed Captain of the *Excellent*, took these developments to their logical conclusion with a system of 'director firing' whereby all ships' guns could be controlled and fired from the aloft position. This was still the germ of a design in 1904, but the principle of central control of all guns had been established and long range accuracy was a practical proposition. This was the decisive factor which led Fisher to inaugurate his new capital ship type.

There is much evidence to suggest that he wanted to do without heavy armour, relying for protection on the ability to hit outside the range at which an enemy could hit.[11] Such a plan would have

HMS *Implacable*, Captain Protheroe 'the bad' cleared for action, Grand Harbour, Malta

come naturally to him: extreme logic, ruthlessness and high drama were the essence of his approach to all questions.

> The first desideratum in every type of fighting ship is *speed*. It is the *weather gage* of the old days. . . . Strategy demands it – so as to get the deciding factor the Battle Fleet quickest at the decisive point; and tactics demand it, to afford choice of range at which the action is to be fought.[12]

He was not able to go so far as to eliminate heavy armour for battleships, and the prototype of the new class, HMS *Dreadnought*, was conventionally protected. In other respects she was a new type altogether with the usual secondary armament of QF guns abandoned for an 'all-big-gun' armament, and a cruiser speed of 21 knots obtained largely by fitting the recently developed turbine engines. Since she had twice the weight of main armament of conventional battleships and could use her speed to choose the range outside the effective range of secondary guns, she rendered obsolete all 'pre-Dreadnought' battleships.

At the same time Fisher produced a similar type of big gun cruiser, which sacrificed thickness of side armour to obtain a speed of 25 knots. This was termed a Battle Cruiser as in addition to its commerce-protection role, it was designed to chase and hold an

An early 'A' class submarine half-submerged alongside a destroyer

enemy battlefleet, or bring a concentration of fire to bear on part of the enemy line. It was probably closer to Fisher's idea of the ideal battleship than the Dreadnought.

At the other end of the scale was the submarine. By 1904 it had developed a periscope, and the original five, built for the Royal Navy primarily to examine ways of defeating enemy submarines, had been succeeded by larger 'A' class boats; these were still under 200 tons and could only make 4½ knots underwater with electric motors, 11 knots on the surface with petrol engines. But, far from revealing how to destroy *them*, exercises had revealed that they could destroy blockading battleships.

One of Fisher's most brilliant protégés, appointed Inspecting Captain of Submarines, had already reported that in war no ship should be allowed within twenty miles of an enemy port defended by submarines. Fisher envisaged larger types capable of defending whole sections of coast and narrow straits like Dover. Meanwhile, much of the eccentricity of the early Whitehead torpedo had been removed by the invention of gyroscopic control; their speed and effective range had been improved to perhaps a mile at 18 knots, and torpedo boats as well as torpedo-boat destroyers had improved in sea-keeping ability. All these developments placed a question mark over the British strategy of close blockade off enemy coasts, and therefore of the battlefleets which were to carry it out.

An early submarine coming alongside

The battleship of olden days was necessary because it was the one vessel that nothing could sink except another battleship. *Now* every battleship is open to attack by fast torpedo craft and submarines . . . a battlefleet is no protection to anything or any operation.[13]

This view of Fisher's at the same time as his development of the ultimate battleship type, was recognition that technological progress was still gathering momentum and that there could be no finality in design. Nevertheless, submarines as yet lacked the speed and range to challenge battlefleets far from their bases, and new large 30-knot destroyers were able to protect battleships from surface torpedo craft. So while it was a correct appreciation for the long term, in the immediate future command of the seas still depended on battleships, and as 'Dreadnought' after 'Dreadnought' followed the name ship down the ways and was commissioned into the fleet in home waters, British naval superiority remained

HMS *Dreadnought*, Fisher's revolutionary all-big-gun battleship

assured. Fisher found a new name for the type – the hard-boiled egg.

> Why? Because she can't be beaten. We shall have *ten*
> Dreadnoughts *at sea* before a single foreign Dreadnought is
> launched, and we have 30 per cent more cruisers than Germany
> and France put together![14]

Percy Scott was appointed to a new post of Inspector of Target Practice to co-ordinate long-distance firings and disseminate new methods, and with Fisher's most trusted lieutenant, Captain Jellicoe, as Director of Naval Ordnance hastening supplies of new range-finders, range transmitters, change-of-range 'clocks' and other gunnery control instruments, there was a revolution in long-range fire similar to the earlier short-range transformation.

To add to the intense rivalry between ships and fleets Fisher and Scott used the national press; scores in the annual 'Battle Practice' were featured prominently in the daily papers. Those officers whose ships excelled were written up like stars; here is *The Times*, 6 December 1906:

> The *Drake* has just completed her Battle Practice and shows the
> most marvellous shooting, shooting which is unequalled in the
> Navies of the world. At a range of four miles, 133 rounds were
> fired and 105 hits were made, or a percentage of 79. . . .

By 1908 targets for Battle Practice were towed, and the firing ship had to open at an unknown distance between 8,000 and 9,000 yards while steaming at 14 knots. The *Excellent* had come into its own. Gunnery officers, who only a few years previously had been hard-pressed to find men or time for training them, from Commanders concerned chiefly with the appearance of the battery decks, found themselves the most important men on board. Gunnery specialisation was recognised as a clear path to rapid promotion.

> It was not so much anticipation of war, but the competitive
> spirit which drove the Navy with a sharp spur to unexampled
> standards of endeavour.[15]

Tactics were now, more than ever, designed to secure gunnery advantage opening at 9,000 to 10,000 yards, closing to 'decisive' range at half that. The main function of destroyers was to prevent the enemy flotilla craft closing within torpedo range of the battle-

Forward turret, bridge and tripod mast for main armament director tower of the battle cruiser, *Inflexible*

fleet, holding the ring while the great gun duels were fought. All ideas of ramming had been discarded with the *Dreadnought* herself. Cruisers and Battle cruisers were exercised with the fleet searching for the 'enemy' force, reporting its composition, course and speed visually through repeating ships, or with the fast-developing wireless telegraphy. Increasingly, as the German navy followed Fisher's Dreadnoughts with larger displacement German Dreadnoughts, and stepped up the pace of German building, manoeuvres were carried out in the grey waters of the North Sea. The ships themselves had been painted grey since 1902 to make them less conspicuous.

The old Navy had disappeared; a new specialist Navy had risen in its place. The old forms were retained: the Gunroom was run on the same robust lines as for centuries past by the senior 'Sub' administering corporal punishment with a dirk scabbard. Junior Midshipmen were still required to stampede from the mess at the words, 'Fork in the beam!', running the gauntlet of a 'whipper-out' as they went. 'Naval men are very like schoolboys,' one journalist noted, 'but in nothing as much as their treatment of the new boy.' Wardroom officers still lived in small, sparsely furnished cabins without heating and with poor ventilation, still bathed in tin tubs with water brought by their servant. In most ships the Captain had the only long bath on board. Gunnery, tactics, blockade and general strategy had joined the fit topics for conversation and were debated with heat. Some officers ran the risk of being considered brainy by studying naval history for lessons to guide them through the shifting sands of technological progress in the manner pioneered by the Colomb brothers. Marriage was still impossible for Lieutenants without large private means, and was generally frowned upon: 'an officer married is an officer marred'; there was no system of marriage allowance, nor any allowance made for married men to see their wives. On an overseas commission they might not see them for four years, and then only for a brief spell before the next commission unless they made their own arrangements for the wife to come out.

Promotion had been speeded, however, for able men and for those with the good fortune and courage to distinguish themselves in action; David Beatty was the outstanding example. Seniority in itself was no longer the only way up, and a start had been made at introducing younger men to Flag rank. Still, the early age of indoctrination in the Service combined with the closed, isolated ambience of the Wardroom contributed in many ships to that old 'formidable atmosphere of seniority and incidence of mere rank,

[229]

The Dreadnought battleship *Colossus* and battlefleet at Scapa Flow

which has embittered and belittled so many lives in the past'.

> To take a little boy of thirteen away from his home and isolate
> him from all thought and development of his generation with
> the idea of getting out of him every ounce of specialised
> efficiency is an austere method of ensuring the survival of a
> certain kind of the fittest . . . there were many other kinds of
> fitness that could not survive that ordeal, and so through the
> years that this fierce winnowing went on, the survivors, as they
> proved, were undoubtedly fit. But how much splendid material
> was not rendered useless?[16]

The men were still subjected to an even tougher physical weeding
from an equally early age. Although Fisher had opened the door to
promotions from senior Warrant Officer to Lieutenant, the path
from the lower deck to commissioned rank was closed to all but a
very few. The pay remained the same, 1s. 8d. a day for an Able
Seaman, rather below similar shore employments; yet there was no
shortage of recruits, because of the security offered by the service.
They signed on for twelve years, with a further period of ten years
to qualify for a pension. They still slung hammocks wherever space
could be found in the labyrinthine steel maze below decks, were

organised in divisions corresponding to the old sailing ship masts, lived out of their 'bags', and ate off collapsible mess tables.

Fisher was instrumental in gaining improvements in messing arrangements in 1907. The system of taking 'savings' instead of rations was replaced by an official obligatory ration of ½ lb fresh meat (or salt meat on long voyages), 1 lb of soft bread baked aboard, 1 lb of vegetables, tea, sugar, condensed milk, chocolate powder, 1 oz of jam or marmalade and ¼ lb of preserved meats, together with an allowance of 4d. per day per man for additional purchases at an official canteen. Out of it all the Cooks of the messes still prepared their traditional hashes: 'Steerage 'ammick' – or pork, currants and raisins laid in a pudding, lashed up in a cloth and boiled; 'March past' – meat placed on a pudding and baked in a dish; 'Three-decker' – slices of beef divided with layers of suet pudding and boiled, 'Oosh-me-gosh' – sliced beef with vegetables; the inevitable 'Figgy dough' or dumplings with currants, and many more. The messes were issued with knives, forks, spoons and crockery plates for the first time as the new system was introduced, and also soup ladles, condiment sets, kettles, meat dishes and other aids to civilised

The watch below

meals. The ritual of the 'grog' issue remained unchanged.

Fisher believed that there had been a vast change in the men of late.

> They are far more discriminating and far more susceptible to want of fairness and far more critical of the qualities of those above them than they used to be, and consequently they are far more sensitive to the whip and spur of discipline than they were, and I personally am convinced that you can nowadays maintain discipline more easily.[17]

Like the new breed of officers they were products of the industrial age; initiative based on craft pride and the fickle demands of sails and natural elements had been replaced by the uniformity and mechanical responses precision machinery demanded of its servants. It had started at the *Excellent* in the 1860s and 1870s; gunnery officers' notebooks now provided evidence that the changes had been thorough and complete: 'Gunlayer – the human machine – training to the point of mechanical and automatic accuracy – HE MUST NOT THINK . . .'[18]

There is little doubt that they were the most meticulously organised and drilled sailors ever to man British fleets. The times for the various drills are even more astonishing than those for mast and sail drill in the Mediterranean fleets of the 1850s. Here are some from 1907: 'Clear ship for Action!' – best cruiser 0m. 36 seconds; best battleship 0m. 45 seconds. 'Out Torpedo Nets!' 0m 36 seconds. 'In Torpedo Nets!' 1m 4 seconds. 'Negative clear for Action!' 0m. 54 seconds. Such results were achieved, like the gunnery records which were bettered each year, not simply by intensive training, but also by immense ingenuity in preparation.

> A guest who had been dining with the Captain one Sunday night inadvertently on leaving, tripped over a rope stretched across the quarterdeck; which releasing some gilguy, instantly resulted in the friend in question being straightway flattened to the deck as awnings, boats' davits, quarterdeck rails, and sky-light covers with an appalling crash, fell prone.[19]

The unfortunate guest had cleared the after end of the ship for action.

The old Navy, the Imperial police force, social 'interest', Sahib, salt-horse Navy did not die without a struggle. Under the lead of

the nation's most social and popular Admiral, Lord Charles Beresford, and with the aid of a school of intellectual officers who believed
– quite wrongly – that Fisher and his protégés were only concerned
with *materïel* and were neglecting the ancient moral qualities which
had raised the British Navy and Empire to supremacy, opposition
to Fisher and all his works rose to a pitch which had, by 1908,
become a public scandal. Fisher's ruthless methods of forcing his
reforms through without consultation with the die-hards may have
been the only way of heaving the Service bodily into the twentieth
century in time to meet the German challenge; whether or not this
is so, he had to do it because he was Fisher.

> I'll alter it all, and those who get in my way had better look
> out. I've ruined about eight men in the last eighteen months,
> and I'll ruin anyone else who tries to stop me. I'd ruin my best
> friend if necessary for the Service.[20]

Many brilliant men from both camps were ruined as the dissension
turned into virtual mutiny by the senior officers of the now-premier
Channel Fleet against the Fisher-dominated Admiralty.

Most notorious of the episodes blown up by the feud was the
'paintwork incident' at the end of 1907. With the Channel Fleet
under Lord Charles Beresford was a cruiser squadron commended
by one of Fisher's loyal supporters, Rear-Admiral Sir Percy Scott.
After exercises the Fleet, returning to Portland, was held up by fog,
and Scott's squadron arrived at noon before the main body under
Lord Beresford. One of the cruisers remained outside the breakwater to carry out gunnery exercises. However, a message from
Lord Beresford ordered all ships to be painted externally for a visit
by the Kaiser, and Percy Scott dashed off a flippant signal to his
cruiser outside the breakwater: PAINTWORK APPEARS TO BE
MORE IN DEMAND THAN GUNNERY SO YOU HAD BETTER
COME IN IN TIME TO MAKE YOURSELF LOOK PRETTY BY
THE 8TH.[21]

Nothing more would have happened had not one of the Channel
Fleet officers heard of Scott's signal a few days later and, construing
the form of words as a pointed insult to Lord Beresford, reported it
to the great man's Flag Lieutenant, who reported it to the Admiral.
For Beresford, whose flagship had been criticised in the press for
coming low on the annual Prize Firing lists, the word 'gunnery'
acted like a red rag to a bull, especially as Scott had a reputation
for turning all his commands into crack shooting ships and was
suspected in addition of being a 'spy' for Fisher.

Inflamed and unbalanced by the bitter quarrel, Beresford sent for Scott and, without allowing him a word in defence, described his signal as 'pitiably vulgar, contemptuous in tone, insubordinate in character, wanting in dignity' and much more besides. Following the private dressing-down, he made a public signal to all ships that the offending message was to be expunged from the signal logs.

This extraordinary rebuke soon became public property ashore, and the sensational press reporting of the whole incident, which lasted well into the New Year, contained scarcely-veiled hints of the real top-level quarrel behind it all. In society, parliament, and Service clubs gossip flourished.

> *Miss Mabel de Vere of Mayfair*
> *Said I really have nothing to wear.*
> *I need a new dress*
> *And must buy one unless*
> *Percy paints me – Lord! Charlie will swear!*[22]

After further storms and heated exchanges in parliament throughout 1908 both Scott's and Beresford's commands were terminated, and neither flew his flag again. Beresford, free from any constraints, renewed his efforts to pull Fisher down, and succeeded in having an altogether unprecedented inquiry into Admiralty policy convened in 1909. As the resulting report failed to back the Admiralty and condemn Beresford's own part in sufficiently unequivocal terms, Fisher himself resigned in 1910.

Throughout this period and the difficult years that followed, the service was saved by a strong core of officers who refused to take sides, but simply obeyed orders and carried out their duties to the limits of their ability – as they had been trained from their first days in the *Britannia*. Epitome of this undemonstrative, dedicated majority was Fisher's successor as First Sea Lord, Sir Arthur Wilson. Under him the violent changes of the Fisher years were absorbed as quietly as the dark grey Dreadnoughts, battle-cruisers and submarines which gradually displaced the older ships in a mighty armada prepared to meet the German challenge.

Was war coming? David Beatty bet me a fiver it would not. He longed for it. We had not fought for a century; it was time we repeated the deeds of our forefathers.[23]

The atmosphere and pride and sense of service of the Edwardian Navy, an unbeatable force which knew it, is captured perhaps best in the fiction of Bartimeus. One poignant tale, *The Legion on the Wall* strikes extraordinarily prescient links between the legions during the decline of Imperial Rome, and the Royal Navy before the First World War. The battle squadrons have returned to their anchorage after the annual war game; the officers relax. After dancing the Lancers with the Gunroom officers, finally whooping across the deck in the grand chain, ending up in a heap of mixed limbs and mess jackets and crumpled shirt fronts; after a cheerful sing-song around the Wardroom piano, there is a final chorus:

> *God of our fathers, known of old,*
> *Lord of our far-flung battle line . . .*

The solemn harmony rising into the night induces a thoughtful mood in two officers pacing the quarterdeck. They discuss the parallel between the barbarians knocking at the gates of ancient Rome, and the news from ashore – 'all these strikes and rioting – class hatred – this futile discussion about armaments . . . lesser breeds without the law generally assuming control'.

> And meanwhile we go on just the same, talking as little as they will let us – just working on our appointed task – holding to our tradition of 'Ready, Aye Ready!'
> But the end is not yet.
> 'No,' replied his companion. He made a little gesture with his pipe stem, embracing the silent battle array stretching away into the night. 'Not yet.'[24]

REFERENCES
AND SELECT
BIBLIOGRAPHY

The references for quotations used in the book provide a list of many of the books which I found most helpful. In addition to those referenced, the following are important. For naval policy and strategy: C. J. BARTLETT, *Great Britain and Sea Power, 1815–53*, OUP, 1963; A. J. MARDER, *British Naval Policy, 1880–1905*, Putnam, 1941; and the five volumes of *From the Dreadnought to Scapa Flow*, OUP, 1961–70. For a fascinating analysis of economic-strategic factors PAUL KENNEDY, *The Rise and Fall of British Naval Mastery*, Allen Lane, 1976; for microscopic analysis of particular areas G. S. GRAHAM, *Great Britain in the Indian Ocean*, OUP, 1967; ANTONY PRESTON and JOHN MAJOR, *Send a Gunboat*, Longmans, 1967; and W. E. F. WARD, *The Royal Navy and the Slavers* (Atlantic only), Allen & Unwin, 1969. For social history MICHAEL LEWIS'S, *The Navy in Transition*, listed below and ADMIRAL BALLARD'S 'The Navy' in G. M. YOUNG (ed.), *Early Victorian England*, OUP 1934, followed by 'Onlooker', 'The Last Fifty Years' in *Naval Review*, July 1966 pp. 211–21. For life at sea there is a host of nineteenth- and twentieth-century naval memoirs (listed at the National Maritime Museum); from among them ADMIRAL SIR REGINALD BACON'S, *A Naval Scrapbook* and *From 1900 Onwards*, both published by Hutchinson in 1925, are good guides to late Victorian and Edwardian ethos, as are the stories of Bartimeus and Taffrail, both serving officers. For the early- and mid-Victorian Navy, Keppel's Memoirs, listed below, and ADMIRAL COLOMB'S biography of Cooper-Key, also listed below, provide contrasting glimpses of hair-raising adventure and *materiel* progress. The latter contains perhaps the best account of the Victorian Navy to be found in a single volume. Another first-hand view is ADMIRAL G. A. BALLARD'S, (eds. G. A. OSBON and N. A. M. RODGER) *The Black Battlefleet*, published by the Nautical Publishing Company and the Society for Nautical Research, 1979. For gunnery progress see the bibliography of my own *Guns at Sea*, John Evelyn, 1973, and for the ships see SIR ALAN MOORE'S *Sailing Ships of War*, Halton & T. Smith, 1926, followed by the bibliography of my own *The Battleship Era*, Hart Davis, 1972.

CHAPTER 1   SHIPS AND ATTITUDES

1 C. BERESFORD, *Memoirs*, Methuen, 1914, i, p. 1.
2 R. C. LESLIE, *A Sea Painter's Log*, 116, cited A. Moore, *Sailing Ships of War*, Halton & T. Smith, 1926, p. 27.
3 C. C. P. FITZGERALD, *Memoirs of the Sea*, Edward Arnold, 1913.
4 HENRY CHAMBERLAIN's manuscript notebook 1840, HMS *Excellent* historical library.
5 J. BRIGGS, *Naval Administrations 1827–1892*, Sampson Low Marston, 1897, pp. 47–8.
6 J. ROSS, *A Treatise on Navigation by Steam*, London, 1828, pp. xi–xii.

CHAPTER 2   MEN – AND A FEW WOMEN

1 H. KEPPEL, *A Sailors Life under Four Sovereigns*, Macmillan, 1899, i, p. 166.
2 P. H. COLOMB in *Navy & Army Illustrated*, June 25, 1897, p. 72.
3 C. BERESFORD, *Memoirs*, Methuen, 1914, pp. 15–16.
4 L. YEXLEY, *The Inner Life of the Navy*, Pitman, 1908, pp. 174–5.
5 AGNES WESTON, *My Life Amongst the Bluejackets*, London, 1909, p. 113.
6 H. E. WOODS, *Spunyarn*, Hutchinson, 1924, i, p. 17.
7 WESTON, op. cit., p. 113.
8 W. P. ASHCROFT, 'Reminiscences', in *Naval Review* January 1964, p. 61.
9 BERESFORD, op. cit., i, p. 18.
10 Health Report, 1840, cited C. LLOYD and J. COULTER, *Medicine and the Navy*, Livingstone, 1963, iv, p. 84.
11 WOODS, op. cit., p. 22.
12 YEXLEY, op. cit., p. 218.
13 G. L. SULIVAN, *Dhow Chasing in Zanzibar Waters*, Sampson, Low, Marston, 1873, p. 75.
14 P. H. COLOMB, *Slave Catching in the Indian Ocean*, Longmans Green, 1873, p. 206.
15 ASHCROFT, op. cit., January 1965, p. 62.
16 LT. COOPER KEY's Journal, 31 May 1843, cited P. H. Colomb, *Memoirs of Admiral Sir Astley Cooper Key*, Methuen, 1898, p. 77.
17 ASHCROFT, op. cit., April, 1964, p. 199.
18 WOODS, op. cit., p. 15.
19 P. SCOTT, *Fifty Years in the Royal Navy*, Murray, 1919 p. 7.
20 ADMIRAL CYPRIAN BRIDGE, *Sea Songs and Ballads* (ed. C. Stone), OUP, 1906, pp. iv–v.
21 ASHCROFT, op. cit., January 1965, p. 64.
22 ibid., January 1964, p. 63.
23 YEXLEY, op. cit., pp. 50–1.
24 ASHCROFT, op. cit., October, 1965, p. 359.
25 ibid., January 1964, p. 64.

26 COLOMB, op. cit., p. 21.
27 ibid., p. 77.
28 YEXLEY, 2 p. 39.
29 ibid., p. 47.
30 ibid., p. 132–3.
31 ASHCROFT, op. cit., January 1964, p. 62.
32 YEXLEY 2, op. cit., p. 134.
33 BERESFORD, op. cit., i, p. 15.
34 ASHCROFT, op. cit., October 1965, p. 363.
35 ibid., April 1964, p. 195.

CHAPTER 3   OFFICERS

1 CAPTAIN SIR E. BELCHER, cited by C. Lloyd, *Mr Barrow of the Admiralty*, Collins, 1960, p. 195.
2 YEXLEY, *The Inner Life of the Navy*, Pitman, 1908, p. 82.
3 T. T. JEANS, *Reminiscences of a Naval Surgeon*, Sampson, Low, Marston, 1927, p. 18.
4 J. FISHER, *Memories*, Hodder, 1919, p. 115.
5 C. L. POPE 'Gun Room Messes of the Last Generation' in *Navy & Army Illustrated*, 18 February 1899, p. 540.
6 P. SCOTT, *Fifty Years in the Royal Navy*, Murray, 1919, p. 23.
7 GEORGE COX (engineer), private journal, 26 May 1869, cited G. COX, *Cox and the Ju Ju Coast; A Journal kept aboard HMS Fly*, Ellison, Jersey, 1960, p. 44.
8 H. KEPPEL, *A Sailor's Life Under Four Sovereigns*, Macmillan, 1899, i, p. 30.
9 SCOTT, op. cit., p. 11.
10 H. E. WOODS, *Spunyarn*, Hutchinson, 1924, i, pp. 20–1.
11 P. H. COLOMB, *Memoirs of Admiral Sir Astley Cooper Key*, Methuen, 1898, p. 9.
12 YEXLEY, op. cit., pp. 197–8.
13 CLEMENTS MARKHAM's description, cited N. Wright, *The Quest for Franklin*, Heinemann, 1951, p. 112.
14 W. P. ASHCROFT, 'Reminiscences' in *Naval Review*, October 1964, p. 441.
15 ibid., April 1964, p. 316.
16 Cited LLOYD, op. cit., iv, p. 45.
17 WILSON, cited ibid., iv, p. 177.
18 PATRICK RILEY, *Memories of a Bluejacket*, Sampson, Low, Marston, 1921, pp. 60–1.
19 WOODS, op. cit., p. 214.
20 JEANS, op. cit., pp. 37–8.
21 ibid.
22 WOODS, op. cit., i, p. 84.

23 cox journal, January 30, 1869, cited Cox, op. cit., p. 9.
24 KEPPEL, op. cit., i, p. 174.
25 SCOTT, op. cit., p. 12.
26 H. H. SMITH, *A Yellow Admiral Remembers*, E. Arnold, 1932, p. 37.

CHAPTER 4   THE COMMITMENT AND THE MEANS

1 J. BRIGGS, *Naval Administrations 1827–1892*, Sampson Low, Marston, 1897, p. 620.
2 Cited H. KEPPEL, *The Expedition to North Borneo of HMS Dido*, London, 1847, i, p. 194.
3 Cited ibid., i, p. 263.
4 ibid., ii, p. 46.
5 ibid., ii, p. 49.
6 ibid.
7 ibid., ii, p. 51.
8 ibid., ii, pp. 57–8.
9 ibid., ii, p. 111.
10 P. H. COLOMB, *Memoirs of Admiral Sir Astley Cooper Key*, Methuen, 1898, p. 178.
11 Cited ibid., June 1848, p. 164.
12 CAPTAIN J. TUCKER to Queen Pomare, 3 October 1843, Public Record Office, ADM, 1, 5547.
13 COMMANDER BOSANQUET to the Secretary of the Admiralty 5 February 1844, Public Record Office, ADM, 1, 5547.
14 ibid.
15 H. KEPPEL, *A Sailor's Life Under Four Sovereigns*, Macmillan, 1899, i, p. 244.
16 BOSANQUET, op. cit.
17 SIR THOMAS PASLEY, cited Colomb op. cit., p. 80.
18 KEPPEL, op. cit., i, p. 202.
19 ibid., i, p. 243.
20 P. H. COLOMB, *Slave Catching in the Indian Ocean*, Longmans Green, 1873, p. 236.
21 KEPPEL, op. cit., i, p. 226.
22 W. P. ASHCROFT, 'Reminiscences' in *Naval Review*, October, 1964, p. 443.
23 LT. J. PASCO commanding HMS *Kite* to Senior Naval Officer, Cape of Good Hope, 6 June 1843, Public Record Office, ADM, 1, 5547.
24 ASHCROFT, op. cit., January, 1965, p. 62.
25 P. SCOTT, *Fifty Years in the Royal Navy*, p. 19.
26 H. E. WOODS, *Spunyarn*, Hutchinson, 1924, i, pp. 40–1.
27 G. L. SULIVAN, *Dhow Chasing in Zanzibar Waters*, Sampson, pp. 64–5.
28 ibid., p. 168.
29 L. YEXLEY, *The Inner Life of the Navy*, Pitman, 1908, p. 78.

30 ibid., p. 82.
31 COLOMB, op. cit., p. 269.
32 ibid., p. 402.
33 'Whitewash' (LT. GLEIG), *The Bogus Surveyor*, London 1887, cited G. S. RITCHIE, *The Admiralty Chart*, Hollis & Carter, 1967, p. 354.
34 F. L. M'CLINTOCK, *The Voyage of the Fox*, Murray 1908, pp. 37–50.
35 ADMIRAL RICHARDS introducing Nares' account of polar exploration, cited Ritchie, op. cit., p. 337.

CHAPTER 5   WIDER YET AND WIDER . . .

1 J. BRIGGS, *Naval Administrations, 1827–1892*, Sampson Low, Marston, 1897.
2 C. C. P. FITZGERALD, *Memories of the Sea*, Edward Arnold, 1913, p. 34.
3 P. H. COLOMB, *Memoirs of Admiral Sir Astley Cooper Key*, Methuen, 1898, pp. 224 and 228.
4 H. KEPPEL, *A Sailor's Life Under Four Sovereigns*, Macmillan, 1899, i, p. 221.
5 REAR ADMIRAL CHADS to Napier 12 August 1854, cited D. BONNER-SMITH (ed.), *Russian War, 1854*, Navy Records Society 1943, p. 95.
6 KEPPEL, op. cit., i, p. 279.
7 Cited LLOYD, *Mr Barrow of the Admiralty*, Collins, 1970, iv, p. 147.
8 SIR ALGERNON WEST, *Memoirs*, cited V. STUART, *The Beloved Little Admiral*, Robert Hale, 1967, p. 159.
9 COLOMB, op. cit., p. 260.
10 KEPPEL, op. cit., i, p. 176.
11 MID. JACKY FISHER to Mrs Warden, cited R. F. MACKAY, *Fisher of Kilverstone*, OUP 1973, p. 20.
12 Reports of Committee of Enquiry into the Naval Estimates 1852–8, p. 15.
13 Trials report, cited T. BRASSEY, *The British Navy*, Longmans Green 1882, i, p. 352.
14 Firing trials, cited ibid., i, pp. 384–5.
15 ibid., i, p. 381.
16 H. H. PAYNTER, 'Battleship Life in the early '80s' in *Royal United Service Institution Journal*, 1929, p. 119.
17 COL. J. STOKES's evidence, First Report of Carnarvon Commission 1811, Q 5240, 5242, Milne Papers, National Maritime Museum, p. 231.
18 COLOMB, op. cit., p. 457.
19 H. H. SMITH, *A Yellow Admiral Remembers*, Edward Arnold, 1932, p. 28.

CHAPTER 6   HIGH NOON OF NAVAL POWER

1 E. CHATFIELD, *The Navy and Defence*, Heinemann, 1942, p. 16.
2 K. G. B. DEWAR, *The Navy from Within*, Gollancz, 1939, p. 21.
3 PATRICK RILEY, *Memories of a Bluejacket*, Sampson, Low Marston, 1921, pp. 3–5.
4 ibid.
5 L. YEXLEY, *The Inner Life of the Navy*, Pitman, 1908, pp. 9–10.
6 ibid., pp. 15–16.
7 H. H. SMITH, *A Yellow Admiral Remembers*, Edward Arnold, 1932, pp. 57–8.
8 GEORGE COX (engineer), private journal, 31 January 1869, cited G. COX, *Cox and the Ju Ju Coast; A Journal kept aboard HMS Fly*, Ellison, Jersey, 1960, p. 10.
9 RILEY, op. cit., p. 74.
10 An Undistinguished Naval Officer, *The British Navy in the Present Year of Grace*, 1885, cited G. PENN, *Up Funnel, Down Screw*, Hollis & Carter, 1955, p. 10.
11 Cited G. LOWIS, *Fabulous Admirals*, Putnam, 1957, p. 32.
12 R. TUPPER, *Reminiscences*, Jarrolds, 1929, p. 11.
13 C. C. P. FITZGERALD, *From Sail to Steam*, Edward Arnold, 1916, p. 130.
14 P. SCOTT, *Fifty Years in the Royal Navy*, Murray, 1919, pp. 39–40.
15 C. C. P. FITZGERALD, 'On Mastless Ships of War' in *Royal United Services Institution Journal*, 1887, p. 117.
16 P. COLOMB on 'Gabriel Charmes' in ibid., 1887, p. 765.
17 A. H. FINCH, 'Destroyer Trials', in *Mid-Tyne Link*, October 1904.
18 OSWALD FREWEN to his father, cited G. P. GRIGGS (ed.), *Sailor's Soliloquy*, Hutchinson, 1961, p. 151.
19 TUPPER, op. cit., p. 108.
20 *The Times*, 28 June 1897.
21 CHATFIELD, op. cit., p. 28.
22 YEXLEY, op. cit., p. 177.
23 ibid., pp. 188–9.
24 SMITH, op. cit., p. 55.
25 B. CURTIS, 'Square Rig' in *Naval Review*, July 1966, p. 237.
26 B. CURTIS, 'Nucleus Crew System' in *Naval Review*, April 1963, p. 168.
27 History of the Benin Expedition, Naval Library P(NS) 221, p. 34.
28 ibid., p. 16.
29 ibid., p. 41.
30 H. W. WILSON, *With the Flag to Pretoria*, London, 1900, I, p. 150.
31 ibid., p. 151.
32 ibid.
33 Letter from LT. ARMSTRONG to Captain Lloyd's father, 14 July 1900, Royal Marines Museum, Eastney, Hants.

CHAPTER 7   WAR NAVY

1 FISHER to 1st Lord (Selborne) 19 December 1900, cited A. MARDER, *Fear God and Dread Nought*, Cape, 1952–9, i, p. 174.
2 G. LOWIS, *Fabulous Admirals*, Putnam, 1957, p. 32.
3 Fisher to Chamberlain, 12 November 1900, cited MARDER, op. cit., i, pp. 66–7.
4 Cabinet Papers, Vol. 59, CAB 37/59, 16 November 1901, cited B. McL. Ranfft, *The Naval Defence of British Seaborne Trade*, D. Phil. thesis, Oxford, 1967.
5 R. H. BACON, *The Life of Lord Fisher of Kilverstone*, Hodder, 1929, p. 170.
6 Notes on a visit to Kiel and Wilhelmshaven printed for Naval Intelligence Department, Public Record Office, ADM 116 940B.
7 BACON, op. cit., p. 115.
8 ibid., p. 133.
9 M. HANKEY, *Memoirs*, i, p. 19, cited R. F. MACKAY, *Fisher of Kilverstone*, OUP, 1973, pp. 225–6.
10 P. KEMP, *The Fisher Papers.*, Navy Records Society, 1960, p. 19.
11 See J. T. SUMIDA, 'British Capital Ship Design and Fire Control in the *Dreadnought* Era' in *Journal of Modern History*, 51, 1979, pp. 205–30.
12 KEMP, op. cit., p. 25.
13 ibid., p. 36.
14 ibid., p. 302.
15 C. V. USBORNE, *Blast and Counterblast*, Murray, 1935, p. 22.
16 F. YOUNG, *With the Battlecruisers*, Cassell, 1921, p. 255.
17 Fisher to Selborne 5 August 1902, cited MARDER, op. cit., i, p. 257.
18 E. ALTHAM's gunnery notebooks (manuscript) Royal United Services Institution.
19 C. CRADOCK, *Whispers from the Fleet*, Portsmouth, 1908, p. 316.
20 BACON, op. cit., pp. 249–50.
21 See P. PADFIELD, *Aim Straight; A Biography of Admiral Sir Percy Scott*, Hodder & Stoughton, 1966, pp. 164 ff.
22 ibid., p. 171.
23 E. CHATFIELD, *The Navy and Defence*, Heinemann, 1942, p. 120.
24 BARTIMEUS, *Naval Occasions*, Blackwood, 1915, p. 58.

ACKNOWLEDGMENTS

I should like to thank the Captain of HMS *Excellent* and Lt Cdr Herbert-Smith for the facilities of the historical library at Whale Island, and for permission to reproduce illustrations from books found there; also the Curator of the Royal Marines Museum at Eastney, and Lt Col. Eagles for permission to reproduce illustrations from the sketchbook of Colonel Field. I am most grateful to Vice Admiral Sir Ian McGeoch for permission to quote from reminiscences published in the *Naval Review*. I should like to thank the following authors and publishers for permission to quote extracts: A. D. Peters and Co Ltd for Arthur Bryant's *Letters, Speeches and Declarations of King Charles II*, Martinus Nijhoff Publishers for G. Symcox *The Crisis of French Seapower*; and the following for permission to reproduce illustrations: National Maritime Museum, pp. 13, 19, 22, 23, 34, 37, 40, 88, 170; Imperial War Museum, pp. 148, 157, 225, 226, 228; HMS *Excellent*, pp. 14, 42, 172, 177, 186, 187, 188, 190, 191, 218; Hulton Picture Library, pp. 27, 63, 84, 99, 112, 120, 123, 152, 182, 214.

INDEX

Acre, bombardment, 90–2
Aden, 92–4, 97
Admiralty Board, 131, 152, 178
Agamemnon, HMS, 133
Alecto, HMS, 132
Alert, HMS, 109
Alexandra, HMS, 156, 157, 159
Alexandria, 89, 171–4, 209
Arabi, Colonel, 171–4
Armaments, 1830s, 7–10, 15; 1850s, 139, 149, 151; 1860s, 152–64; 1880s, 169–71, 173; 1900s, 209
Armour, 142, 150–68, 194, 209, 223
Armoured batteries, 142
Armstrong guns, 152–3, 163, 169
Asia, HMS, 38
Assistant Surgeon, 55, 68, 70, 150
Atlantic fleet, 222
Auckland, Lord, 131

Barnaby, N., 163–4
Bases, 1, 83–4, 92–3; *see also under individual names*
Battlecruiser, *see* Cruisers
Battleships, sailing, 2–3, 7–8, 17, 85, 135–7, 226; screw, 101, 133–7, 142–3; armoured, 142, 150, 154–66, 193–4; pre-Dreadnought, 193–5, 209; Dreadnought, 224–7, 234
Beatty, Capt. D., 229, 234
Beaufort, Admiral, 16
Benin, expedition, 203–7
Beresford, Admiral Lord C., 21, 233–4
Beresford, Sir J., 15
Blackbirding, 201
Bluejackets, 4, 18–50, 71, 116, 122–5, 140, 180–6, 205, 230–2
Boatswain, 13, 64, 68
Boatswain's Mates, 38, 41, 46
Boer War, 24, 207–8, 219
Bolt, G., 24
Bomarsund, 137–41
Bosanquet, Commander, 109–13
Bounty, 106, 116
Boxer rising, 208
Breech-loading guns, 153, 156–7, 167–8
Britannia, HMS, 188, 220, 234
Brooke, J., 100–6
Brownrigg, Captain C., 53
Brunel, M., 158

Camperdown, HMS, 199–200
Cape of Good Hope, 84–5, 108, 125, 201–3, 209–10, 222
Captains, 38–9, 43–4, 46, 51–82, 97, 106, 109, 116, 149, 185, 189, 195, 229
Captain, HMS, 158–9
Carpenters, 13, 64, 68
Challenger, HMS, 128
Channel fleet, 209–10, 222, 233
Chaplains, 68, 71
Charts, Admiralty, 3, 125–6, 129
Chatfield, Admiral, E., 176
Chatham, 20, 212, 222
Cherry, Commander, G., 82
Chichester, Captain E., 53
Childers, HMS, 81
China, 94, 143–4, 208
China station, 96, 150, 209–10, 222
Christmas at sea, 38
Clerks, Captain's, 54, 68

Colomb, Captain J., 191–2, 193, 229
Colomb, Admiral P., 20, 41, 62, 137, 191–2, 193, 196, 229
Colonies, scramble for, 175
Commanders, 45, 62–3, 73, 81, 185, 189, 197, 227
Competition, 15, 21, 45, 61–2, 191, 197, 227, 232
Conway, HMS, 98
Cooking, *see* food
Cooper-Key, Admiral, 62, 107
Cormorant, HMS, 74
Corvettes, 10; steam, 143, 194
Cost of Navy, *see* Naval Estimates
Cowper-Coles, Captain, 158–9
Crimean War, 130, 135–42, 150–1, 178
Crossing the line, 38, 39
Cruisers, 4, 192, 194, 209–13, 222; battle-, 224, 229, 234; *see also* Frigates, Corvettes, Sloops

Dacres, Admiral Sir S., 55
Dance and skylark, 33, 77
Defaulters, 53; *see also* Punishments
De Grey, Lord, 15
Destroyers, 193–4, 211–12, 222, 225
Devastation, HMS, 159–60
Devonport, *see* Plymouth
Dido, HMS, 100–5
Discipline, 25, 40–8, 51, 61, 182–5, 232
Divisions, 45, 231
Dover, 209, 225
Drake, HMS, 227
Dreadnought, HMS (1879),

INDEX

160–2, 166; (1905), 224–9;
see also Battleships
Drills, see Competition
Drink, 23–5, 29–31, 41–3,
50, 57, 68, 73
Dublin, HMS, 108
Duke of Wellington, HMS,
133, 136, 137–9
Dundas, Admiral Sir W., 136
Dundonald, Admiral, 136

Education of officers, 177–8,
188–9
Egypt, 87–91, 93, 171–5
East India Company, 83, 94,
149
East Indies Station, 85, 89,
96, 125, 150, 172, 210
Elgin, Lord, 146
Empire of the Oceans, 1, 4,
87, 175
Entente Cordiale, 216–18
Engineers, 13, 59, 150, 177,
186–7, 195, 211, 220
Engines, see Steam power
Erebus, HMS, 126–7
Ericsson, J., 13, 158
Excellent, HMS, 14–15, 18,
64, 92, 152, 177, 185, 218,
223, 227, 232

Far Eastern Fleet, 222
Fire control, 223, 227
First Lieutenant, 40, 44, 64–
5, 73, 81, 100, 201
Fisher, Admiral Sir J., 57,
193, 209, 212, 215–23,
230–4
Fisher reforms, see Naval
reforms
Fitzgerald, Captain C., 191
Flag officers, 63, 81, 106,
189
Flogging, 41–3, 51, 180–5
Food, 27–31, 38, 68, 72–3,
122–3, 203, 231
Fore-bitters, 36
Foreign Intelligence
Committee, 178
France, 17, 84–9, 94, 97–8,
108–13, 122, 130–3, 135,
138–46, 150–6, 168, 171,
175, 192–7, 211–17
Franklin, Sir J., 126–8
Free trade, 83, 85–7, 94,
125, 130
Frigates, sailing, 10; screw,
133, 143, 168; armoured,
150–3, 194

Gatling gun, 169, 174
Germany, 5, 216–18, 229,
233, 234
Gibraltar, 84, 209
Gladstone, W., 96, 171, 175

Gloire, 154
Graham, Sir J., 131
Grand Fleet, 222
Graspan, battle of, 24, 207
Grog, see Rum
Gunboats, 13, 139, 142–3,
144, 168, 222
Gun drill, 14
Gunner, 14, 24, 45, 64, 68
Gunnery Lieutenant, 64,
190, 227
Gunroom, 57–60, 72–8, 229,
235
Guns, see Armaments; and
see under makers' names
Gunvessels, 143, 149–50

Half pay, 62–4, 189
Hall, Captain W. R., 178
Harpy, HMS, 114
Head money, see Bounty
Heneague, Captain, 187
Hewett, Admiral Sir W., 59
Hindustan, HMS, 188–9
Home Fleet, 2, 7–10, 16–17,
209–11, 222
Hong Kong, 143, 150
Hong Kong, 143–4
Hope, Admiral Sir J., 146
Hornby, Admiral Phipps,
193
Hotchkiss guns, 169
Hyacinth, HMS, 95
Hygiene, 26–7, 57, 69, 114,
140

Immortalité, HMS, 53
Impregnable, HMS, 179
Inconstant, HMS, 191
India, 86–9, 92–4, 97–8,
145–9, 171, 197
Indian Mutiny, 145–9
Industrialisation of Navy, 1–
6, 13–17, 130–5, 136–7,
139, 143, 150–6, 164–5,
176, 185–6, 190, 210, 215,
218, 226, 232
Inflexible, HMS, 163–5, 173
'Interest', 54, 61–4, 189
Ironclads, 154–66, 172
Investigator, HMS, 127

Japan, 4, 149, 215
Jellicoe, Captain J., 227

Kagoshima, bombardment,
149
Kelly, Captain, 98
Keppel, Admiral Sir H., 20,
81, 99–108, 114, 134, 140,
143–5
Kinburn, Fort, 142
Kite, HMS, 117–18
Kroomen, 115
Krupp guns, 169

Lahej, Sultan of, 93
Lancaster guns, 152
Lemon juice, 31, 128
Lieutenants, 55, 62–5, 81,
116, 149, 189, 195, 229–
32; see also First
Lieutenant
Lime juice, 31, 128, 204
'Liners', see Battleships
Lloyd, Captain, H. T. R., 208

Machine guns, 169, 174
McClintock, Admiral L., 60,
127–8
McClure, Commander, 127
Madagascar, 98
Mahan, Captain A. T., 196,
209
Malta, 197
Manning, see Recruiting
Marines, 24, 28, 51, 64, 66,
72, 138–40, 145, 171, 180,
187–8, 203–5, 208, 220
Marine Society, 19, 24
Marlborough, HMS, 64
Marriage, 24–5, 64, 229
Master, 55, 60, 81, 106
Master at Arms, 31, 46, 179
Master's Mate, 55, 59–60,
64, 189
Mate, see Master's Mate
'Materialists', 220, 233
Mauritius, 85
Maxim gun, 169, 202, 204–6
Mediterranean station, 1, 26,
79, 85, 88–9, 135, 150,
172, 196–7, 199–200, 208,
209–20, 222
Men, see Bluejackets
Midshipmen, 38, 51, 40–60,
69, 71, 189, 229
Milne, Admiral Sir A., 57,
192
Muscat, Sultan of, see Sayid
Said

Napier, Admiral Sir C., 90,
136–8
Napoleon III, 130, 142, 150–
1
Napoléon, 133
Navigating Lieutenant, see
Pilot
Naval Brigades, 3, 138–40,
143–9, 171–5, 185, 202–8
Naval Defence Act, 193, 196,
209, 215, 219
Naval Estimates, 15, 83–4,
130, 193, 196
Naval history, 71, 192, 196,
229
Naval Intelligence
Department, 178, 213
'Navalism', 4, 196
Naval reforms, 220–33

Nordenfelt guns, 169, 174
North American station, see West Indies
Northwest passage, 126–7

Oceanography, 128–9
Opium wars, 95–7, 143

Pacific Station, 150, 200–1, 210, 222
Pakenham, Captain, 212
Palmerston, Lord, 87–92, 95–8, 107, 111–13, 120
Parker, Admiral Sir W., 136
Parsons, C., 211
Pasco, Lieutenant, 117
Patronage, see 'Interest'
Pay, 18, 62–4, 68, 178, 230–1
Paymaster, 150, 190
Peel, Captain E., 140, 145
Peiho forts, bombardment, 146–7, 208
Pekin, 208
Petty Officers, 18, 24, 28, 31, 44–6, 60, 68, 71, 116, 178, 183–8
Phlegethon, 104
Pilot, 55, 66
Piracy, 2, 30, 85–7, 97–106
Plymouth, 20, 25, 84, 177–9, 187, 212, 222
Police, Ships', 44–8, 176, 180–1
Policing, 1–3, 149, 200–7, 221
Pollen, A., 223
Portsmouth, 20, 25, 54, 84, 187, 212, 218, 222
Powerful, HMS, 207
Promotion, 54, 62–3, 116, 189–92, 197, 227–31
Protheroe, Captain, 207
Punishments, 40–4, 51–3, 61, 180–8, 230
Purser, 48–9, 57, 68, 81, 150, 190; see also Paymaster

QF guns, 169, 193–4, 207, 209

Ramming, 155, 192
Rates, see Battleships, sailing; Frigates, sailing
Rattler, HMS, 132
Rawson, Admiral, 202–6
Recreation, 33–41, 74–9
Recruiting, 18–20, 178–80
Reed, E., 158–60, 164, 173
Religion, 24–6, 71
Rimington, Commander, 74–6
Rocket, Congreve, 119, 204

Ross, Sir J., 16
Royal Marines, see Marines
RNR, 178
Royal Naval College, Portsmouth, 54; Greenwich, 177
Royal Naval Engineering College, 177, 187
Royal Navy School, 19
'Royal Sovereign' class, 193
Rum, 25, 29, 31, 38, 43, 183
Russia, 5, 17, 85–8, 92–4, 97, 130–2

Sailing Master, see Master
Sailors, see Bluejackets
Sails, 11–12, 164–8, 176–7, 190–1, 197, 231
St George, HMS, 201–7
St Jean d'Acre, HMS, 134
Sayid Said, 86
Schoolmaster, 55, 68–71
Scott, Captain, 128
Scott, Admiral Sir P., 59, 223–7, 233–4
Scurvy, 31, 69, 128
Sebastopol, 135, 141, 142
Seamanship, 1, 10–15, 20–1, 25, 78–82, 176, 180–1, 191, 232
Seine net, 30, 78
Seriff Sahib, 104
Servants, 72, 76
Seymour, Admiral Sir E., 208
Seymour, Admiral Sir M., 143–6
Sheerness, 25, 212
Ship construction, 1830s, 8–9; 1860s, 150–68; 1900s, 212
Singapore, 94, 96, 100, 222
Slave trade, 3, 13, 30, 60, 83, 87, 97, 109–25, 201
Sloops, 10, 85, 194
Slops, 68
South American station, 85, 150, 210, 222
'Starting', 41, 45, 180
Stead, W. H., 193
Steam power, 1, 12–16, 92–4, 125–6, 130–8, 142–3, 149, 160–4, 187, 190–1, 194–5, 212
Stopford, Admiral Sir R., 90
Stokers, 186
Sub-Lieutenant, 189
Submarines, 213, 225, 234
Suez, 92–3, 172–5, 197
Surgeon, 68–71, 81, 114; see also Assistant Surgeon
Sveaborg, bombardment, 138, 141

'Symondites', 9, 12
Symonds, Sir W., 9

Tactics, 1, 15–17, 71, 82, 137, 155–6, 167–8, 176–7, 191–3, 199–200, 219, 224, 227–9
Tahiti, 108–9
Telegraphs, 150, 206
Terrible, HMS, 207, 208
Terror, HMS, 126–7
Thomson, Charles, 128
Thorneycrofts boats, 168
Thouars, Admiral, 108
Thunderer, HMS, 160–1
Tientsin, 146–8
Torpedo boats, 168–74, 193–4, 210, 213, 225–7
Torpedoes, 166–9, 177, 192, 225–7
Torpedo Lieutenant, 190
Trade protection, 4, 10–12, 192–4, 209, 213
Trincomalee, 83–4
Tryon, Admiral Sir G., 199–200
Tucker, Captain, 108–9
Turkey, 87–90, 97, 135, 142, 149
Turrets, 158–63, 194
Two-Power Standard, 2, 17, 83, 193, 208, 213

Uncar, 109, 112–13
Uniform, 48–9, 81, 122, 181–3, 190, 204
USA, 4, 85, 94, 110–13, 122, 215–16

Venereal disease, 24
Vernon, HMS, 177, 218
Victoria, HMS, 199–200
Victualling, see Food
Volage, HMS, 95

Wardroom, 72–6, 186, 235
Warrant Officers, 24, 31, 51, 55, 66, 68–9, 116, 230
Warrior, HMS, 154–5
West Indies and North American station, 85, 150, 210
Whale Island, 218; see also Excellent, HMS
Whitehead, see Torpedoes
Whitworth guns, 152
Wilson, Admiral Sir A., 214, 234

Yarrow boats, 168

Zanzibar, 202